Avery Press

NewYork • London

The Rules of Action

The Rules of Action Second Edition, 2014.

This book is a work of fiction. References to real people, events, establishments, organizations, products or locales are intended only to provide a sense of authenticity, and are used fictitiously. All other characters, and all incidents and dialogue, are drawn from the author's imagination and are not to be construed as real.

Cover design: Brandon Stout.

Cover photograph: Javier Vargas. Photograph reproduced with permission.

Author photograph (at back): Troy Aossey.

Avery Press, USA.

Manufactured in the United States of America.

Copyright © 2014 Landon J. Napoleon

All rights reserved

ISBN: 0988651963

ISBN 13: 9780988651968

The Rules of Action

LANDON J. NAPOLEON

"Briskly told and well-drawn… this legal thriller (*The Rules of Action*) does what many courtroom-based novels and television shows do not: It stays true to the actual practice of trial law… A fast-paced tale of justice in action and a remarkably accurate portrait of a trial lawyer's daily grind… Prospective law students are frequently encouraged to read law-student memoirs or legal hornbooks, but for a realistic view of litigation and a great deal more action, they'd do well to add this legal thriller to their reading list."

—*Kirkus Reviews*

"*The Rules of Action* is one of the most compelling and entertaining books I have ever read on the strategy and gamesmanship of the legal process."

—Grant Woods
Former Arizona Attorney General

Praise for *Burning Shield: The Jason Schechterle Story*

"A maimed cop fights to regain his life in this inspiring true story… Landon J. Napoleon, the author of several crime novels, is skilled at painting a scene in slangy strokes while balancing plotlines… this true story reads like a novel."

—*Kirkus Reviews*

"*Burning Shield: The Jason Schechterle Story* is a powerful, inspiring story of one man's will to survive and to thrive in the face of horrific injuries. It is also a keen look into the workings of our police men and women and the close bonds that knit them together. We admire them, and we especially admire Jason Schechterle."

—Janet Napolitano, former Arizona governor (2002-2009) and
Arizona attorney general (1998-2002)

"Sad, exciting, life-changing and emotional, *Burning Shield: The Jason Schechterle Story* is an amazing story of one man's triumph over tragedy with the support of an entire community."

—Jack Ballentine, former homicide detective and
author of *Murder for Hire*

"Jason Schechterle's life has been one of joy, tragedy, love, and hope... This man is an inspiration and his story must be read and shared."

—Derrick Hall
President & CEO, Arizona Diamondbacks

More praise for Landon J. Napoleon's debut novel *ZigZag*

"*ZigZag* is one of the boldest and most original first novels to appear in a long time. It's also very funny, in a way that only the raw street-song of truth can be funny. Landon J. Napoleon has written a gem."

—Carl Hiaasen

"A remarkable debut portraying the inner life of a disturbed ghetto teenager as he attempts to grow up in the frightening world he's inherited... An unaffected, moving, astonishing insight into the heart of a troubled, silent genius."

—*Kirkus Reviews*
(starred review)

"... this mixture of comic adventure and paean to the values of volunteerism is a vivid read and impressive debut novel."

—*Library Journal*
(starred review)

"...affecting first novel that explores the survival of the human spirit in an atmosphere of deprivation and cruelty."

—*Publisher's Weekly*

"...Landon J. Napoleon's first novel is an affecting work."

—*The Dallas Morning News*

"Landon J. Napoleon conveys the strength of the human spirit through his wonderful creation, and in the process tells an engaging and enriching story."

——*Barnes and Noble Discover Great New Writers,*
1999 Finalist

Books by Landon J. Napoleon

Nonfiction

Burning Shield: The Jason Schechterle Story

Novels

ZigZag
Deep Wicked Freaky
The Rules of Action
The Flatirons

www.landonjnapoleon.com

For the girls—Amy Lynn,
Avery Jane and Riley Ann—
for everything

Author's Note

THIS SECOND EDITION INCLUDES a new cover design as well as editorial refinements and polish.

While this book is a work of fiction, it is inspired by the real life and decades-long career of a prominent trial attorney. After interviewing this attorney for a magazine article in 2004, we struck a connection and, eventually, the idea for this novel emerged. That initial seed was the beginning of five years of research and writing that became *The Rules of Action*.

In the end, however, the characters, names, and legal situations created herein are fictitious and wholly products of the author's imagination.

If in one day, one hour, everything could be arranged at once.
The chief thing is to love.
—Fyodor Dostoyevsky

Acknowledgments

THE FOLLOWING PEOPLE WERE ALL INSTRUMENTAL, to one degree or another, in helping me research, edit, fine tune and complete the first and second editions of this book. Many hearty thanks to the entire supporting cast:

Literary Support: Philip Hobsbaum and Willy Maley, my first and best mentors at University of Glasgow; Martine Bellen and Jim Moore for wordsmith support; Eagle-Eyed Lisa Fontes, my sister, for the final proofread of this edition; Mark Caccamese, aka Max Daniels; Javier Vargas, a new friend in Argentina who shot the second edition cover image; and Brandon Stout for finding said photograph and creating the stunning design.

Legal Advisors: Dr. Terrence Brown, J.D., who so thoroughly vetted the medical passages; Lawyer Shannon Clark, who helped me shape the narrative; Debbie Francis; Lawyers Katherine Hughes and Steve Tucker, for patiently answering my endless questions; Intellectual Property Attorney Brian LaCorte, for key insights on life as a lawyer; Retired Judge Dan Nastro, for allowing me to sit in and soak up the mediation process; Maricopa County Superior Court Judge Doug Rayes and his staff, for granting me interviews and an enviable front-row seat throughout jury selection and a trial; and Richard Rea, for taking me inside the mind of a first-rate defense attorney.

Larger realm—A special note of love and thanks to my late mom, who cemented my career path when she signed me up for my first writing class one Colorado summer (1975) and instilled in me a great love for writing and books; and to her mother, my grandmother Ann, who demonstrated true unconditional love, eloquently taught me the difference between a "twin-quin" and a "trifecta," and used her extensive connections at the Cloverleaf Kennel Club dog track to get me a job there during my freshman year in college.

And most of all, to the man who lived these events with passion and purpose and inspired the main character, thank you for bringing me into your world, sitting with me for endless hours, days, weeks, months and years to relay your life and work, and always advocating for me as an author. I am forever grateful for our collaboration and creation, our many moments of laughter and, now, our ongoing friendship covering more than a decade. WTF, eh?

Prologue

Phoenix, 1970

THE 25-YEAR-OLD LAWYER CONNOR J. DEVLIN drew a breath, rose from his chair, and, for the first time in open court, said, "Objection, your honor." It was, in the young counselor's estimation, one for the books, a truly laudable missive.

"Overruled." The gray-haired judge slowly turned, frowned, shook his head, and sighed. He looked like a wrinkled dog sniffing the air, and even when he wasn't annoyed, which he was now, his face was always crumpled into a grimace. The judge took in the young lawyer—tall with longish hair and thick sideburns, impeccably dressed in a plaid jacket and dark pants, and ill-prepared to an astonishing level—and sighed again. In a more seasoned lawyer, the honed swagger would be a solid asset. But in this young rogue, it only accentuated his lack of ability.

The bailiff looked up and stopped rustling papers at his desk. The clerk and court reporter both sat motionless in the uneasy silence. The only sound Devlin could hear was his own heartbeat and the fluorescent buzz above his head. The judge finally said,

"Counselor, will you be getting up to speed anytime soon, or will each statement from your mouth continue to be ill-timed, inappropriate, and ineffective?"

Other than the uniformed deputy the gallery was empty, but Devlin heard a chuckle from the prosecutor's table. Perhaps the parade-route planning to herald this new career had been a bit premature.

"Yes sir, your honor."

"Yes sir, you will continue to be ill-timed, inappropriate, and ineffective?"

"No sir. I mean no, your honor."

"I should hope not. And if you must object again, turn the volume down a notch or two. I'm certain I look frail and aged to you, but my hearing is quite good."

Another snicker.

As Devlin slid back into his chair even his client, whom Devlin had met twenty minutes ago as they entered the courtroom together, was shaking his head and whispering, "The hell kind of jive-ass lawyer you anyway? Damn torture watching your honky ass."

"Yeah," Devlin whispered, "For you and me both, pal." Just a week removed from passing the bar and becoming an official lawyer, each time his apartment phone rang the sound brought forth a brilliant specter of possibility. Real cases and clients, and problems that needed solutions. As a kid, Devlin didn't have a singular career vision, but he certainly never wanted to be a lawyer. Growing up in Buffalo, New York, a hard 1950s town, the oppressive weather had a looming presence that paralleled the Korean War and the clamp-down of the Eisenhower years. The overall bleakness was a common bond: The townspeople braved, collectively, the gloomy pallor and Arctic fury alongside the fear of imminent Communist invasion. Spawned by sub-zero reality, Buffalo's barstool-and-bowling culture forged a gallows humor embodied in its official town slogan, philosophy, and all-around response to anything: *What the fuck*. By age 10, every kid in Buffalo had heard, learned, and begun using, at least with friends, every varied nuance of those three words. Watching this current debacle unfold triggered the old standard.

What the fuck, Devlin.

Like most law school graduates, he had imagined various scenarios for his first case. Perhaps the inaugural foray would be a stunning settlement bringing justice and riches to an impoverished victim. Or maybe a front-page trial with all the Perry Mason theatrics, wherein a hard-nosed Devlin cracked a key witness during a deft cross.

In each imagined scene, an ivory-tower grandeur and gentlemanly protocol infused the proceedings. There would be eloquent and nuanced discussions of courtroom strategy over hand-wrapped cigars and single-malt swirled in crystal snifters. This all transpired against a backdrop of leather-bound law books, the light playing off the luster of cherry and other fine woods oiled to luxurious perfection. And, ultimately, triumph on the courtroom stage. However, the reality of how this disaster began three hours ago was 180 degrees from those pristine visions.

When Devlin answered the phone, anticipating great possibilities, what he got instead was a high-profile, high-dollar, and highly inebriated lawyer. Devlin checked his watch: 10 a.m. Tuesday seemed an odd time to be blasted, even to an Irish-Catholic kid who found the barstool at 14 and spent his youth prowling Buffalo's blue-collar nooks and crannies. Devlin, while working part-time as a bouncer as he studied for the bar exam, had met this currently addled lawyer at work, and they had struck up an ongoing banter. Now the grizzled veteran was saying he needed the kid to take a case, and Devlin was buoyed and even honored. He pledged to the seasoned pro, in his most solemn and respectful voice, that he would not let him down, and that diligence would be the watchword.

"Good for you, kid, good for you," the veteran said laughing, "because you're due in court for jury selection in an hour."

"An hour?"

"Yes (*burp*) you am. You step in, you handle it. I'll owe you one, kid. You make your mark in the legal game when it's fourth-and-twenty. Not when the bases are empty."

The lawyer could be excused, in his condition, for mixing his metaphors. Then he laughed and added, "I'd say this qualifies, kid. Hey, you could start a new firm: Diligence and Watchword. People will come out of the fucking woodwork on that one."

"I've never tried a case—"

"Passed the bar, right?"

"Yes but—"

"Then the state of Arizona says you're a lawyer, right?"

"Right, but I've never actually tried a case—"

"First time for everything."

"But I don't know the rules of evidence as they apply to trial—"

"First time for everything."

Devlin paused, a sick feeling in his stomach, and then added, "Sir, with all due respect, I don't even know who your client is or what the case is about. I've never even been to the courthouse."

"First time for everything." Then the lawyer added this reassurance: "Kid, like you said, it's fourth-and-twenty. You're coming off the bench because (*burp*) one client's like their needs are what you represent for the good of the (*extended pause*) responsibility. Cheers, kid. I salute you." And then the superstar lawyer was shouting directions to the downtown bar.

"Sir, please, I really don't think... Sir? Hello?"

All Devlin could hear were muffled shouts and the gritty opening refrains of "American Woman" by The Guess Who. Then raucous laughter and unmistakable bar-room shouts. Either the lawyer had passed out cold and slid down the wall, or he had re-joined the revelry without hanging up the pay phone receiver. Devlin took a deep sigh and grabbed a legal pad.

It was a five-minute blast from his apartment to the tavern. In any other city he might have walked it, but the triple-digit September heat killed that idea. Besides, with his new ride he wouldn't be walking anywhere. After graduation, he'd traded in his Corvette for a vehicle more befitting a barrister: a brand-new 1970 black Lincoln Mark III with its block-solid V8 power plant. There was also the unmistakable and Rolls-Royce-inspired grill, headlight covers, and the standard fake spare-tire bulge on the rear deck. Inside, the car was loaded with power everything, trim panels in rosewood laminate, and an eight-track tape player. Heading south on Central Avenue, Devlin passed a billboard with a twenty-foot-tall Elvis Presley: The King's first tour since 1958 was kicking off in Phoenix tonight, and Devlin had tickets. The King's return, at least, softened the blow of The Beatles unraveling a few months back.

Once his eyes adjusted to the dingy ambience, Devlin scoured the red vinyl booths and then the few faces staring from stools. He looked again, and then a third time. And the lawyer was not there. Devlin was off the hook. He'd just stay away from the apartment until after jury selection began, and the lawyer would have no way of calling him. Devlin would say he frantically searched every bar within a three-mile radius. That should do it. Relieved, he headed for the restroom.

Before he pushed open the men's room door, Devlin heard muffled grunting and shouts like two bears fighting in slow motion. He stepped in, walked toward the stall, and, fearing someone was being mugged and beaten, pulled open the door. What Devlin saw instead was the high-profile attorney standing with his bare and very hairy ass center stage. Devlin couldn't see the woman, but it was easy to deduce that she, too, was standing, bent over and clinging to what had become her porcelain ballast amid the thundering frenzy. Devlin swallowed back an acid sickness in his throat and turned to start out.

"Devlin?"

Silence.

"Devlin, that you?"

Devlin said, "Yes sir," as the lofty law school vision began dissolving at a frightening pace.

"Good work, kid," the drunk lawyer said, his hips never breaking rhythm. "Brief you the case a minute."

"Can we not have the talking, please?" the woman said between thrusts, a reasonable request but one unlikely to restore whatever scintilla of dignity might have been present before Devlin arrived. Devlin stepped out and waited in the dark hallway that had a Buffalo vibe he knew well: that clawing beer-and-smoke stench masking the vague desperation of dreams unfulfilled, The Fifth Dimension thumping out "Let The Sun Shine In." Devlin could still hear them rutting as he reviewed the succession: (a) summoned to a toilet stall; (b) witnessed the lawyer's hairy backside; and (c) forever scarred with displeasing visuals lodged in his mind.

From that inauspicious beginning, Devlin's first case plummeted to its nadir. About all the drunk could tell him was that the client, a colored guy, was charged with carrying a concealed weapon. The veteran lawyer dug a very thin file folder from his briefcase, handed it to Devlin and, literally, gave the client's new lawyer directions to the courthouse.

"Let's see, what else?" the lawyer said, swirling his glass and studying it as though the amber liquid were some oracle of knowledge. He was visibly swaying and looked as though the next thing from his mouth would be vomit. But instead, all he said was, "Well, fuck it. Go win the case, kid."

Although being in a real courtroom to try an actual case was heart-pumping excitement at first, now Devlin just wanted it to end, because he fully realized how clueless he was. The judge had pretty much nailed it. *Ill-timed. Inappropriate. Ineffective.* Devlin's only saving grace was his fierce intent to help the client, but that resolve faded when even the client jumped ship. After nineteen years of formal education, Devlin didn't know what the hell he was doing. Finally, mercifully, the proceedings ended. The sum total of his effort: a pony-tailed Girl Scout trying to seal off Dick Butkus on an end-around might have fared better. *Objection, your honor!* Devlin could only shake his head as he gathered the papers he had spread for appearance's sake.

As the civil and criminal justice system wound down for the day, Devlin stepped from the Maricopa County Superior Court complex into the searing September heat. He wondered whether the drunk lawyer was conscious, and how he'd take the loss. From where he was standing, Devlin looked across the street to glowing red neon: *AAA Bail Bonds.* He smiled. First in the phone book and ready to serve. Like all young upstarts, Devlin knew that every criminal case logged into the system required a preliminary hearing, and preliminary hearings required lawyers. Get in with the right bail bondsman—bingo, a steady stream of bread-and-butter billings. There were other ways to get referrals, but the bulk came by way of the bail bondsmen, the gatekeepers as the accused's first point of contact. Devlin studied the neon sign as his plan began to formulate: He wouldn't trample through the front door of AAA Bail Bonds with the herd of frothing lawyers. Instead, he'd ask around and see who was running the show at AAA Bail Bonds. Then he'd find a way to make his entrance memorable.

"Hey kid."

Devlin turned to see the prosecution lawyer who'd just decimated the greenhorn's first attempt at practicing law. Without breaking stride, and with an underling in tow, the victor smiled and said, "Preparation is not a punch line; it's a way of life." Then he laughed and, as if on cue, the young associate laughed, too.

Devlin could only shake his head. For now, he had his bar number and case #1 in the books. He might be 0-1, but he was also on the map as an official lawyer, a free-wheeling raconteur, an East Coast transplant in Barry Goldwater Land. *Perfect*, he thought. He laughed to himself and felt a surge of energy.

They'd see the Irish kid in court again.

GAMBLING, the 76-year-old widow Ann Pearson liked to tell her friends at the dog track, was God's way of giving old women a good time. Ten years ago, in 1965, when cancer cut down Ann's husband Charlie, she stumbled upon dog racing as an unlikely escape for her bottomless grief. Of course, her foundation had always been, and would continue to be, her daughter Kay and her Catholic faith. For Ann, these meant a twin ritual.

Every morning at six, the phone rang and Ann answered with, "Good morning, dear." On the other end was her only child, a university librarian who adored her parents. After her father's death, Kay began this daily tradition as a way to keep tabs on her mother's well-being. Gradually, these chats became comforting to mother and daughter alike.

Then, after hanging up, Ann dressed for church and ventured onto Phoenix's six-lane boulevards in her white Plymouth Valiant. Destination: the chapel across the street from the university library where Kay worked. Ann had two bumper stickers that the desert sun had nearly rendered illegible: "*Today is a gift—That's why we call it the Present.*" And: "*I might be slow, but I'm ahead of you.*"

Ann Pearson didn't march lockstep with everything the church professed, but she loved the comfort, peace, and meditative quality of that hour each morning. She sat in the front pew and was first in line for Communion. After, she'd linger and talk to friends. While her church routine helped after Charlie's death, she still needed something to fill the long, empty days.

Gambling with her Social Security check, it turned out, was not only tolerated by the management at Desert Gardens Senior Living, but openly encouraged, endorsed, and even facilitated with daily noon-departure bus trips. Like loitering hordes of teenagers, the aged needed places to congregate where they weren't in the way of productive, wage-earning adults. One such location was the Royal Palms Kennel Club, a cavernous and sagging facility near downtown Phoenix. For Ann Pearson, the gambling trips began simply as something on the daily calendar, a diversion to occupy wide blocks of time.

On this day, March 19, 1975, another balmy afternoon in Phoenix, Ann Pearson was three races into the matinee schedule when—although she had promised herself she would spread the action in hopes of playing all week and through the weekend—she couldn't resist going in heavy.

CC's Colorado Can-Do.

Three minutes to post.

He was a young pup and a 40-to-1 long shot that no one appeared to be on to except Ann Pearson—courtesy of a tip from the dog's owner. There were only a few others lucky enough to be in this hallowed of innermost circles within the dog-racing fraternity. This dog was, Ann thought, as sure as these things get.

She had been working the program around this race for days. So when she stepped to the window, she pushed across a good chunk of what used to be her Social Security check to box-and-wheel CC's Colorado Can-Do every way she could. Just thinking about the trifecta payout—she was guessing $2,000-plus—made her heart race. On a good weekend run she could double or triple her meager government dole. When the picks ran cold, she still showed up for the comforting routine, laughter among friends, the bus ride back and forth, and staying up on the various dramas in the lives of the track waitresses, janitors, and ticket-takers. If there was one venue in greater Phoenix that promised human drama, in all its comedic and tragic forms, it was the Royal Palms Kennel Club. The place was daily Shakespeare, performed for $2 a bet: *Friends, Romans, countrymen, lend me your ears; we have a photo finish.*

Once she had her betting slips in hand, Ann quickly tucked them in her black purse that was big enough to hold two watermelons. Per her own longtime ritual, she would not look at the tickets again until the race ended. Avoiding the usual area where her friends gathered—One-Armed Lucky and Vera were here today—she retreated to a table near a monitor. This was another rule: she never watched the race live through the large, smeared windows; she preferred the inside monitors, by the betting windows, that eliminated the long walk to the seating area.

Two minutes to post.

She wiped her palms on her stretch polyester pants. The first pain flashed through her chest, barely perceptible, a piercing twinge so brief she didn't break her gaze locked on the monitor.

One minute to post.

The next pain was deeper and drew a hand to her chest. *That didn't feel right*, she thought.

Post time.

Betting windows closed. As the tightness subsided, she glanced at the board and saw that no one was on to her pup. All the money was on the favorite, Pop's Big Red Suburban, which watered the payout on that dog down to twenty cents on the dollar. Ann smiled at her good fortune. She watched the grainy video image as the handlers pushed the muscled, 80-pound greyhounds into steel boxes. CC's Colorado Can-Do drew box eight, which gave the dog an uncluttered line into turn one. Ann was predicting a box-to-wire lap, a ten-length crushing. The trifecta might even top $3,000!

"Here… comes… Dynamo!" came over the loudspeaker in a static blare, Dynamo being the motorized approximation of a rabbit that always bobbed just beyond reach of the exuberant dogs. Ann leaned forward and stared at box eight, her mind still distracted by the tightness in her chest.

"Get the break, get the break," she repeated aloud, her index finger and thumb rubbing rosary beads. As Dynamo whirred through turn four, the metal gate snapped opened and eight muzzled greyhounds burst forth, digging hard, a flurry of dirt roiling behind the tight pack as the dogs raced at thirty-five miles per hour down the front stretch.

"Yes!" Ann yelled as CC's Colorado Can-Do broke clean and drew a bead to the inside just as Ann had mapped days ago. Going into the dangerous turn one—where speeding dogs often bumped and rolled each other right out of contention—CC's Colorado Can-Do was in perfect position, tight on the rail, and already had clawed out one length on the pack. Ann's genius, it seemed in that instant, was forever solidified and would soon unleash its full bounty. Her legend among the eclectic clutch of dog-racing regulars would only grow.

But Ann Pearson did not see any more of that race. She didn't see that her long shot of long shots faded severely on the backstretch, dropped to mid-pack, got pinched hard on turn three, and ran wide to the wall. She didn't see that CC's Colorado Can-Do finished dead last, some twelve lengths back. She couldn't have known any of that, because the third wave of pain put her on the floor and rendered her unconscious.

Part I

The Lawyer

Chapter One

AT THE SAME MOMENT ANN PEARSON was leaving the Royal Palms Kennel Club in an ambulance, Connor J. Devlin loosened his tie and walked across Madison Street. In Maricopa County, justice was meted out in this fifteen-square-block area of downtown Phoenix. From Washington Street to Jackson Street, and east to west from First Avenue to Seventh Avenue, every building existed solely for the purpose of processing and documenting the machinations of law. Devlin had just spent a long day hustling among various courtrooms, shuffling paperwork, representing clients chained at the wrists and ankles, and now he had a bead on the red neon glow that he'd first seen five years ago: AAA Bail Bonds.

There were bail bond offices all over downtown Phoenix, coming and going in the desert like ambling coyotes, but only AAA Bail Bonds had One-Armed Lucky as proprietor, permanent fixture, and undisputed kingpin in springing the accused. Not only did One-Armed Lucky know every prosecutor, defense attorney, and judge, he had the scoop on street urchins and sleazebags, dirty cops and straight-up solid detectives, hopheads and dealers, pimps and whores, snitches, bailiffs, court clerks, newspaper reporters, paralegals, judges' secretaries, judges' secretaries' lovers, and the administrative staff down to the hair-nets scrubbing lunch plates in the court complex cafeteria. Anyone wanting to touch the pulse of crime and punishment in greater Maricopa County came through the doors at AAA Bail Bonds and therein sought the sage counsel of

One-Armed Lucky, aptly named for the limb he left in a Vietnamese jungle. The oracle, however, was also suspicious by nature and selective in dishing his street buzz, and, although many tried, few lawyers made the cut for Lucky's coveted client referrals.

So after starting 0-1, the initiate had simply observed from afar for a few weeks. Devlin watched how on Friday afternoons, sometime after five, One-Armed Lucky dragged a wooden stool outside, set up his little radio, leaned against the brick wall of AAA Bail Bonds, and pulled a cold bottle from a white five-gallon bucket of ice. Sometimes he sat there and drank alone; other times various acquaintances, friends, and random interlopers joined him. However, after watching this regularity for a month, Devlin had never noticed a single suited lawyer amid these clutches—there was his back door. Six weeks after first seeing flickering red neon, Devlin wheeled an obvious U-turn at AAA Bail Bonds and parked the gleaming black Lincoln Mark III in full view of the social circle.

Cold bottle in hand, One-Armed Lucky was already assessing the tall kid in the suit climbing from the shiny ride as Led Zeppelin's "Whole Lotta Love" thumped from the radio at Lucky's feet. For most lawyers, bail bond offices were hit-and-run, résumé-building stops on the way to more worthy legal pursuits. Few wanted to make a career of languishing with One-Armed Lucky types and the lifetime lackeys they bonded out. Lucky took offense at this snobbery and, accordingly, shunned lawyers almost without exception.

So the first thing One-Armed Lucky noticed was, unlike all the other bookworms who came sniffing around in their expensive suits, this one had a different air. Subtle, but hey, it was there. The suit was as hip as any One-Armed Lucky had seen, and that ride: straight-up fat city. But it went deeper, something about this cat: The kid moved with a street sensibility Lucky could have smelled three blocks from here, something he rarely saw in lawyers who existed in the rarified spheres of academia, unrealistic theoretical stances, and silver-spoon-in-ass aristocracy. This kid, though, had some gutter time under his belt before he got packed off to some fancy law school. And when Lucky extended his left hand, his only hand, Devlin deftly reciprocated with his own left, thereby avoiding the awkward, left-right twisted mess of a handshake that normally ensued. Sure, the kid needed some track time. But a little polish, Lucky decided right then, and there was Earl-the-Pearl potential all over this one.

"Nice to finally meet a Big-Time Lawyer," he said. "Don't see too many of you come through this way. And nice ride, Big-Time." And from that first meeting, One-Armed Lucky never referred to the lawyer by anything other than that nickname.

Lucky offered a cold one. Devlin flipped a plastic milk crate and sat across from Lucky. Lucky was older than Devlin by almost ten years, but looked much older with his thinning hair already speckled gray. The hard life and a war had beat Lucky down and left deep tracks in his face. As they jawed for two hours that first night, it transported Devlin to his youth: the pungent denizens, the excitement and rebellion in the bowels of Buffalo's icy downtown streets. At sleazy strip clubs like The Stage Door, One-Armed Lucky might have been a regular with his hardscrabble tales straight off the pages of the Mickey Spillane potboilers Devlin loved to read as a teenager. Sitting there against the dirty brick wall with the one-armed bandit, Devlin felt the comfort of going home.

Lucky asked a lot about Buffalo. Devlin said he lived on a street like everyone else: two-story houses stacked in tight rows, attic and a basement, backyards barely big enough to hang the laundry. He told Lucky about his old man, the first Connor J. Devlin, a looming figure in both stature and fear potential at six-foot-three and 250 pounds. The bail bondsman and the lawyer mused about both having fathers who never saw the ninth-grade. Devlin's came over on the boat, ran booze with Joe Kennedy, and married a Jewish woman, making Devlin officially Catholic and, unofficially, Jewish. Lucky's patriarch never got near a boat, ran dope with Bobby Goodspeed, and married a white Christian woman, making Lucky officially Negro and, unofficially, Negro.

Devlin's old man eventually parlayed the bootlegging proceeds into a legitimate and profitable chain of grocery stores across the Northeast. Then his father launched into the stratosphere of local Buffalo celebrity by helping the city land its beloved Bills football team in 1959. The boy Devlin rubbed shoulders with George Halas and ate dinner with a long list of gridiron legends. Lucky had nodded, then pointed his bottle at the young lawyer he'd known less than an hour. "You still trying to get out from behind your old man's big shadow."

From there, the Friday twilight confab evolved into a weekly practice. In turn, it wasn't long before One-Armed Lucky put Devlin on the coveted referral list for AAA's clients. With no county or state grand jury system, each criminal case went before a justice of the peace to determine initial probable cause. And each of those preliminary hearings required people like Devlin. Thanks to One-Armed Lucky, the kid was on the map.

Devlin's first official job was with Grant & Ross, a low-key operation consisting of the two namesake partners and an office manager named Nadia Flores. In actuality, the duo didn't so much hire Devlin as rent him space in their cramped office on Central Avenue. Although they allowed him to add a nameplate to the firm's door, the large chunk of oak between their names and "Connor J. Devlin" left no doubt as to the corresponding hierarchy of the partners and the upstart. In size, general ambience and vague odor, Devlin's office might easily be confused with the janitor's closet. There was a battered, gray steel desk, which looked like a retired battleship that had seen one too many tours of duty, and two mismatched bookcases filled with outdated statute books. No window. No secretary. Not even enough room to bring in a client (Devlin himself could barely squeeze around to sit behind his own desk). And Devlin would never determine the source of, nor be able to scrub clean, the smell that landed somewhere between dirty socks and week-old Chinese takeout. But the gig was a start, one that required Devlin to hustle up all his own clients. For $100 he'd do traffic tickets. Wills and divorces: $20 a pop.

Then one Friday while waiting for Lucky to finish processing a bond, Devlin crossed paths with Trevor Walsh, a hot-shot Maricopa County prosecutor everyone in the legal arena knew by name because of his savant-like prowess. When Walsh wasn't pulverizing defense strategies and the unsavory clients behind them, he was drinking, fucking, and parlaying (usually in that order, and, at certain synchronous zeniths, all three simultaneously). Walsh's legend around town ran the gamut from Herculean booze binges to rampant sexual conquests and five-figure gambling swings. But somehow the addictive insanity never dampened Walsh's prosecutorial zeal and ability: He'd already tried and won twenty-two murder cases by the time he was 30. A mark of 22-0 was three careers for most prosecutors. Because the mere mention of Walsh deflated defense attorneys before they'd even opened a client's file, everyone—his overlords and peers at the county attorney's office, and even judges—gave Walsh a reluctant free pass on his other meanderings. Some reasoned that Walsh drank and chased women like an aberrant hyena as the only way to level out all the splatter, spaghetti photos, and twisted gore he'd digested into his persona. Others said Walsh was born crazy and canned criminals because it was just malicious fun, a grown-up version of ripping legs off live grasshoppers. Either way, everyone gave Walsh astral marks as a lawyer and a wide berth in every other arena.

But from the first moment, Devlin's own blue-collar DNA somehow clicked with this fascinating rogue. Devlin came of age under a steady drumbeat of paternalistic terror—of God, his father, and the priests (normally in that order but subject to change depending on the hour or the day)—and the immigrant-Irish mantra that success only came through service to others and an unrelenting work ethic. Crazy as he was, Walsh seemed to have that same driving core and ravenous dedication to the greater good. He and Devlin shook hands at AAA Bail Bonds as Devlin shared his quick bio, the sum total of which was a shiny new degree from USC law school. Devlin didn't mention what one of his law professors had said about the first paper he wrote—*The worst piece of dribble ever penned by a law student purportedly fluent in the English language*—or that he'd graduated in the lower third of the small class of thirty-five. Nor did he mention the disastrous start to his legal career.

"Welcome to the real world, kid," Walsh said, thirty-five and ten years older than Devlin. "Out here it's all meatball justice. And just like there's no such thing as algebra in the real world—trust me, you'll never see another fucking polynomial as long as you live—there's no such thing as nuance and strategy in this type of law." Walsh paused. "Factoring polynomials. Remember that shit?"

Devlin nodded and laughed. There was a palpable energy around Walsh, like some exposed live wire that might spark an explosion in the next moment. The crackling energy Walsh emanated was intriguing and infectious.

"What the fuck is a polynomial anyway? And why do we care? That would be my first executive order as president: no more polynomials. Just line them all up and let every kid ever tortured by that lunacy take a crack with a baseball bat." Walsh grunted some deep laughs. "What the hell was I saying?"

"Nuance. Strategy."

"Right. Think of it this way," Walsh said, smiling. "Nuance and Strategy are like two German whores after a long night of drinking beer: They might look good, but you'll regret it if you start in with those two. You dig?"

Devlin dug and nodded, but Walsh wasn't done.

"Forget nuance and strategy, kid, and forget the truth, too. 'Truth' is their foxy cousin: just another whore with better make-up, but don't be fooled; she has crabs, too. I don't care which side you're on, grinding down these perps doesn't have anything to do with what they teach at law school. Your job, on the defense side, two words: Reasonable Doubt. I don't care if the other side has a color photograph of your client and ten witnesses with 20/20 vision to corroborate. All you should be looking for as you enter that courtroom is your best friend, and his name is Mr. Reasonable Doubt. He's there waiting in every case if you look hard enough."

Devlin had never heard it put that way in law school, or any time since.

"And while you're at it, kid, you can start wrapping fish with pages from your *Law Ethics 101* book, because there is no such thing in the real world. I'm not talking about disbarment stuff, but look, there's the way it is out here, and then there's the way it is out here. You get my drift? One more thing, kid; just make sure you're never surprised in court. Surprise is death."

Months later, Walsh pushed his boss too hard on some issue and snapped the tenuous look-the-other-way thread that had saved him a thousand times before. Just like that, the untouchable and still-undefeated prosecutor had been summarily canned. A week later he called Devlin, whom he'd seen around court and taken to lunch a few times, with the unlikely scenario of hanging a shingle together. Devlin was flattered and, equally, terrified. But other than giving him the malodorous office space, Grant & Ross were doing little to guide the young lawyer. Of course, while Walsh's undeniable powers in the courtroom would be a rare tutelage, the senior lawyer's volatility and raw proclivities might likely attach a guilt-by-association cloud to the unknown Devlin. But then again, if Walsh could hold it together 9-to-5 without spinning out of orbit, he would be an unequaled mentor. Walsh & Devlin was in business.

Devlin moved out of his janitor closet and into an office with a window. Because of his storied prosecutorial career, Walsh suggested billing Walsh & Devlin as criminal defense. Working the other side all these years, Walsh knew what made scumbags and perverts tick, and the dirty thoughts they conjured while you were sleeping. He knew every sleazy lawyer sleight-of-hand and snake-oil trick ever played. A further incentive in switching sides, for Walsh, was the chance to go head-to-head with the meatball clods—his words—who had fired him.

Trailing Walsh those first days and weeks in court was a rude wake-up call. Unlike what happened on *Perry Mason*, the life of a lawyer and the justice treadmill did not revolve around a single, dramatic trial. Concurrent to whatever big trials were underway, each judge had a daily docket of fresh defendants making their initial appearance within twenty-four hours of arrest as required by law. By 8:45 a.m. outside the central court building, there was a line fifty people deep waiting for the building to open. Devlin and Walsh were there among a disproportionate number of women—the mothers, wives, sisters, aunts, and girlfriends whose men were now in the system. Also clustered about were the attorneys from up and down the legal hierarchy, PAs and public defenders and high-dollar lawyers from firms big and small, all of them waiting with over-stuffed case bags and file boxes at their feet. It was not glamorous, but gritty and rife with unspoken anxiety.

Meanwhile, hours earlier at 2 a.m., guards had roused the defendants on that day's docket and transferred them from jail to holding cells at the courthouse. They were individually handcuffed and chained to each other at the ankles and collectively shuffled into the courtroom in an awkward bouncing motion. Thanks to sleep deprivation, by 10 a.m., seated in the jury box in striped pajamas, the defendants were sallow and looked heavily medicated. As a group, they were nameless, numbered, and dubbed "the morning chain." They were also the prospect pool from which Walsh & Devlin would draw new clients and, hopefully, a robust revenue stream.

A single judge and staff may process more than 1,000 such defendants through one courtroom in a year, so the morning chain was a hectic, revolving-door mishmash that at first unnerved Devlin. In every courtroom, he and Walsh swept in with all the other lawyers and stood at the back, milled about, gossiped, studied thick files, read case papers in the gallery, told bad jokes, and whispered to clients. The lucky few defendants had hired lawyers like Walsh and Devlin, but most had a public defender who was juggling thirty-five, forty, fifty cases at once. The chances of winning at trial for these indigent and accused, with a lawyer who barely knew the defendant's name and only the basic facts of the case, were almost nonexistent. The full power of legal training and educated counsel for these clients usually began and ended with "Take the plea."

In those early days, another oddity that struck Devlin was the scale and bare aesthetics of most courtrooms. Again, his brilliant law school visions had been recast in dour undertones. Everything—the height of the judge's bench, the witness stand, the jury box and gallery—was much smaller than he'd envisioned. The cramped courtrooms were windowless and cast not with long shafts of rich sunlight, but rather a fluorescent, yellow pallor delivered from tubes with a grating buzz. Additionally, the walls and jury box were covered not with venerable, aged cherry or masculine, well-oiled dark oak, but government-issue, plastic wood laminate with an obscene sheen never seen in nature. The gallery, too, from which the public was free to observe the USA's open system of justice, amounted to only three rows that might hold thirty people squeezed uncomfortably. It was into these sterile venues that Walsh and Devlin ventured each morning, sometimes only getting a client's file as they walked into the courtroom.

Frustrating, too, was the compressed time allotted each case. Devlin usually glanced through the file for the basic facts minutes before speaking to the judge. Never once did he have the luxury of actually studying a case, ferreting out its nuances, and then developing a strategy the way they had done in law school. Just like Walsh had said about the two German prostitutes: forget it. Devlin often had the nauseating sense of trying to put together a 500-piece jigsaw puzzle on a roller coaster before the ride ended. Then, finished or not, the judge was already making rulings and scheduling hearings. Five minutes later the train left again, and Devlin had a new puzzle, his stomach in knots as the cars ratcheted skyward. He rode those trains all day, five days a week, and by Friday night the puzzle pieces, whiplash turns, and unfinished images all blurred together into a patchwork of fatigue, frustration, and, increasingly, victory.

Gradually, Devlin fell in step with the pace and short-handed vernacular of the morning chain. Beneath the swirling chaos and confusing staccato, he started to see a steady thread of order. From sheer necessity, one of the first things he developed was rhythm, the subtle foundation upon which he started building effective cross-examinations. As defense lawyers, Walsh and Devlin had the legal luxury of not having to prove a single fact. All they had to do was attack the prosecutor's witnesses effectively and open the door for Walsh's old pal Mr. Reasonable Doubt.

At first Devlin's questions were too winding and complicated. Walsh assailed him: *Only ask questions that a witness could understand and answer while he's lighting a coffin nail and watching a ball game. Drinking a beer and eating a burger. Banging the old lady and handicapping a dog race.* Any question too complicated to answer while otherwise occupied was a waste of time. From there, Devlin found rhythm by learning to alter the volume and tenor of his voice. The rate of speech. The order and wording of questions. The ease, fluidity, and variations of physical movement between glancing at his notes, asking questions, listening to responses, picking up exhibits, and looking toward the judge, gallery, and jury.

A pause for effect.

A good rhythmic cross flowed with a simple ease between counselor and witness.

Devlin learned, too, to keep his own clients off the stand. Rare were the defendants who could bolster their own cases. Yet every single one of them begged Devlin for that chance. Defendants were bursting to tell their side and shine the glorious light of truth on their case. To trumpet their innocence. To reveal the real version of the blatant lies put forth by crooked cops. To expose the obvious frame-up to the judge, jury, and the world beyond the courtroom doors. To sweep aside the suffocating legal posturing and simply proclaim, "I didn't do it!" But that very eagerness was the reason Walsh and Devlin kept their clients parked at the defense table, mouths ball-gagged and duct-taped.

Nonetheless, there were those rare times when it was unavoidable. Prior to those instances, usually in whispers at the defense table, Devlin distilled his witness preparation down to its bare-bones essence: *Being on the witness stand is not a conversation. Listen to the question, answer it, and stop talking (Walsh's words: shut your dirty hole). Don't offer follow-up or any clarification. If you don't understand a question, say so. If you can't remember something, say so. If you need a drink of water, say so. If you get confused or don't know what to say, just say, "I can't recall."*

Trevor Walsh was the unlikely mentor who had crafted the young talent into a capable pro. And rounding out the unlikely twin tutelage was the kingpin himself down at AAA Bail Bonds.

"SO this broad you been seeing," One-Armed Lucky said, offering Devlin a cold can of Olympia. "Big-Time's holding out on me. How many years I been knowing you? So she's a fox? Bonanza Brothers tell me you're rock solid with a *Playboy* Playmate, huh?"

Devlin nodded, took a slug of frosty beer, and let the bubbles tickle the back of his throat. "Not technically."

The Bonanza Brothers owned AAA Bail Bonds. Even though the two Mexicans had zero resemblance to Dan Blocker or Michael Landon, they were brothers, and "Hoss" was fat and always wore a white cowboy hat; his lean brother translated easily to "Little Joe."

"Now what do you mean? Either she is, straight up, or she ain't. You can't out-lawyer me on this one, Big-Time."

"Come on," Devlin said, "you know I don't kiss and tell."

What he had with Jessica Jean was schoolboy-fantasy stuff, and worthy of the most lurid and graphic shop talk. But Catholic guilt never died. Devlin was neither married nor was he intending nuptials. Sure, he was between the sheets with a *Playboy* bunny on Saturday night like 007, but, unlike Bond, he'd be at mass on Sunday to balance the ledger. Any gloating or locker-room banter could only tip things the wrong way. To a twenty-something from a blue-collar blip on the map, Jessica Jean was a VIP pass into Hugh Hefner's odd subculture, a mixed bag of contrived exclusivity, cheesy dinner jackets, and deep cleavage. And therein were the straight C-listers from all walks, the ones who had never fully peaked and didn't yet realize they were already slipping further down the it-factor hierarchy.

"Come on now, Big-Time. We got roots we been putting down here a long time. Give me more than that."

"OK, yes, she's a bunny, but not a Playmate."

"What you mean, Big-Time?"

"Well at the Playboy Club, right, the waitresses wear the satin ears and… you know." One-Armed Lucky didn't need a color chart. "Those are the bunnies. The Playmates are the ones in the magazine."

"So basically," Lucky surmised, "it's like baseball."

"Objection. Relevance?"

"Baseball. You got all them bunnies working in those clubs, you know like single-A, double-A ball, and then all that feeds into the majors. All those bunnies working for nothing wages and then bam, they get their shot at the money and fame of being a Playmate."

Devlin loved the banter and the way Lucky's mind processed the abstract, his thinking never constrained by the boundaries and conventions of educated lawyers. Few Harvard Law superstars could draw the same dotted lines as Lucky.

"Never saw it that way, but OK."

"But what we on about, counselor? Bunny, Playmate. Broad's a straight-up deuce, right?"

"You would be correct there," Devlin said.

Lucky lingered in his boobs-and-hairspray fantasy and then, "Hallelujah, brother."

They both laughed and tapped their beers, their Friday night equivalent of an affirming hug. They were both good in their own skin, and let the silence hang there and then extend into a long pause. Silence. Beautiful, powerful silence. Devlin had learned quickly that no technique elicited information better than the unbearable vortex of protracted nothingness. In court. On the witness stand. With other lawyers. Even in bed with women. Just shut up, and all the secrets started pouring forth. Worked every time. But here, the gaps elicited no such gnawing urges to babble.

Instead, time here became the perfect triumvirate for Devlin. First, the talks decompressed things for Devlin, from juggling his caseload in court all week to keeping tabs on Walsh's whereabouts. Second, Friday nights were Devlin's weekly jolt back to Buffalo, his access point to the street-savvy outcasts, hairy-knuckled drunks and lunch pail clock punchers, the huddled masses yearning to plead. But third and best of all, the weekly enclave was pure ritual. To a Catholic—practicing, non-practicing, skeptic, or believer—nothing soothed more than ritual. Friday nights at AAA Bail Bonds didn't replace Mass, but always felt equally sacred.

Some weeks Devlin might arrive and see fifteen guys, all blacks, gathered around the bucket. As he took a cold can or bottle, whatever might be on sale that week, Devlin always pressed a $20 bill, left hand to left hand, into One-Armed Lucky's palm. It was their unspoken agreement. Devlin never suggested that One-Armed Lucky go buy beer. One-Armed Lucky never asked to be reimbursed for the beer, nor did he ever feign resistance or thank Devlin for the money. The cold beer and money just changed hands, a fluid and flawless element of the ritual, and then they sat and talked. While his legal peers—court reporters, clerks, judges, lawyers, and administrators—were all clogged in traffic and racing to get home to their weekend suburban bubbles, Devlin leaned against the brick wall at AAA Bail Bonds, content, savoring his real-world course on human nature. One-Armed Lucky, it turned out, was a one-man litmus test and focus group.

Although he barely finished high school, Lucky had a razor sense of which way a case might go given the facts. Devlin would run through his docket and give updates from the previous week on the fate of the real-life characters and their respective dramas unfolding in court. And One-Armed Lucky took it all in like a Broadway theater critic who'd then deliver his review verbally: always direct, honest, and amazingly accurate.

It was dark now in the slot between the two buildings where they sat. "Me and Julio Down by the Schoolyard" by Paul Simon was playing on Lucky's battered and paint-splattered radio beneath his stool. Devlin sat opposite on a plastic bucket, his back to the eclectic next-door restaurant that served everything from black-eyed peas and collard greens to tacos and beef stroganoff. There was light coming from the twenty-foot opening to the street, and there was a steady, white-noise hum from rush hour.

"You believe in God, Lucky?"

"Depends what you mean God. Old white man with a beard throwing lightning bolts and helping ballplayers hit home runs?" Lucky shook his head. "That ain't my God."

Devlin laughed.

"Why you bringing God into it anyway?" Lucky asked.

"I'm just saying, if God can forgive every last lowlife we try to help, well... I don't know. Maybe people *can* change." Devlin paused and stared at his bottle. He drank little, other than nursing a single beer each Friday night.

"I know what you saying, Big-Time, but really change? I ain't seen it much the people be coming through here." It was dark now, a rare chill in the desert air.

"Yeah, you've bonded out a long line of petulant little trolls."

"Now you know I ain't know that word, but I get your drift, Big-Time."

They watched a dirty cat meander through the space between the buildings, stare at them briefly, and then shuffle around the corner.

"But check this out, Big-Time, I think I might have another one for you. You been crying about wanting more personal injury stuff, right, getting out of this game because you're too good for us lowlifes?"

Devlin laughed. "Well, now that you put it like that."

Indeed, the clock on Walsh and the criminal grind had expired. Weeks had turned into months, and months into years. From drug raps to kidnapping and even a few armed robbery and murder cases, the stench of criminality was growing around Devlin like a diseased second skin. He spent his days in and around clattering jails listening to tired excuses, lame-brained rationalizations, and ridiculous lies. Like Walsh always said, no one, not even cops or lawyers, lied as much as criminal defendants. And, Walsh laughed, defendants weren't nearly as good at it as cops and lawyers.

Devlin began seeing how Walsh, once a good Mormon, had found the hard edge out of necessity. In that same way, in the rare spare moment when he had time to consider such things, Devlin knew the constant criminality would eventually blunt his own natural sense of empathy. Working in Walsh's world had been a beneficial baptism by fire, but the lofty ideals Devlin had conjured in law school—amending the pain of society's marginalized outcasts—had been muddied and given way to this revolving-door hustle of trying to beat the rap. Again, Walsh nailed it: meatball justice. Five years in, Devlin had the *Playboy* bunny girlfriend and the growing respect of his mentor and peers, but his fledgling legal career was, at best, skidding sideways.

"Well, some time back I bonded out this guy name of Dubrow. Pretty much a dead-ender, nothing violent, just drug charges stacked up on him until it was time—you know how that goes—pin the tail on the donkey. Forget his first name. He eventually did his stint and been out now awhile. Anyway, his brother Rick called the other day asking if I knew any good lawyers. Something about his mom getting herself killed in a car accident and maybe there was a case there with the car was bad or something."

"And?" Devlin said, playing into it.

"Yeah, told him I only know one dead-ender can barely find his own ass in the morning. But a good lawyer? Hell no."

Devlin smiled and stood. "Go get the phone number, you one-armed freak, and stop wasting my valuable lawyer time. By the way, don't you have something better to do on a Friday night than sitting here with a wannabe in a suit?"

"Oh me? Hell yeah," Lucky said, standing. "Heading to the track tonight to meet up with my friend. She been there all day working the program. Damn if she don't know those dogs cold."

"Yeah, you mentioned her before. You've been friends for what, years now, right? What's her name again?"

"Annie. Or Ann."

"That's right," Devlin said, his memory kicking in at the mention of her name. "Ann Pearson."

Chapter Two

THERE WERE CERTAIN CLIENTS that walked through the door with an intangible, white-light, jury-appeal halo shimmering above their heads. One look, and a good lawyer knew those clients would instantaneously trigger the magic word—*settlement*—from across the aisle. Then there were those potential clients so utterly unlikable, or with character defects or criminal records so damning, that a savvy lawyer would not run the risk of parading them before a jury. Since the early debacle, Devlin's ability to assess potential clients had improved immensely. And like most clients, the two people seated before him, at first glance, didn't seem to fall into either of these two extremes.

Within minutes of meeting Rick and Lucy Dubrow, a brother and sister, they were landing somewhere just south of the middle. Sure, Devlin would have to work a little to polish some rough edges and present them in the best possible light, but they probably wouldn't be a liability, either. Without knowing much else about the people in front of him, these first impressions were usually remarkably accurate, because those in the jury box made similar unconscious, and immediate, intuitive judgments. Devlin had learned that in most cases, a juror's initial, gut reaction to a defendant would match that juror's final vote in deliberations.

Through all his work with a wide and colorful cross-section of clients—One-Armed Lucky's troubled masses, wary cops, and run-of-the-mill folks befallen by everything from dog bites to niggling red-light/green-light bumps and bruises—Devlin had refined his ability to present himself to prospective clients. It was one of those areas that received only cursory mention in law school but was, perhaps, one of the most critical in building a real practice. With eight billion lawyers in the naked city, there was enormous competition to pull in great cases. The world's most brilliant lawyer, without good clients and great cases, Walsh had once said, was like King Kong without an Empire State Building: no legacy.

Especially now, as he drummed up more personal injury cases, Devlin fully grasped the importance of the first visit, even the first moments, with a client. Far from the meat grinder of Walsh's world, Devlin enjoyed one simple luxury with these cases: the time and space to simply sit, listen, and ask good questions. This wasn't the time to throw around his résumé, which was heavy with defense work and light on plaintiff cases anyway. Nor was it the time to bring up contingency fee agreements or to start calculating 1/3 of a settlement. Long before any of that, he needed to understand the client situation, their condition, and any immediate needs.

A case, at its core, was just a problem that needed to be solved. No sense in getting caught up in conjuring exotic flavors of icing if he didn't have a decent cake. This was the time, he'd learned, to summon all his personality, experience, and empathy to exude a professional and calming presence. If at all possible, he liked to first meet clients here, at his office, which he'd furnished and decorated to be a citadel of common denominators. Every client he met could look around the room and find at least one object of interest, curiosity, or commonality.

There were framed photos: the Hawaiian Champ flanked by two would-be promoters, a boxing experiment gone bad when he and Walsh tried to let this kid Dallas Klotz box his way to $5,000 in legal fees. (They never saw dime one.)

Devlin and his father with George Halas.

Devlin as physical specimen, 210 pounds of rippled fury, in his own Notre Dame boxing days.

A Super Duty TransAm and the second addition to his car collection (now totaling three with his daily driver): a 1962 Chevy 409 two-door coupe.

An old black-and-white of Devlin with his cousin Andrew Goodman just before Goodman left for Mississippi, eleven years ago, where he was murdered along with two other civil rights workers in the big case that drew national attention.

There were also newspaper clippings: As Eugene McCarthy spoke during the Notre Dame commencement, a photographer took a front-page photo of Devlin reading a newspaper while everyone around him sat riveted to McCarthy's words. There was a signed football from the great American hero O.J. Simpson, who'd dined several times at the Devlin family table.

The other thing Devlin had learned is that clients, just like Walsh said, lie like everyone else up and down the legal system. Usually unintentionally, but sometimes not, they embellish, skip things, or just don't know the true facts of their own case. Devlin always signed up new clients with the unspoken caveat that he'd need to confirm their concerns, suspicions, and facts as true before proceeding. Anyone could walk into his office and spin a great tale; corroborating and proving that tale in court was another matter entirely.

After getting the number from Lucky on Friday and an initial phone consultation yesterday, Devlin had scheduled this meeting with Rick Dubrow, 37, a welder, and his younger sister Lucy, who worked as a secretary at the power company. Their older brother Bob, the one Lucky had bonded out some time ago, would not be able to attend the meeting but would be the third named plaintiff in any action filed. Devlin's office was at the back of the building and large enough that it doubled as his conference room, with a small, oak table by the window. Rick and Lucy, neither educated beyond high school, were soft-spoken, deferential, and courteous. As they talked Devlin continued his silent, and now-automatic, jury-appeal assessment. Couldn't say absolutely yet, but so far, so good.

"I know this is a difficult time with the loss of your mother," Devlin said, "and I want to extend my deepest sympathies to you."

"Thank you," Lucy said. "We been to two other lawyers, but they didn't really seem too interested in what we got to say."

"But they was different from this one here," Rick said, sitting cross-armed, an odd third-person choice of words. Back to jury appeal, the heart and soul of any plaintiff's case: Devlin saw a good chance to do some light probing, open-ended, see how Rick handled himself. Devlin nodded. "You say they were different. How so?"

"They was big fancy lawyers. Nose in the air. Too good for us even though we ain't country or nothing like that. Hell, we as city as they come, but they still looked at us like we was dumber than a bucket of dead monkeys."

For that very reason, Devlin was careful to always park his ride behind the building, well out of sight. No need to risk rubbing people the wrong way, especially at the outset. Thanks to a run of good billings, he'd traded in the rolling luxury of the Lincoln for the high-speed precision of a brand-new 1975 ice-blue Porsche 930. Zero to sixty in under four seconds, it was a limited-production European model. For a plaintiff's lawyer, the effective timing and use of ego and flash was simply another tool in the practice of law. Meeting prospective clients was usually not the time for wielding that particular tool. "And you don't see me that way?"

"Nah," Rick said, shaking his head.

"What do you see that's different, Rick?"

"I dunno, really. Just that feeling you get when you meet someone. Either you is or you isn't, and you isn't."

"What he's trying to say is you treat us like we ain't worthless just because we don't got money and fancy college degrees like you," Lucy said.

"Fair enough. And understand that whether a certain lawyer takes your case or doesn't take your case is nothing against you. What I think is a great case might be very different from what another lawyer thinks is a great case. Don't take it personally."

"Hell no we don't," Rick said. "But the day is young, so you still got plenty of time to jack things up from here to Yuma and back."

The needle on the likability meter wasn't necessarily plummeting, but it certainly wasn't peaking to the warm-and-fuzzy side, either. While Rick Dubrow would never be mistaken for an international diplomat sent in to unravel a delicate conflict, simple and direct witnesses with a common man's appeal often did very well on the stand.

"Fair enough. So, Lucy, we spoke on the phone, and I know this is painful, but why don't you tell me again what happened. Take your time. I'm going to make some notes. Rick, you can add anything you'd like. And then we can talk about whether I think you have a strong case and next possible steps. Sound fair?"

They both nodded without looking at each other. As Lucy began to relate the story, Devlin picked up on something that he previously hadn't connected: They hadn't looked at or touched each other, nor had they spoken directly to one another since they first came in the office. And at the conference table, they sat on opposite sides with their chairs turned toward the lawyer. Perhaps it was nothing. But for two grieving siblings suffering the common loss of their mother, they seemed oddly disconnected.

The general facts were straightforward and, from where he sat, coalesced into a defective-tire case. Mildly intriguing, but certainly not a leap-out-of-your-seat stunner. And Devlin's intuition wouldn't let go that something wasn't quite right about these clients. He just didn't know what yet.

Lucy continued: Last year, Rick Dubrow bought a 1974 Monte Carlo coupe from Big City Auto Sales. The window sticker on the vehicle classified it as a "new dealer demo," which explained the 1,100 miles on the odometer. A month later, he was driving his 82-year-old mother, Claire Dubrow, north to Denver to visit friends. Also in the car were Lucy's two children, 9 and 12. Just west of the Arizona-New Mexico state line, the front passenger tire blew. The Monte Carlo veered, skidded off the pavement, and flipped upside-down in the highway median. Claire died at the scene. The children survived their physical injuries, but still suffered lingering emotional trauma. Rick Dubrow crawled from the Monte Carlo with a six-inch gash across his head, a broken right arm, and a twisted spine that made it painful to sit and would steadily degenerate for the rest of his life.

As Lucy continued her story with unnecessary details, Devlin started making a list on his legal pad. He might or might not take the case, but he was already thinking through the preliminary foundation. To conclude the meeting, Devlin asked for some time and said he'd be in touch in a week or two with a decision. Then he made some phone calls to at least corroborate the basic facts. Three weeks later, Lucy and Rick Dubrow returned to the office and officially retained Devlin in their wrongful death case against Big City Auto Sales. Devlin picked up a bottle of Black Velvet, Lucky's favorite, and dropped it by one afternoon with a note saying thanks. Lucky was gone, so he leaned the bottle on his chair.

The next months and into summer went by in a flash. In April, President Ford gave a speech declaring the Vietnam War was finally over, and the U.S. was cutting off all aid to the Saigon regime. Helicopter evacuations carried on day and night while North Vietnamese troops circled the outskirts of Saigon, but people were still having trouble believing the news. Going back to France's occupation in 1945, Vietnam had been a thirty-year lesson in human misery. Devlin wondered if it would ever end. But then it happened, April 30, Saigon officially falling and newspapers declaring that the Vietnam War really was over. Not that the U.S. had won, but that its involvement was at an end as the last U.S. Marines left the U.S. Embassy. For Devlin, the war's end would take some time to fully sink in. One of his buddies from Notre Dame had died there, and three of his friends, including Lucky, had come back minus various limbs.

By June, Devlin was digging up the paper trail that would become ammunition in bringing the suit against Big City Auto Sales. And there was always paper. Death certificates. Medical records. Vehicle sales agreements. Letters. Typed notes. Handwritten journals and notebooks. Notes under magnets on refrigerators. Random thoughts scribbled on random scraps of paper balled up in trash cans. File folders full of invoices and agreements. Carbon copies of old receipts. Phone bills. Most defendants left a paper trail as voluminous as Walsh's discarded betting tickets.

As obvious as it sounded, Devlin needed Claire Dubrow's death certificate. Then he'd order the medical records of Rick and the children involved in the accident. He left a message to have Lucy mail a copy of the sales agreement on the Monte Carlo. He would need to buy back the smashed vehicle from the impound yard and get it towed to the garage he'd rented to store the TransAm and Chevy 409. And of course he'd have to find an expert to examine the tires. His secretary Nadia Flores, whom he'd stolen away from Grant & Ross, typed and mailed all the requests. By the time Devlin received all the documents it was almost mid-year. With step one covered, Devlin decided to bring in a private investigator for the first time.

"He's a tough grunt," Walsh said with a mouthful of hot dog and French fries. Walsh was dropping out of sight regularly now, sometimes for weeks, before resurfacing. Devlin knew better than to ask. He didn't tell Walsh that he was looking for office space and, when the timing was right, would be hanging his own shingle. Devlin might have moved with more immediacy had he known this: Each time AAA Bail Bonds referred a client to Walsh & Devlin, Walsh was throwing a ten-percent taste of the retainer to the Bonanza Brothers back at the Ponderosa. Illegal as hell. Devlin would never learn of Walsh's side deal, which wasn't surprising considering Walsh had side deals stacked on top of side deals. But Devlin did often wonder how the new firm on the block had landed such plum clients. For his part, Lucky didn't know about the arrangement either.

"You want information," Walsh said, "you want someone to get inside a mark's life, you need someone to do unsavory things that need to stay off the record? Then you call Max Daniels. You want a bullshit bedtime story about unicorns and rainbows, then don't waste his time."

Max Daniels, according to Walsh, was a real-life Travis McGee except, being in Arizona, he didn't live on a boat. Instead he had a modest house on thirty acres south of Phoenix surrounded by a thick grove of orange and lemon trees. He apparently also had a small fleet of vehicles, was well-stocked with munitions, and had a northern and similarly remote outpost in the mountains near Flagstaff. Previously he'd been a cop for ten years, but had been creatively unemployed for the last fifteen years. He'd parlayed his acumen for sniffing out deals, and had apparently done well in real estate. Additionally, over the past ten years or so he had earned a reputation as the best investigator in the desert Southwest. From Moab to Durango, Santa Fe west to Yuma, Max Daniels was number one. For the right fee, he'd bounty-hunt and skip-trace, too, which he'd done several times for Lucky.

Devlin studied the business card Walsh had just given him. They each had a hot dog and were standing near turn one at the Royal Palms Kennel Club. The card just had "Max Daniels" and a phone number. No address. No title. No credentials. But Walsh swore by him. And just as it had always been with his mentor, Devlin admired Walsh's no-nonsense expertise and equally feared its possible ramifications.

"He's above-board, right? He's not going to do something to get me disbarred?"

Walsh was engrossed in watching the pack of dogs that had just left the starting boxes.

"Come on, you little bitch. Get the rail, get the rail." Then, without looking at his protégé, he said, "Relax, kid. He's not a hit man or anything. He just gets things done. And he's clean. Trust me."

Later, over beers with Lucky, Devlin got further validation that Max Daniels was his guy.

"He was just here today," Lucky said.

"Really?" Devlin said, surprised he'd never crossed paths with this guy.

"I had him chasing down someone who jumped bail. Bloodhound stuff."

"He get him?"

Lucky smiled. "Max Daniels always gets them. Get this: Somehow he tracked this pencil neck to a broad's house in Oregon. Word is Daniels has someone at the phone company who dumps records for a little dust on the side. Anyway, Daniels walks right up to this guy while he's eating a hamburger in a packed restaurant, starts talking some bullshit like he knew him from high school and before the poor brother even knows what's happening, Daniels just slips the cuffs on him real quiet and smooth."

"You're the second person inside a week who says he's good."

"What case you putting him on?"

"That Big City Auto Sales thing. It's probably nothing, but I want someone to dig around a little and see if there's anything we're missing."

"You gotta watch them tires," Lucky said, working a toothpick with his tongue.

"How so?"

"Tires could be tricky," Lucky said. "If I'm the defense, I attack there. I say there ain't a lick of evidence those tires killed your client, but there's a million other possibilities. How could new tires on a new car just blow out like that?"

Devlin had already considered that defense. "I know. But that's the case. That's why I need to find out everything about those tires. Maybe we're missing something we can use."

"I'm just saying, Big-Time. If the tires are your case, then your case is shit. Those defense guys got a whole filing cabinet labeled 'How to Fuck Up Someone's Day.' How about my boy Dubrow? Solid?"

"I wouldn't go that far. They're OK, but not great." Indeed, some deeper fissures had started to appear in the Dubrow triad. First, Devlin learned that the three siblings were embroiled in some petty family feud that had gone on for more than a decade. That was the tension he first noticed in his office when they wouldn't look at or speak directly to each other. Then Lucy told him that older brother Bob, Lucky's original contact, was a cocaine addict and, basically, homeless, which explained his absence from the initial meeting and every one since. Now Devlin was wondering what else he'd find. Part of his strategy in hiring Max Daniels, unfortunately, was to investigate his own clients. The lawyer could probably handle whatever came up, but he needed to know now. He couldn't have any revelations popping up for the first time during a deposition. What had Walsh said? Surprise is death.

"No offense here, Lucky, but they're not educated or white-collar professionals who lost the family breadwinner; they're three blue-collar types who lost an elderly mother. I'd say these clients are a push at best and perhaps a liability."

"No offense taken, Big-Time. I know how the gears turn in the law machine. Least they white as Wonder Bread. You'd really be in a world of hurt you had a dead Aunt Jemima."

"You know I'm not like that."

"I ain't saying you, Big-Time. I'm just saying. 'Impartial jury' my black ass."

"You know, Lucky, Walsh always says there's no such thing as a perfect case. Great cases—with all the facts and evidence lined up in 100 time-stamped and hermetically sealed glass containers—can still be lost. And cases that stink like my first office over at Grant & Ross are routinely resurrected and pulled into the win column."

One-Armed Lucky took a slug of beer. "Yeah, I'll give you that. But at the same time you can only put so much makeup on a whore before you take her home to Mama. And she ain't no dummy, Big-Time."

Devlin laughed. "You'd make a helluva lawyer, Lucky. What's up in your world, anyway? You been throwing all your hard-earned money at those dogs?"

Lucky looked down at the cracked asphalt, shaking his head. "I ain't told you about that?" Lucky already knew he hadn't said anything to the lawyer or anyone else because the full impact of Ann's death had really hit him hard. Instead, it was easier to avoid the subject.

"Shit, Big-Time. I ain't been playing the dogs as much. Just ain't been the same. Remember my friend, one I always told you about?"

Devlin paused and then, "Yeah. Ann Pearson."

Lucky nodded. "She done had some health problems all along. Her heart mostly. Damn if she wasn't the nicest lady you ever meet. I seen her give away her last dollar to help someone more times than I can remember. But ain't none of us seen this one coming."

Chapter Three

"WE NEED TO GO FULL SPEED AHEAD on this," Devlin said. Life and a crushing caseload had somehow delayed this call for months. It was early August, and Devlin was scanning the newspaper as he talked on the phone. Teamsters Union president Jimmy Hoffa had apparently vanished, broad daylight, from a restaurant parking lot in suburban Detroit. Weird. Devlin was briefing Max Daniels on the Big City Auto Sales case. "I need to know everything there is to know about this vehicle and its history. Think you can dig that up?"

"Definitely. I know people in the car business who know people with that kind of information. I'll prepare a full history on the vehicle from the time it rolled off the line in Detroit."

In Arizona, a state with comparative negligence, more than one party could be assigned liability, so Devlin was casting a wide net. And the name of Devlin's net was Max Daniels. "Perfect."

"Then there's the matter of my fee," Daniels said.

"Right. How's that work?"

"I bill my time at $85 an hour plus expenses."

"That's a bit steep, isn't it?"

"No, but there's more. I'll need a $1,500 retainer up front. The retainer's non-refundable and non-negotiable. You pay me, I do the job right, and you win a big settlement. Am I expensive then? No. Go hire some cut-rate hack and lose the case, then call me and we'll have a nice talk about price versus cost. You know that saying about stepping on dollars to pick up dimes?"

Devlin knew. He punched some numbers on his new Texas Instruments. Just to hire Daniels could easily run a few grand. Plus there'd be other expenses for expert witnesses who could talk intelligently about things like the vulcanization of rubber. And he'd have to pay any travel and lodging expenses for these experts. Just ballpark, he could see easily sinking $10,000 in this one before day one in court. That was a truckload of dough on one case. Walsh would never go for that, not with his slash-and-burn approach to the law that had served him so well. So if Devlin pursued this, he'd be all in and on his own. His father's mantras bubbled up in his mind: *Your work is to serve. Service is your work.* The old man had always driven the kid to find ways to out-smart, out-dress, and out-maneuver his peers. And if that didn't work, dad invoked the old "out-Irish" them, which meant working until everyone else has dropped. But still… "I don't know. I might be getting in too deep on this one, you know, cost-wise."

"I got a two-drawer filing cabinet here at my place. The top drawer is marked 'My Shit,' and the bottom one says 'Your Shit.' I don't ever open the bottom drawer. See what I'm saying?"

"I hear you," Devlin said.

"Now my man Lucky says all you need is one big case to blow the doors open. It falls back on you. You going to be just another lawyer lost in the big city, or are you going to step up when you get your shot? Is this your shot? I can't say. But if it is, you're talking to the right guy to get your case in order."

Devlin considered it.

"Look, kid, there was this old codger lawyer I worked with on a big case who was riding the fence like you're doing here. I looked at the old man and said, 'Show your opponents death, and they'll always accept sickness.' You bring me on, and I'll be your fucking grim reaper. You can count on that. You with me here?"

In that moment, five years of being a lawyer flashed through Devlin's mind. The first disastrous case and the smug asshole outside the court. Walsh's razor-edged brilliance. Now Max Daniels. Devlin grabbed a legal pad and scribbled it down for the first time:

The Rules of Action
#1 Preparation is not a punch line—It's a way of life.
#2 Never be surprised—Surprise is death.
#3 Show your opponents death, and they'll always accept sickness.

"Still there, partner?" Max Daniels asked.

"Yeah, just thinking," Devlin said.

"Thought I smelled cat piss cooking on the stove."

Devlin had, at last count, fifty or so cases on his docket. The red light/green light stuff he could do in his sleep. Then there were maybe ten cases—the ones stacked around his living room and bedroom—that required more energy and diligence, with a commensurate payday potential. But he had yet to land the singular big one, something north of six figures. Maybe this was the turning point.

At the outset, even with degrees from Notre Dame and USC, it was no secret that Devlin didn't have the grades or academic standing for the big firms. Besides, he was just wired differently than the people who got the stuffed-shirt gigs and judgeships. He'd never told anyone, but Devlin barely made it into law school. The night before the LSAT, he ended up out with his roommate, drunk, and only got a single fitful hour of sleep. After trudging across the ice-crusted darkness that is South Bend in November, just before the proctor distributed the LSAT, Devlin had felt a sick nausea rising into his throat. Helpless, he had lifted the classroom window to let the frigid air swirl around his head. The icy blasts were the only thing that had kept him balanced, just barely, in some state of quasi-equilibrium. He had taken the entire exam like that, his head at the window like some sick hound on the way to the vet. The results were corollary and abysmal, and would require suffering through a second attempt. The test scorers, he envisioned, must have huddled around his answer sheet, in uproarious laughter, and wondered aloud how the esteemed and hallowed University of Notre Dame had turned out one of the dumbest would-be lawyers in history.

"All right, let's go all in," Devlin said into the phone receiver.

"That's the spirit, kid."

"Yes it is," Devlin said. "Now find me something that cracks this thing open." Devlin hung up and, minutes later, the phone rang.

"What it is, Big-Time."

"Lucky, my friend, how the hell are you?" Lucky, in the years they'd known each other, had never called. Further, he'd never spoken to Devlin beyond the small perimeter where they convened their Friday ritual.

"I'm cooking with gas, brother, cooking with gas. You?"

"Me? Same old fucking grind."

"You go to bed with whores, Big-Time, guess what?"

"I know, Lucky. I was just telling your old lady that this morning."

"You watch your mouth about my old lady, Big-Time."

"Hey, no fooling, I was just talking to your guy Max Daniels. Just put him on that Big City Auto Sales thing I was telling you about."

"That's cool beans, Big-Time. Cool beans indeed."

"So what's up? We doing beers on Friday? Sorry I haven't been around. Been up to my ass in it."

"Oh yeah, I hear you loud and proud. That's why I called, Big-Time. Just wanted to make sure you coming around Friday."

"OK, yeah, no problem. I'm there." In Lucky's world there was no such thing as formal invites, calls to confirm, RSVPs. If you showed, you showed. If you didn't, well, catch you next time. Something was up.

"All right. I'll see you Friday then, Big-Time."

"Lucky, c'mon. We known each other how long? Talk to me."

After a short pause, Lucky just said, "Look, something's been on my mind. Just eating away, you know? The more I think on it maybe there's a good case in there for you. You know her. Well, you don't know her, Kay's her daughter... look, not on the phone. I told her I'd get her the best, and that's you, Big-Time. I think this one here might be your first big shot. Just come on Friday, and I'll explain."

Part II

Discovery

Chapter Four

BEFORE DAWN ON A COLD JANUARY MORNING, with 1975 officially in the books, the phone rang in Devlin's bedroom. In the early darkness, a woman with tousled blonde hair answered. She was wearing a white tank top and blue panties, and her name was not Jessica Jean. The fling between the young lawyer and the Playboy bunny had run its natural cycle and faded with no official end. The blonde nudged Devlin: "Hey. Phone."

Already jolted awake by the ring, Devlin took the receiver. After less than a minute, he said, "I'll meet you at the office then." He handed the receiver back.

"Everything OK?"

Devlin sighed. He glanced at the clock: 3:45 a.m.

He'd met her a month ago, at The Wellington. Now she snuggled up against Devlin and kissed him on the forehead as he pushed the covers aside.

"Where you going?"

"I'm up now. Apparently Max Daniels lives by a different clock than the rest of the world. I'm going for a run and then to the office."

"Who's Max Daniels?"

"Guy I work with. Let's meet everyone at The Wellington later and grab dinner."

She nodded. Then she pulled the tank top over her head. "Sure I can't entice you to take today off?"

Devlin smiled. There was just enough light to cast her form. But hearing from the private detective had already started the gears turning in his mind. If ever there were early indications of a case starting to take over the totality of one's being, his next statement was strong evidence: "Hell of an offer. But I need to get going on this thing."

She nodded. He kissed her again, got up and slipped into his gray sweats.

He'd just bought his first place, a three-bedroom, two-bath townhouse in the tony suburb of Scottsdale. For the princely sum of $85,000 he had a resort golf course as his backyard, a small swimming pool and Jacuzzi, and a garage for the Porsche. He was keeping his two collectors, the TransAm Super Duty and the Chevy 409, at a rented garage in downtown Phoenix near his new office: Devlin & Associates. There weren't really any associates, at least not yet, but it had a nice ring. Upon hearing the news, Walsh had groused and grumbled like he always did and then acted like he didn't care either way. But privately, to himself and others, he admired the kid and pegged him to go far. Now a soloist, Devlin had locked on to the Big City Auto Sales case as his rainmaker. He needed a breakthrough case—a David versus Goliath headline grabber—to establish himself a formidable thorn under the saddle of the corporate establishment.

Although no early bird by any stretch, he'd fallen into a diligent routine: at the office by 9 every morning and full-bore until midnight. If he wasn't in court, or meeting with prospects and clients, he was out trying to generate new clients and juggling his current cases. The stacks of work had encroached into his home and now formed piles, by case, on the table, floor, and furniture. He carefully navigated that paperwork in the dark, left through the sliding back door and cut across the wet grass at a quick clip. He could see his breath in the morning cold. He stopped near a golf green to catch his breath and stared at the jagged silhouette of the desert mountain in the darkness. Hunched over, his chest burning and heaving from the sprints, Devlin paused in the cold silence and then darted off again into the chill air.

Later that morning at the office, Devlin shifted in his chair and checked his watch again. Max Daniels had uncovered some intrigue in the Big City Auto Sales case. He would be here any minute, at the red-brick building on Third Avenue, to divulge his findings. Then Devlin saw a 1964 convertible Chevelle roll up, cherry-red and gleaming in the sun. Even with the winter temperature only in the 40s, Max Daniels had the top down. Devlin watched Daniels carefully park the car and get out with a large envelope in his hand. He was short with a slight frame, but walked like a Marine with a direct order from up the chain. He wore a weathered brown leather jacket to buffer the cold. He was clean-shaven with a flattop, which trumpeted to the world his disdain for the hippie milieu. With that look, Max Daniels could only be one of two things—ex-military or ex-cop—and you didn't want to lock horns with either. Devlin had never met him, and he liked Daniels immediately. Minutes later, after routine pleasantries, they were seated at the conference table in Devlin's office. Daniels looked around and nodded.

"Glad to see you're into muscle cars, too."

"Your Chevelle's amazing."

"I know. To be honest, when I first saw you I was picking up the whole peace-and-love, lawyer thing. Your hair, the sideburns. No problem if that's what floats your boat, live and let live. But the cars. That's good."

"Well, I'm champing at the bit here to find out what you've got."

"Oh, you mean this?" he said, holding up the envelope, smiling. "Yes. This is very interesting indeed. Turns out your big case here might be an even bigger case."

"Oh?"

"Yeah. This particular vehicle has a fascinating and particularly sordid history. Let me lay it on you. First of all, the car was actually stolen off the dealership's lot some months before your client, Rick Dubrow, bought it."

"Stolen? No shit?"

"Indeed. Some hippie hopheads took it on a joy ride that culminated in southern Arizona with a high-speed police chase, which ended when the driver veered into the desert and grounded the Chevy on a sandbar."

Now Devlin was bristling with energy. "None of this was ever disclosed."

"Hold on, counselor. It gets better."

"Better?"

"Better as in call-the-other-side-and-tell-them-to-get-out-the-checkbook better."

"OK, so tell me."

"When the cops searched the vehicle, the trunk was full of assorted shotguns, drug paraphernalia and the fresh carcasses of three jackrabbits. Back seat had several pillows and blankets, and there were human feces nearby in the bushes. Apparently the new owners had converted the back seat to a master suite. Who knows about the jackrabbits, maybe they preferred wild rabbit stew to more traditional fare. Either way, the police had to get a tow truck to drag the car off the sandbar and haul it back to the impound lot."

"Unbelievable. I can't believe the dealership didn't disclose any of this to the customers, sales staff, nothing."

"Then Big City Auto Sales, the rightful owners, pay to have this blood-stained bucket towed back to Phoenix. They hose off the dust and jackrabbit entrails and put the car back on the lot as a new demo."

"How'd you find out all this?"

"Hold on. There's more."

"More?"

"I nosed around a little to see what we could find out about those tires. Turns out they were worn down to nothing, but never replaced. And none of the salespeople knew any of this history. There was no mention of dead jackrabbits, high-speed chases, bongs, or any of it. Nor was the vehicle given anything more than a cursory inspection. Call it in, counselor. That's B-I-N-G-O for you."

At its essence, the law of negligence was not complicated. Sure, there were twists and turns, but for the most part Devlin dealt with facts, theories, and hypotheses. This information turned upside-down every fact, theory, and hypothesis he'd had in this case and made the whole thing pulse with new possibilities. Devlin thought he was just dealing with some defective tires. But from a liability standpoint, Max Daniels had just handed him the keys to the top desk drawer at Big City Auto Sales.

"Now, of course, for all of that to be of any use to us, as you already know, counselor, you need records and documentation—" The phone rang.

"Sorry," Devlin said. "Give me a second."

"Big-Time, where you been at? Ain't seen you in months."

"Lucky, sorry, man. I've been buried."

"I still got that case I want you to look at. You gotta be coming around."

Devlin remembered now; Lucky had said something about a case. And Devlin had promised he'd show, but hadn't. "Lucky, I'm with someone just now, but let me get back to you."

There was a pause. "OK, Big-Time. But I need you to do me a solid here and at least look at this one."

"You got it, Lucky. I promise." But all he could think was that with this new information from Max Daniels, all available energy would be re-directed to nailing Big City Auto Sales. If Lucky's case was decent, Devlin would do him the solid by referring a good attorney. When Devlin finished the call, he apologized and motioned for Daniels to continue. Daniels held up the thick envelope.

"As I was about to say, it's all in here. My interview notes, photographs, towing records, the supposed vehicle inspection report they did at Big City Auto Sales. Of course, for the record, you'll have to follow up everything in your depositions."

"Of course. Mr. Daniels, you're one helluva private investigator. How did you get all this?"

Max Daniels just smiled and stood. "Counselor, I'm off to Vegas."

"Vegas? What's in Vegas?"

Max Daniels was already at the door. "In my world, counselor, discretion is a key discipline. But let's just say it's business and pleasure. And the pleasure portion begins in the Chevelle with the 300 miles of desert asphalt between here and there."

"Nadia has your check up front," Devlin said. "Thank you. You'll be hearing from me again."

"Yes I will," he said, nodding.

After Daniels left, Devlin pulled out a legal pad and started scribbling notes. His shoddy tires case, a bottom-rung product liability play, had just evolved into all-out fraud. And malicious fraud was much further up the spectrum on two critical counts: burden of proof and payday potential. Devlin's brain was out-racing his note-taking ability: He'd need to get his hands on that Monte Carlo, which would mean buying it from impound and moving it to his collector storage garage. He would have to call around and find the best possible tire expert to do the analysis. He'd tell his new expert to pull the tires and microscope them from every angle. He'd use his connections with the police to find out who'd worked the case when the car was stolen and on the subsequent joyride, which would involve multiple jurisdictions. He wanted to talk to all of those cops.

When he looked at his list, he could see his costs doubling and tripling right there on his legal pad. Originally he'd earmarked ten grand including trial and appeals, which was more than he'd ever spent in one go. But looking now, his best guess was that he was already closer to $15,000 just to get through discovery. A trial, with paid experts and all their attendant travel expenses, might double that amount. One of Walsh's broken-record admonitions was never bet with scared money. He'd implored his protégé to apply the craps-table dictum in the practice of law: Never try a case or represent a client if you weren't willing to go all the way. To play now Devlin would have to bring a bigger stack of chips and get comfortable with the idea of pushing the entire lot to the center. All of it, assuming he won, was recoupable at the conclusion of the case. But from where he sat, even full of confidence, a victory was still a big assumption.

He opened his calendar, flipped ahead to June, and circled his birthday. He gave himself that deadline, the five or so months before he turned 31, to prepare this case, write the complaint, and file the lawsuit. Even if he or Daniels turned up new tidbits after that, he could file an amended complaint since Arizona was a notice-pleading state. Then he'd wait the customary thirty or sixty days for the defense to answer the complaint, and it would be on. He could barely stand the thought of waiting another six months to do his first deposition in his first big case. Devlin & Associates was about to go head-to-head with the big boys.

That Friday, as promised, Devlin parked the Porsche at AAA Bail Bonds and walked between the two buildings. Somehow, five months had slipped by without a Friday confab. Lucky was on his chair, beer in hand, chair balanced against the brick wall, and he reached in the bucket when he saw Devlin. After exchanging the beer and money, Devlin sat on an upside-down five-gallon can. Now that he was accustomed to the desert clime, January in Phoenix meant there were some days where it almost felt like winter. Today was one of those days, with the high stuck in the 40s.

"I got this case," Lucky said, which was a very uncustomary opening salvo. Usually the conversation began with small talk about the weather and then meandered very slowly, taking in everything from women to sports, and whether this cat Jimmy Carter stood a chance against Ford. They'd muse about American muscle versus foreign sports cars and how they should make more films like *Three Days of the Condor*. Only then would they move to the main event, in which they discussed all things legal including Devlin's cases. And there were several juicy topics on the legal agenda as the year of the nation's bicentennial opened: would-be assassin Sara Jane Moore, who tried to kill President Ford, was up for sentencing on January 15. One-Armed Lucky and Devlin had made a friendly wager on what sentence the judge would impose. And there was the Patty Hearst trial, which was set to begin at the end of the month. But tonight was different.

"... it's just been bugging me bad, Big-Time."

"Tell me what's up."

"Well that's the problem. I mean, don't get me wrong, something stinks here. But I don't know if it's a case you can win. Or if it's even a case. But it just keeps eating at me, you dig?"

Devlin nodded. That was always a good sign, like in the Big City Auto Sales case, when the facts and characters and events gnawed away and wouldn't let up until the idea became more of a quest. It was that energy, those heightened levels of fury and rage and indignation, that would fuel a plaintiff's lawyer through the grind of litigation. Walsh had warned Devlin that marginal cases produced little such fervor and, usually, commensurate results. As his mind spun away, he realized he couldn't help himself now: Everything was playing through the filter of the Big City Auto Sales case and how to win it. But even more than that: how to expose the arrogance and indifference that killed Claire Dubrow. There was no way his psyche had room for Lucky's case no matter what, but Devlin would find a way to let him down easy.

"Well, let's back up," Devlin said. "We've both got a cold beer. Why don't you just tell me what happened first, and then we can talk about whether or not there's a case."

It was the standard soliloquy Devlin had now recited to dozens of potential clients. When he'd met Lucky, Devlin could count his cases and clients on one hand. Through their ongoing and unlikely repartee, One-Armed Lucky had grounded the lawyer in a comforting equilibrium. Devlin acknowledged, to himself, this warm glow of giving back some measure of what the one-armed witticism machine had imparted.

"OK, Big-Time. I'll just tell it like it happened."

Chapter Five

IT WAS OBVIOUS THAT THE DILAPIDATED Royal Palms Kennel Club rarely, if ever, took from profits to pay for capital improvements: parking-lot potholes big enough to swallow a VW Bug; peeled paint on top of older peeled paint; leaky toilets that emitted animal-in-distress squeals with each flush; and windows cracked by bored teenagers wielding pellet guns. But hard-core dog-racing veterans like One-Armed Lucky never once noticed the dated color palette or missing design aesthetic, nor did they ever once pine for silent plumbing. They flocked to the track with an unmatched and singular purpose: to bet the dogs and make their fortune. To be certain, none of the regulars had ever personally witnessed a new fortune generated trackside, but there were always a few "friend-of-a-friend-of-a-friend" rumors that fed the ubiquitous gold fever. And so, without exception, nothing pierced this stoic vision and common bond.

So, oddly, it was here—among the choking fog of cigarette smoke, the missing-finger heroes and glory-days stories of long shots picked cold, the molded, sticky plastic chairs and canned pomp and circumstance, the lines ten-deep at the betting windows and the grimy floor powdered in a confetti of hunches unfulfilled—that One-Armed Lucky made his closest friend: the church-going widow Ann Pearson, the woman everyone knew by her kind words, broad smile, and undeniable knack for picking winning dogs.

Buzzing with the energetic laughter of someone half her age and always looking for a good conversation, Ann Pearson never considered herself old or pondered her own demise. She did not ruminate on the meaning of life, complain about the stifling desert heat, or bemoan the state of near-bankruptcy that was her constant companion. She was too busy for all that.

For its part, the Royal Palms Kennel Club was a strange and inspiring confluence. Of course she would never fully put aside the pain of losing her husband Charlie ten years prior, in 1965, and she would never deviate from her rock-solid faith and conviction that she would eventually be reunited with her love. Nor would she ever shake a vague sense that she really shouldn't be at places like this, and so therefore she continued to give away any winnings to her friends and the church.

After Charlie died, keeping her normal routine imparted at least a modicum of normalcy. After getting up just before 5 a.m. and saying her prayers, she would prepare a breakfast of two scrambled eggs, buttered toast, and one cup of black coffee strong enough to make a cowboy grimace. She ate by the sliding door to the balcony, where she could watch the hummingbirds frequent two red feeders she kept brimming with sugar water.

Unable to bear all the reminders in their apartment, Ann liquidated what little belongings she had, which she'd whittled down to what would fit into her Plymouth Valiant, and moved into Desert Gardens Senior Living, a nine-story apartment building in a Phoenix suburb. She only brought her clothes and shoes, a framed photo of herself, Charlie and their daughter Kay—Ann and Charlie had tried, unsuccessfully, to conceive more children—and a box of other memorabilia. In those first weeks alone in her small, furnished studio, Ann cried off and on every night. She was unprepared for the shock of widowhood and further saddened by the undeniable doom of being surrounded by people waiting to die, many of them parked all day in wheelchairs up and down the hallways like cars abandoned in a snowstorm. Ann clung to her daughter, her faith, and her church for sustenance, but she needed something to occupy the long, lonely days without Charlie. That's when Ann discovered her new hobby.

Bound as she was by unplanned earthly circumstances, the dog track helped her forget and nudged her back into feeling alive again in a way she couldn't have predicted. At the Royal Palm Kennel Club she simultaneously found an extended family—a scattershot and dysfunctional clan whose members covered the entire spectrum of intelligence, sobriety, and general mental stability—and a hobby that got her intellect humming once again.

With each $2 bet, there was the palpable possibility that life-changing riches might pour forth on that very race. But more importantly, especially during that first year of milestones after Charlie's passing—his birthday, Easter, Christmas, Thanksgiving, the anniversary of their first kiss on her dad's old tractor in a Kansas cornfield—the routine itself, like her scrambled eggs and morning Mass with Father Martin, had become constant companion, trusted friend, and soothing balm. Then, with a tip from One-Armed Lucky, Ann banked her first $100 jackpot. Truly, for someone who came of age during the Dust Bowl, her win felt as though the heavens had broken loose and bestowed all the riches in the world upon Ann Pearson. Of course, her well-entrenched sense of duty and service reminded her of Father Martin's admonishment to tithe. True to that intention, by the time the bus rolled up to Desert Gardens, Ann had given everything away except $20, which she tucked in her purse for the collection basket the next morning. Ever so slowly, week by week, through all the races and odd characters she met, as she won big and lost bigger and never quite got back to even (and believed she was up overall), the angst and grief gently ebbed away. Incredibly, Ann Pearson had survived the first year of her greatest loss. Unbelievably, it was dog racing that had brought her back from the brink.

Back at Desert Gardens Senior Living, she started giving unofficial clinics to her wheelchair-bound comrades. They listened intently as she explained the difference between a "daily double" and a "twin quin," a "win, place, and show," and a "trifecta." A few of the seniors even understood, but mostly they just listened with rapt attention because Ann's enthusiasm was sufficiently captivating. For those unable to leave the building due to their health, Ann became unofficial bookie and placed bets on their behalf. Of course Ann never took a piece of anyone's winnings; she was just glad to spread the joy she had discovered. For someone stuck on a fixed income and in a wheelchair, the excitement of winning $25 was a meaningful boost. Oftentimes if Ann took a bet and the dog lost, she'd lie and pay the person back as though they'd won.

Like needlepoint with profit potential, she loved the quiet meditation of studying the dog-racing programs. She punched the oversized buttons on the big

Texas Instruments calculator and computed race-time averages and studied box-position tendencies. She looked for trends from the different breeders, kennels, and bloodlines. She drew careful conclusions, all with marginal results: matinee versus night preferences among the dogs; summer versus winter; male versus female; litter size and the type of food each kennel used. She compiled career trend lines on all the dogs and compared the data against the historical charts at the back of the program. She created a dog-weight and box-position grid and looked for ideal combinations. All of Ann's efforts attracted an entourage of fifteen or so hardened track regulars who hovered around her for inspiration, tips, and the possibility of absorbing some of Ann's winning energy simply by general proximity.

The Holy Grail for all concerned was hitting the trifecta (picking the dogs finishing 1-2-3 in order). After such a payout, Ann would retreat to the women's restroom. Ann always wore pantyhose and polyester slacks because the layered combination kept her warm, especially when the summer AC could chill down to the bones. But as she discovered, the pantyhose doubled as a private vault to stash winnings. Once ensconced in a restroom stall, she would stuff hundreds and twenties inside the waistband of her pantyhose for safekeeping. Not even a dope fiend with a gun, she figured, would go there. These moments were truly heart-pounding, pulse-racing, trembling-hands glorious. One night she stuffed $6,000 cash in her pantyhose and, as she did each time a big winner came up, she steadfastly resolved to pay off all the overdue bills. No more debt. Free and clear. Then she'd spend a few extra minutes thanking Jesus, Mary, and Joseph for her good fortune, promising to share her bounty with the church, and, just in case, doing a rosary and several Hail Marys. Before leaving, Ann always tucked away some money (in a zippered purse pocket) to send Kay, who worked as a librarian at the university in Flagstaff three hours north of Phoenix.

Then, once back among her gambling cohorts, all equally dedicated to this road map to riches, the true celebration would begin. Immediately, the rush of her inherent generosity swept away any prior resolve to repay her own debts. The first three gifts always went to her closest track companions. First, she would give One-Armed Lucky a $100 bill so he could enjoy his favorite meal at the track, a mountainous slab of prime rib called "The Big 21." Although Ann had never had a colored friend, they immediately hit it off as he took the time to teach Ann the inexact art of picking dogs.

Rounding out the threesome was Vera, a slumped-over little woman from Brooklyn who had a manic energy that sped forth in a rapid-fire stream of dialog and a quick, rocking shuffle everywhere she went. She would never sit with the other two, but instead paced back and forth, asking if anyone needed anything from the snack bar, introducing herself to anyone who made brief eye contact, and talking non-stop for hours.

From there, Ann doled out gifts to her other more casual track acquaintances, hangers-on and young men in suits who loved the old lady who could pick the dogs. Ann would tip the waitress $40 for bringing her a watery $2 Coke, and she'd throw in another $40 and tell the waitress to buy something nice for her kids. At the end of those big nights, she'd take the entire entourage out for a meal and drop $200 at a mediocre diner for lukewarm steak and eggs and cold pancakes drenched with maple syrup. The next day, back at Desert Gardens Senior Living, she'd go room to room and regale her adopted family with the entire story about the hunch weeks before, the clandestine and chance encounter with the dog's owner near the hot dog stand, the intricacies of her various bets, the minute-by-minute build-up to post time, the unbelievable race and, of course, the big payoff. The amount won was always unintentionally rounded up and inflated out of sheer enthusiasm. An $870 winning daily-double ticket became a cool grand back among the seniors. In reality, even with the big spikes the running total was a net loss, but no one wanted to be bothered with such pedantic bookkeeping drudgery amid the euphoria.

Ann would continue to hand out money to anyone who asked, and tucked cash under the pillows of those who couldn't because of their respirators. The day after a big win, she would drop $500 in the collection basket. It was a tidal wave of goodwill, laughter, and excitement that washed over Ann and everyone around her. And each time, usually within 72 hours, the winnings would be gone. The various bills never got paid as she had intended during the frenzy of stuffing cash into her pantyhose. No money had been saved for a rainy day. But it didn't matter to Ann or anyone else. The glow from that big win would linger for weeks, within Ann, throughout the senior apartments, and among her track friends. Ann's theatrics infused a rare, hopeful energy among the seniors and track regulars who had all taken hard hits in life and, on the bad days, just wanted to give up. A big win, though, was like an unexpected visit from a loved one. Any such break in the monotony erased the gloom, at least momentarily, and then lingered up and down the halls at Desert Gardens Senior Living. And although Ann didn't realize it, trying to inject logic and predictability into what was uncontrollable—eight eager greyhounds running around a dirt oval—was her way of easing Charlie's departure.

DEVLIN finished his beer and shook off the chill evening air. Even in his suit jacket, it felt damn cold. The Buffalo transplant, however, refused to wear an overcoat even if he could see his breath. He rubbed his hands together and blew in warm air. He liked the way Lucky's expression softened, in a way he'd never seen, when the bail bondsman mused about his friendship with Ann Pearson.

In this moment, Devlin wished he could stop the story right there, with Lucky and Ann carving out their innocent little corner of fun and peace. But he knew he couldn't. Happy endings rarely required the services of a lawyer: Devlin got called when people were in pain and surrounded by mounting problems. Devlin had learned to appreciate this brief silence, before he heard Act III with its chilling dénouement of suffering, indignity, and, often, death. Devlin savored the silence for a few moments longer. Then he took in a deep breath of cold desert air, looked at Lucky and smiled: "Just tell me what happened, brother. I can't help if I don't know what happened."

Chapter Six

ON MARCH 22, 1975, less than 72 hours after passing out at the dog track, Ann Pearson was in a Phoenix Municipal Hospital bed straining to remember the name of the U.S president, the one Johnny Carson always teased for being clumsy. She could see the face in her mind, but couldn't quite call up the name. Dr. Wayne Michaels was giving his standard CAO exam times three—conscious, alert, and oriented—to determine her lucidity.

"Do you know where you are?"

She shook her head.

"You don't know where you are?"

Still shaking her head, eyes closed, she struggled to say, "Ford."

"That's right," said One-Armed Lucky, snapping his fingers and smiling. "She got it." Vera nodded and smiled.

"Let her answer, please," said the doctor.

"Doc, if it was me," offered Lucky, "forget about the civics questions and ask her who she liked in the ninth last week. You'll see her mind's lined up right."

"The ninth?" he said. "Baseball?"

Vera shook her head and held up the racing program she pulled from Lucky's back pocket: "Dogs. She bets the dogs."

The doctor glanced back at Ann, then at her odd duo of support. He motioned with his hand and said, "Let's step out here."

Three days ago, One-Armed Lucky, Vera, and the other regulars had all rushed to Ann when the news of her fainting rippled among the bettors. Lucky had stood and watched the paramedics load Ann onto the gurney and, although she was unconscious, took her hand and promised he would be there when she woke up. Then there had been a round-the-clock vigil of dog-track regulars. At first there were ten people, one of whom didn't even know Ann; he was drunk and still holding an empty plastic martini glass from the track as the entourage entered the hospital.

As the group waited for any news about Ann's condition, most openly smoked and talked greyhounds until the nurse made them leave for being too loud. The martini man had wandered onto another floor and passed out in a supply closet. Near Ann's room, eventually the excitement and the crowd both dwindled until it was just One-Armed Lucky and Vera. At least one of the two had been here, twenty-four hours a day, ever since. Meanwhile, after two days of missed morning phone calls, Kay panicked, packed a bag, and drove from Flagstaff straight to Desert Gardens Senior Living. None of the staff there knew of Ann's whereabouts, which baffled Kay, so she started calling hospitals until she found her mother. Kay walked up just as the group stepped into the hall. It took a few minutes to sort out the introductions, but Kay was more concerned with seeing her mother.

"OK," the doctor said, huddling with the group. "Let me tell you that your mother is still very disoriented. The first thing we always worry about is a possible stroke, but her CT was negative. We also want to make sure she didn't damage her myocardium—you know, a heart attack. Right now she still has low blood sugar. We did find a UTI, which is an infection we're already treating. That's very common in the elderly, especially here in Arizona. It's quite easy to become very dehydrated and somewhat altered in mental status with a UTI, although generally we don't see full passing out. And even with the IV fluids she's still dehydrated. Some good news is that neither the heart monitor or the EKG show any signs of an arrhythmia, or heart rhythm problem, to explain why she passed out. And there's no evidence of an interruption of blood flow to her brain."

Kay was in tears, unable to speak.

"Doc, we ain't so hip with all this medical talk," said One-Armed Lucky. "Can you boil that down to plain talk?"

The doctor nodded. "Look, basically she's a little better than when she got here, but she's sure not ready to go home yet. We suspect that the infection might be what's making her sick and such, but she needs lots of rest and fluids, and to be monitored until she's back up to strength."

"So, meaning what?" Kay said.

"Meaning we've ruled out the life threats such as stroke, heart attack, or like-threatening arrhythmia, but she's still sick and is not completely out of the woods yet."

Vera had already wandered off; Lucky silently considered the doctor's words. Kay shook her head in disbelief.

"I'm referring her to a nursing home where she can regain her strength, get fully rehydrated, and make sure there aren't further complications. That was a pretty good tumble she took. We just need to move slowly here and make sure she's OK before we send her home."

"That's cool beans," One-Armed Lucky said, shifting his weight and cracking his knuckles. "We just want to make sure she all right. We got you, too." He put an arm around Kay's shoulder and squeezed tight.

Later, the discharge summary for Ann Pearson included the following quickly scribbled notes by Dr. Michaels: *heart S1S2, regular rate and rhythm, no murmurs noted... disoriented, no sensory or motor deficit appreciated. Discharge and transfer to skilled nursing facility.* Then, buried in the summary, was the reference to a "stage 2 decub on buttocks," a small, relatively benign pressure sore he wanted monitored. The sore, he noted, was about the size of a nickel, and for that he prescribed an ointment to be applied every three days or as needed. He wrote orders for a three-day course of antibiotics for the UTI, an egg-crate mattress pad, a restricted diet and high levels of fluid intake to rehydrate Ann's body. He wrote and signed these diagnostic instructions for the benefit of doctors and nurses at Mercy Care Center, a nearby nursing home where he expected Ann to convalesce under watchful eyes in the coming weeks.

"Wish... you kids wouldn't fuss... over me," said Ann, eyes barely open.

"Mom, stop it," Kay said. "I'm here now, your friends are here, and we'll fuss as much as we want."

One-Armed Lucky walked over and put a hand on his friend's shoulder. "Now Annie, you got to listen to your daughter and the doc. They being straight up with you now. You do what they say, and we'll have you back at the track before you can say 'box-and-wheel the two dog.'"

"That's right," said Vera.

"Straight up," said One-Armed Lucky.

Ann shook her head and tried to say something, but no words came out.

"Mom, just relax. It's OK."

"You're old lady because you're smart," said Vera, pointing to her head. "You got the brains. Look at us; we ain't got the brains."

"Speak for your damn self, woman," said One-Armed Lucky. "I graduated high school. You graduate high school?"

"I been working since the eighth grade in my mother's restaurant in Brooklyn. Didn't have time for no school. Used to cook all day—"

"Well there you go," Lucky said. "Besides, brains is a whole lot more than how much school time you done got. That's for damn sure."

"Some nice tea, dear?" Vera asked.

Kay looked at them and smiled. Only her mother would find and befriend such an oddball duo. And then she said a silent prayer of gratitude that they'd been there for her mother right when it happened.

Later that day, at Kay's insistence, One-Armed Lucky and Vera tagged along when Kay followed the ambulance to Mercy Care Center. Kay took command of the wheelchair from the EMT and walked into the facility at 6 p.m. Immediately Kay smelled a foul odor and looked around the empty lobby. She could see that One-Armed Lucky smelled it, too, but neither Vera or her mother seemed to notice.

"Damn," One-Armed Lucky said. "Someone need to take out that garbage." He pinched his nose closed like a child.

"Garbage, what garbage?" Vera said, shuffling toward the front desk and nosing around like she'd lost her watch. Her voice echoed down the long hallway.

"Doc said couple weeks tops, right?" said One-Armed Lucky. He reached down and squeezed Ann's shoulder. Kay turned her head and was unable to fight back the tears.

The next three days at Mercy Care Center seemed, thankfully, relatively uneventful to Kay and Ann's cohorts. The two had pledged to Kay that someone would visit Ann every day, and one or both dutifully kept that promise. One-Armed Lucky had become the official conduit for keeping the Royal Palms Kennel Club regulars updated on Ann's condition, and he talked to Kay two or three times every day. Kay remembered her mother talking about Lucky many times in their early morning updates, and now she too had found it easy to put her complete trust in him. When the two talked, it was often Kay's jokes that boosted Lucky's spirits rather than vice versa. As part of the new routine, he or Vera stayed with Ann while Kay ducked out for a quick shower back at Desert Gardens. Bedside, he talked to Ann in a low voice even though she had been nodding out most of the day.

"You remember that time old Clancy hit the trifecta, $800, and lost the damn ticket on the way to the betting window?" One-Armed Lucky shook his head as he laughed. "I think you hit that one, too, Annie. In fact, basically you picked it for him, and he still couldn't get it right. Who loses an $800 winning ticket on the way to the window?" She hadn't said a word since he'd arrived. Her face was white, her normal energy buzz drained away somewhere. One-Armed Lucky hated this place.

"Where's the damn doctors, anyway? And nurses? Can't they see you thirsty? And it's cold in here."

Ann barely shook her head, no, her eyes closed. But Lucky was not satisfied and returned five minutes later with a glass of water. "Here you go, Annie." She took one small sip while he tucked the blanket up around her neck.

"Didn't see one damn doctor, and when I asked that nurse, the sister, to get some water she told me to get it my damn self. You believe that? But Doc said you'd be out soon. Ain't that right Annie?"

He sat bedside, not saying anything, until Ann was fast asleep again. When Kay reappeared, her hair still wet, she and Lucky exchanged silent smiles and hugs. Lucky rubbed Ann's face with the back of his hand and kissed her on the forehead. Then he stepped out and started down the hall. As he was leaving, Lucky noticed a nurse sitting in the corner knitting or something, but she didn't even look up. Kay, meanwhile, was in tears again and sobbed into her mother's shoulder.

Neither the daughter nor Ann's two closest friends could know that things were taking an ominous turn, and that Ann would never again be fully conscious. In a matter of days, emergency personnel would rush Ann Pearson in an ambulance, clinging to life, from Mercy Care Center back to Phoenix Municipal Hospital. Dr. Wayne Michaels, upon seeing the women he'd discharged only days prior with a decent prognosis, would be aghast at her condition. There would be an emergency surgery, but none of it would be enough.

On the morning of April 4, 1975, Ann Pearson died in her sleep. She was alone in her room at Phoenix Municipal Hospital, at 5:30 a.m., and didn't feel any pain as she quietly slipped away. Two ICU nurses ran into her room as soon as they heard the monitors, but Ann was already gone.

Chapter Seven

A WEEK AFTER BEERS WITH LUCKY and hearing the Ann Pearson story, Devlin couldn't put it off any longer. Using one of the new push-button phones, he punched in Kay Pearson's number in Flagstaff to tell her that, unfortunately, she did not have a wrongful death case against Mercy Care Center. In explaining the delicate legal whys, he would use all his tact and diplomacy to not minimize her great loss.

After a bit of probing from Devlin, Lucky had remembered that Ann had a history of diabetes and blackouts. *Strike One.* She'd also relayed to Lucky that from her 40s onward she'd have severe fainting episodes that doctors could only vaguely diagnosis as "spells, probably heart-related." *Strike Two.* And since her husband's death, both the frequency and severity of these spells had begun to increase. No less than five times she had been to the edge of the abyss. In one of those instances, she lost her vision entirely for three days. In another, she blacked out and fell down a flight of metal stairs at the apartment building. *Strike Three.*

Through it all, some deep, genetic urging dragged Ann back from the brink. And so, for years, doctors had been giving her the same ominous diagnosis: (1) the end could come at any time; (2) the next "spell" might likely be the last; and (3) just to be safe, make sure your affairs are in order. But stubborn to the core, Ann had dismissed all of it and gone about her life.

As vibrant and likable a person as she seemed to have been, what Devlin saw was a 76-year-old woman with a history of health problems who, apparently, died from exactly what doctors had been predicting for years. And while Lucky said repeatedly that something wasn't right about the nursing home, there was little legal precedent to go after them. *Prove that a nursing home had killed an already-frail elderly woman in its care?* They'd laugh him out of the courtroom, out of town, and probably out of the legal profession altogether. Devlin couldn't even classify this as a long shot, because there wasn't a single legal foothold to begin being building a case. But, of course, when he heard Kay Pearson's quivering voice full of equal amounts of grief, despair, and rage—the emotions especially raw through the first year of grieving—Devlin couldn't quite pull the plug. At least not yet. He'd let her vent some of that pain and perhaps walk her a step or two in the healing process. Then he'd decline.

"… I just kept asking myself, 'How could this happen? Maybe a hundred years ago, but in 1975? How could my mother be gone like that in such a short time? How?'"

Dealing with the bereaved, Devlin had learned, was delicate territory. It required a deft touch to balance care and compassion with the cold, clinical realities of evidence and law. For the survivors who lost loved ones, death was always a shock, and always painfully swift.

"It does seem unfathomable," said Devlin. "How long did you say she was in the hospital?"

"Sixteen days total between Phoenix Municipal and Mercy Care Center and then back to Phoenix Municipal."

Lucky hadn't mentioned this little tidbit about the back-and-forth, which further muddied any potential case. "So she was admitted to the hospital, sent to Mercy Care Center to convalesce, and then returned to Phoenix Municipal?"

"Right."

Pinning the responsibility for Ann Pearson's death on a nursing home was beyond impossible, and bordered on insanity. But trying to allocate blame to one or both of *two* defendants was, well, a ludicrous legal proposition. But instead of stopping right there and taking the opening she'd given, Devlin said, "I see…," a lawyer variant of the standard Buffalo truism: *What the fuck.*

"To tell you the truth," Kay continued, "I didn't get really angry until I went to the nursing home and for some reason they wouldn't give me Mom's chart. I don't really know anything about medical stuff, but I thought that was odd. My mom just died, I just want her chart, and they wouldn't give it to me? Her sole heir?"

"Mercy Care Center wouldn't give you your mother's medical chart? And you identified yourself as her daughter?"

"Yes. Showed the nurse my driver's license. She knew. They're hiding something. I just know it." Yes, Devlin thought, they might be hiding Jimmy Hoffa, too, but without evidence he was powerless. He had true sympathy for her unbridled pain, and understood the need to somehow wrench back some control over the unexplained blackness that had swept through Kay's existence.

"What might they be hiding?"

"I think they neglected her care, and that sore she had on her bottom? The doctor even said he'd never seen anything like it."

"The doctor?"

"At Phoenix Municipal."

"Now we're back at the hospital." Devlin pictured himself as one of the confused jurors trying to follow the convoluted story. If you lose them, jurors simply check out and stare at your suit lapels, as though they're right with you, for the rest of the trial. But in reality, they're thinking about the next break, what's for lunch, the weather, and when they can get back to their life minus the lawyer tedium and tales.

"He discharged her with a clean bill of health," Kay said. "It's in her chart."

"You have the chart?"

"Yes. Then she goes to Mercy Care Center to convalesce, nothing major. Except ten days later they send her back to Phoenix Municipal in an ambulance with that huge, infected sore. The hospital did all they could, but it wasn't their fault. The nursing home is what killed my mom while she was there. That's why they wouldn't give me the chart until I refused to leave without it. Something's definitely fishy."

Yes, Devlin was thinking, but the nursing home did, in fact, eventually give her the chart, which meant they probably weren't hiding anything incriminating. And the hospital did their best to save this elderly lady. The delay in turning over the chart, Devlin guessed, would turn out to be a normal and documented protocol for closing out the file of a deceased patient. Which brought them back to the beginning: There was simply no case here. So it was inexplicable that Devlin found himself saying, "Kay, I will definitely look into this. The first thing I need you to do is send me both of the charts. Just make copies; you keep the originals. I'm also going to send you a form called 'client authorizations for records.' Just sign it and send it back in case there are other documents I need."

"So you're my lawyer?"

He knew it was too late; he'd opened the little door of hope just enough that closing it on her now was going to be extremely difficult.

"Well, let's take this one step at a time," he said. "I'm certainly going to see if there's anything we can do to help you get some closure and honor your mother's memory. Let me check it out and get back to you."

"OK. I'm counting on you. We can't let them get away with this. They killed my mother."

Devlin wished he could say something definitive to assuage her pain. "Let's see what I find out and go from there."

With most of his mind and energy already allocated to the Big City Auto Sales case, Devlin formulated his plan: First he'd order Ann Pearson's death certificate (stranger tales have been spun wherein the deceased has, *voila!*, risen to walk again). Then the autopsy report. Once he got the medical charts, he'd find an expert pathologist to help pinpoint the cause of death. With that expert's sign-off that Ann Pearson died of heart failure and all her other cumulative maladies, along with no inconsistencies in her medical charting, Devlin would feel confident telling Kay that there simply wasn't a case. He'd be able to tell One-Armed Lucky he'd done everything in his power to help.

He played it out in his head: time allotted to mail things back and forth… order those documents and get up to speed on the medical side… track down an expert. Devlin gave himself three months, tops, to close this one out, and move on to bigger things: Big City Auto Sales.

Chapter Eight

WHEN THE LIGHT TURNED GREEN, Devlin punched the Porsche 930 accelerator. "Stranglehold," from Ted Nugent's solo debut, was pumping through the car's speakers. Windows down, sun blazing, it was a glorious, fresh February day in Phoenix. Devlin reached over and ratcheted the volume. The Porsche wouldn't even officially hit the U.S. export market for a couple months, but Devlin had garnered one of the few advance European prototypes after the car's debut at the Paris Auto Show.

Like other astute drivers of high-end machinery, Devlin understood and respected the car's lethal twin traits: lightning-fast ability and balls-out fury. With a voracious power plant squeezed onto a short wheelbase, the Porsche was prone to unwieldy and lethal over-steer.

Further complicating the equation was the sheer torque of the turbocharged engine, which lagged at low RPMs and then erupted with incredible blasts of horsepower. To stabilize the car, Porsche used a whale-tail rear spoiler to create more down force at the back end, along with flared wheel wells to boost the car's width and grip. But still, under its exotic curves this machine was an angry beast that was thrilling and killing without remorse. To uninitiated rookie drivers, the first taste of the German turbo blast instinctively led to easing off the accelerator pedal, which only further devolved the car's precious traction and stability. Consequently, Devlin had been reading about newbies wrapping 930s around power poles and into oncoming truck grilles, within days of purchase, and a growing list of product liability lawsuits from the families of dead drivers.

Devlin knew from his racing days back in Buffalo that acceleration increased, not decreased, traction. And keeping the Porsche at high revs minimized the turbo lag. With that acumen, he'd yet to see a sports car on the road that could stay with his 930, but the Porsche always demanded equal amounts of skill, fear, and respect.

At the Maricopa County Medical Examiner building, Devlin parked and went inside to find his new forensic expert. While the Pearson case would be a one-off and in the books soon, it had also motivated Devlin to track down a good pathologist who could unravel the medical vernacular on malpractice cases and, most importantly, appeal to jurors. Ford Rockwell was that person.

Devlin had actually cross-examined him a number of times from the defense side when one of Lucky's miscreants had done something stupid, which was often. Rockwell, an up-and-comer in the ME's office, was equally entertaining and unflappable on the witness stand, a rare combination that always impressed Devlin. Rockwell was a handsome cat, with short black hair and a neatly trimmed black moustache that turned down on both sides all the way to his jaw. Many people told him he looked like the tough guy from the film *Deliverance*, Burt Reynolds. Devlin saw a passing resemblance to the actor, although Rockwell was a much leaner and less muscled version.

When Devlin checked out Rockwell's credentials he found a veritable genius. Turned out Rockwell did his undergraduate studies at Dartmouth in biology *in three years* and got nothing but A's. *What the fuck.* Four years at Notre Dame and all Devlin could do was scrape out a degree in Russian literature (the easiest major he could find) and almost throw up on his LSAT. After getting his bachelor's degree, Rockwell went on to Harvard for medical school and eventually became triple board-certified in pathology, dermo-pathology, and neurology. Now, after the same amount of time Devlin had (ostensibly) been a lawyer, Rockwell was chief of pathology in the ME's office. With his photographic recall, Rockwell immediately remembered the tall, spirited lawyer with the long hair, thick sideburns, and quick wit. He told Devlin he'd be happy to review the case, and asked to see Ann Pearson's autopsy and medical charts. Additionally, he wanted to get cuts of the tissue slides to review.

Devlin was champing to get Rockwell's sign-off on Ann Pearson's cause of death so he could turn his entire focus back to the Big City Auto Sales case. Max Daniels was still ferreting out the documentation they needed, and the detective's meter was happily clicking away. Meanwhile, the Dubrow trio was getting harder to manage. Rick still didn't have a job and had continued to hit up Devlin for nickel-and-dime bridge loans to stay afloat, which Rick said to just deduct from their settlement. Devlin had fronted him a few hundred here and there to keep Rick's electricity and phone turned on, but he couldn't keep running a tab.

Lucy, meanwhile, kept asking why it was taking so long and, even though they hadn't even officially filed a lawsuit, wanted to know when she would get her settlement check and about how much would it be, you know, ballpark? The third sibling, Bob, at least, wasn't bothering the lawyer because he'd been on a month-long coke bender out in Apache Junction, a dusty outpost east of Phoenix. Devlin had about nine months invested already with these clients and, best scenario, another six months if the case settled. If it went to trial, he'd be babysitting for another year or two. In other words, closure on Ann Pearson would free up some much-needed energy to move Big City Auto Sales along as fast as possible.

Fifteen minutes later, however, things took a decided U-turn when Ford Rockwell said, "You're barking up the wrong tree, counselor." It was uncanny, but Rockwell even smiled like Burt Reynolds. The guy was just so damn likable and brilliant and had none of the false modesty or arrogance of most superstar expert witnesses. Devlin couldn't wait to get him before a jury some day.

"What do you mean?"

"What I mean is they killed her."

"Wait a minute. Killed her? Whom are we talking about here?"

"The nursing home..." Rockwell flipped open the file and read the name. "Mercy Care Center."

As smart as he was, maybe Rockwell had missed something. "Are we talking about the same case? Ann Pearson?"

Rockwell looked at the folder and nodded. "Ann Pearson. You want a Grape Nehi?"

Devlin shook his head. Rockwell lived on the stuff and, subsequently, always had a purple tongue. Devlin would have to talk to him about that if he were ever prepping him for trial. "Talk to me here. Killed her? I thought we said this was routine heart failure, right?"

"No," he said, popping the top off the bottle and taking a long drink. "You might have said that. I never said that. I would never draw such a conclusion before I reviewed the physical evidence. How could I, without a scientific basis?"

"Yeah, but *killed* her? C'mon, doc. You can tell that just from an autopsy and her charts?"

"Well, I read everything. And technically you are correct because, eventually, everyone dies of arrhythmia, or heart failure. In our last moment, the heart stops and, that's it. *Bedtime for Bonzo*. But in this instance, there's more. Much more. It is my theory that the pressure ulcer she developed, in a time span of only ten days, caused sepsis, or widespread infection, that literally permeated her blood."

"Permeated her blood? Jesus. And you're saying that killed her?"

Rockwell nodded and pointed his Grape Nehi at Devlin. "Exactly, counselor."

In medical law, the seminal evaluative tool is the patient's records and charts. There is a medical explanation for every problem, and every medical explanation is subsequently a potential legal minefield, with various competing theories. In the courtroom, Rockwell's theory would be attacked by a qualified defense expert with a contradictory and equally certain position, drawn from the same records and charts.

"OK, assuming your theory stands, can we prove this? That they killed her during those ten days?"

Rockwell nodded. "That, of course, will be difficult. Can we prove that the widespread sepsis, as a result of the nursing home's neglect, was the direct cause of Ann Pearson's death?" Rockwell considered his own question. "Don't know. You can certainly make that case."

"But will a jury buy it?"

"That would be your arena, counselor."

"But you've testified a fair amount. What's your gut feeling?"

"I guess I'm not so sure. Might be a stretch for a jury to pin this on anyone considering her age, various co-morbidities and fragile health prior to the event. And I don't know; is there any precedent here for going after a nursing home?"

"Not really. And even if there were," Devlin said, "there's the elephant in the room we haven't discussed."

"Collectability," Rockwell said. "They solvent?"

Devlin nodded. "Surprisingly so. When I checked it out, the good news is that this little outfit Mercy Care Center is one of seventy such facilities operated by a privately owned corporation called Flynn Enterprises."

"I'd bet this Grape Nehi that Flynn Enterprises has some decent liability coverage."

"Yeah," said Devlin. "And you know the bad news, right?"

"Yeah. I will tell you that in the few medical cases in which I've testified against institutional defendants, the plaintiff's side got crushed. It wasn't even close. On the other side, I've seen cases where juries awarded very large amounts of money in malpractice suits. Much more than in automobile accidents and personal injuries. But I don't know that I've ever heard about a nursing home case."

"So what you're saying is your batting average as a medical expert is zero. Now I'm really screwed." Devlin smiled.

"Not really. Just like the pitcher in baseball, the lawyer takes the win or loss, not the expert witness. Maybe they were just all minor league lawyers." They both laughed.

"Help me out here, Ford. Should I back off? Too big of a mountain to climb?"

He finished his Grape Nehi and let out a long, low burp. "Medically you have a good case if you focus on the sepsis created by the infection. Not only do you have a good case of abuse and neglect, I'd categorize this as criminal neglect. A sore of that depth and scope could only develop to that extent if left totally unattended for a period of many days. Like I said, they killed her. And if that's true, regardless of how daunting a corporate defendant might be, how can you not take the case?"

Devlin knew he was right, but he was already $10,000-plus into Big City Auto Sales with nothing filed yet. Perhaps he could refer the Ann Pearson case and take a back-end. At least that way her daughter would have her shot at justice, and he would be freed up for his big case. But, clearly, Devlin knew being a lawyer was never that neat and clean.

"Thanks, Ford. I'll be in touch, let you know what I decide."

"Sounds excellent. Great to see you again."

Back in the Porsche, Devlin sat and stared at the steering wheel. He'd come here to close this case out. Now this little stunner: *Did they really kill that woman by letting her stew in her own infection day after day? Like Kay said, could that really happen in 1975? And was this done with malevolence? Were there other people out there right now suffering similar fates? Do we live in a society where people are left to die like this? Makes you wonder.*

Devlin kept his anger in check because, for now, there was still a part of him that couldn't believe things had played out with such blatant disregard for Ann Pearson. He started the Porsche, grabbed first gear, and blasted away. He couldn't push away the gnawing intuition that something was starting to stink and, if so, this case could only get bigger, more complicated, and more expensive. Not to mention the damn thing was unwinnable. That's what he got for going to the best, an unearthly egghead like Ford Rockwell.

Going back some ten months, Devlin had been down fifty different trails looking for information to build his Big City Auto Sales case. He'd racked up a lot of miles on the Porsche chasing leads and interviewing cops, making trips to the Motor Vehicles Department, and running down documents. Most importantly, he finally had possession of the Monte Carlo, and his tire expert lined up and flying in next week. Based on the tire analysis, he could draft and file the lawsuit within the next ninety days and begin deposing witnesses. But now this surprise twist. If he wanted to sleep at night, Devlin only had one choice. What he needed was to go do a little more digging, undercover, to see firsthand what went really on at this Mercy Care Center.

Chapter Nine

MERCY CARE CENTER was in a quiet historic neighborhood near downtown Phoenix. Lined with 1920s houses and towering oaks and sycamores planted by homesick Midwesterners, the area was a throwback to Devlin's own childhood digs. He drove the street once, scouting out Mercy Care Center, and then parked two blocks away and walked. He didn't want any questions about the car (and the rare Porsche always generated questions), who he was, or why he was there. Ditching the 930 was a good start on all those fronts. He'd also dressed down—a tie-dyed T-shirt Jessica Jean had given him that he'd never worn, shorts, and flip-flops—and hadn't shaved all weekend in anticipation of this investigative excursion. Rather than some nosy and intimidating litigator, he looked like a gangly college kid. Just another visiting grandson. And just in case, he was even prepared with an alias: Dallas Klotz, aka The Hawaiian Champ, the boxing bust he and Walsh had backed. Devlin was certain no one had ever heard of that chump.

From the outside, nothing seemed amiss. The grass was brown, but so were most lawns in February except a few rich folks and the resorts that went to the trouble and expense of over-seeding with winter rye. The facility was a converted, solid-block house that could stand fresh white paint, but certainly didn't appear to be a den of human suffering. Attached to the original house was an extended addition. The red-pitched roof looked solid and watertight. From all outside appearances, there were certainly worse places to while away the Golden Years.

But when Devlin pulled open one of the two double doors, he was immediately hit with a stinging smell that fell somewhere between cat piss and vomit. He closed his eyes and literally recoiled at the stench before stepping inside. He was standing in what must have originally been the living room, with a large fireplace, sparse but well-appointed furnishings, and a metal reception desk that reminded him of his battleship at Grant & Ross. The room was spacious, painted hospital-white, and devoid of any palpable life spirit.

"Hello?"

There were several doors, one to his immediate left and two back behind the desk, all closed. He chose the closest door, which opened to a long hallway. The smell was still stinging his nose, but was already less offensive. In thirty minutes, he thought, he probably wouldn't even notice it, which is how patients and staff must acclimate. The hallway, too, was ostensibly white but both the walls and linoleum had a dingy, yellowish hue. With each step, his flip-flops stuck and peeled away from the sticky floor.

"Hello?"

The person slumped in a wheelchair at the far end of the hallway, man or woman, didn't respond. Devlin looked into rooms as he passed, all of which were offices. One or two had the lights on, but the rest were dark. All were in various states of disarray. When he reached the wheelchair he knelt down and saw that it was an elderly man, unshaven, and either asleep, unconscious, or dead.

"Sir? Hello?" There was hardened, green snot caked around both of his nostrils. A long string of continuous drool went from one corner of the man's mouth down to his chest, where it commingled with his thick, gray chest hair and the yellowed gown. And judging from the smell, the large puddle beneath the chair was the man's urine.

"Jesus Christ. Is there anyone here to help this poor guy?" Devlin reached out and gently shook the man's arm. "Hey, pal? You OK?"

The man's eyes opened slowly, and he smacked his lips before saying, "Not going to tell you again."

"I'm sorry?"

"You heard me. Don't you talk back to me." He stared at the floor with a heavy scowl.

Devlin looked around again for a doctor, nurse, someone. "I'll see if I can get you some help, pal."

"Not going to tell you again."

Devlin stepped through another door, which opened to a large infirmary ward. There were probably twenty beds squeezed together and lining the perimeter. About half the beds were empty. At least two people were snoring loudly. Some sat upright in their beds. Others lay on their backs and stared at the ceiling. Still, not a single doctor, nurse, or staff person in sight. The room had an eerie starkness to it, with an energy that felt more morgue than hospital. The smell of death, Devlin thought, is what hits you when you open that front door.

"What do they call you?"

Devlin turned. It was a gray-haired, thin man with a pleasant smile sitting up in bed. "I'm… Devlin. Nice to meet you." If there was one thing these people needed, it was some real human connection. Using the alias now seemed silly and unnecessary, and might somehow lessen the interaction.

"Devlin, my boy, Edward William Macintyre. But my friends call me 'Fast Eddie.' Top of the morning. I think fast, talk fast, and eat fast. I used to drive fast, drink fast, and buzz through the dames fast. But I got two words will slow everything down real quick: 'I do.' The old ball-and-chain sort of puts the brakes on, if you know what I mean. Now I just sit here thinking fast, a million ways to get the hell out of this place. Goddam prison in here."

"Hey, there's a guy out in the hallway I think needs some help or something?"

"Yeah? Well, get in line. Look around. Who in here doesn't need help? Jesus. They just park us in here to die, and if that doesn't take the cake, I don't know what does."

"Should I go find a nurse or—"

"Don't bother. They'll be around eventually. That's probably just old Ben anyway." Devlin looked toward the hallway, unsure what to do.

"I'm not going to tell you again?" Eddie said.

Devlin nodded. "Yeah, that's him."

"Son, please, sit." Fast Eddie motioned to the empty bed next to his.

"You don't mind?"

"Mind? If you don't stay willingly, I'm going to handcuff you there just to break the damn monotop… monolop… monolot—"

"The monotony?"

"The boredom!" Fast Eddie snapped his fingers. "Great minds think alike, eh partner?"

"Yes they do. Where you from, Eddie?"

"Fast Eddie's the name, son. Fast Eddie. Dublin. Born and raised. Grew up on a dairy farm but never wanted to be around cows my whole life. They don't smell too good, and the conversation's all one-way. Know what I mean? I was all about the dames and the high life. Came to America with my mate John. The Windy City. The second city my ass, Chicago's my kind of town. Son, you know what a 'flapper' is?"

"Like a dancing girl?"

"Not like a dancing girl, they *are* dancing girls. Not to mention drinking, carousing, necking…phew, those American lassies was crazy as Aunt Millie after she got head-kicked by that Holstein. I got a job in a bank, Devlin, 1923, and boy oh boy was I Mr. Big Shot. I was too young for the first WW and too old for all the rest of them. I never hurt nothing in my life except about a thousand wee lasses and their white-picket dreams, at least until I met my Sadie. Holy Moses, son, those was some crazy times." The spirit in Fast Eddie's words contrasted with his sunken eyes, the heavy dark circles, and the deep yellow pallor of his face. Fast Eddie's spirit was willing, but his body didn't look like he'd see next month.

"Look at this stinking place, son. It's like the ship of death sailing to the ends of the Earth. Don't ever end up here, my good boy. You see other people getting old but you never think you're going to be one of them, you know what I mean? Then one, two, three, you're sitting here in your own piss wondering where the hell your life went. Someone should tell you right at the start not to waste one precious minute, because it all blows by so fast. You go to college, son?"

"Notre Dame."

"Oh sweet Jesus, Mary, and Joseph, he's one of ours. He's a regular Knute Rockne, this kid. Notre Dame? What sort of work you do, Devlin?"

Devlin considered it and then said, "Like you. Finance. Investments." With a nose for the deal, it didn't seem like a deception. No need to raise any questions about a lawyer nosing around. To many, a lawyer asking questions could be like a trip to the dentist.

"Brilliant. How about the wee lasses? You stacking them up and knocking them down? Do it while you still can, son, I'll tell you what. Next thing you know your best friend there will look like a month-old beef stick someone left in the sun."

After another fifteen minutes of similar banter with Fast Eddie, Devlin still hadn't seen a single doctor or nurse. One of the patients across the room was moaning and calling out, "Nurse… nurse… nurse…" Devlin pried himself away from Fast Eddie, promising he'd stop back before he left, and walked through a door that opened to another large ward with twenty more beds. This ward smelled worse, like actual fecal matter, and was at full capacity. The desperate faces staring back at Devlin were all, like Fast Eddie had said, those of passengers booked on the Ship of Death: one-way passage to the end. Finally, Devlin spotted a nurse at the back of the room. His rage was at full throttle.

"Excuse me, nurse?"

Without turning from the patient, she said, "Busy. I'll get there when I get there. This is what happens when staff shirk responsibility. Sick. If she's sick I'm Ellen Burstyn, and *Alice Doesn't Live Here Anymore*." She was tending to an IV, and Devlin spotted an Isaac Asimov paperback under her arm. She wasn't carrying any kind of clipboard or patient charts.

"Excuse me, there's a man up front I think needs some immediate—"

"Immediate what?" she said.

"Help. Medical attention."

"Yeah, and look around," she said, turning now. "There's 51 people here need immediate…well, take your pick. And what do you see? That's right, you see one of me. Now let's do some calculating…OK, don't add up now does it? So if you'll please stop wasting my valuable time I said I'll get there when I get there." She turned back to the IV.

Devlin put a lid on it, quelled the surge of anger and disbelief. "If you're short-handed, perhaps I could help?"

She spun back around. "Who exactly are you, anyway? Are you even authorized to be in here?"

Good question. He'd only been wandering around for how long without anyone noticing? "I'm just here to visit."

"Visit who?"

"Well, my uncle. But I like to make the rounds, too."

"Which one's your uncle?"

"Mr. Macintyre."

"Who?"

"Fast Eddie."

She rolled her eyes. "Oh, that one. All right, Fast Eddie junior, you really want to help, then go in the cafeteria and help with breakfast. Least you'll be out of my damn way."

With each subsequent room, the befuddlement and desperation in the patients worsened. After helping spoon runny eggs, shriveled bacon and burnt toast on the line, Devlin moved from table to table and, literally, helped people eat their breakfast. Many didn't seem to have the ability to even lift the plastic fork or spread jam on their toast. Others had difficulty drinking the orange juice or lukewarm coffee. The ones who could eat finished with egg stuck to their lips and faces.

Then he sat and, like AAA Bail Bonds on a Friday night, held court. First there were three people, and then two more shuffled over, and another in a wheelchair. Within five minutes, there were ten elderly people crowded around Devlin, all craving conversation, stimulation, and informational tidbits from the outside world like prisoners doing life sentences. He told them about the Winter Olympics that had just started in Innsbruck, Austria. Then he got stuck trying to explain the geographical proximity of Austria to Australia, the understanding of which was wholly unsuccessful for several befuddled residents. He switched gears and told them stories about the nights prowling Buffalo in the Cadillac. He told them about his college days at Notre Dame and driving around with his roommate everyone called Frankenstein, and how they named Frankenstein's pink 1954 Buick "The Womb." A couple of the old folks even laughed.

As he sat there and talked and connected with them on a human level, he thought about Ann Pearson. He pictured her among this clutch, cut off from everything she loved and herded around like livestock. He thought about her languishing in one of those foul-stenched wards, in pain, unable to move or ask for the help she needed. He thought about being abused in the worst possible way, simply ignored, while that robotic charge nurse gave each patient a cursory check before moving on to the next. This place was nothing more than a warehouse for the living dead. Unfortunately, even with that and Rockwell's theory, the facts still didn't seem to warrant a case. Regardless, Mercy Care Center had planted a seed of rage in Devlin's core. True to his word, Devlin stopped at Fast Eddie's bedside before leaving. "What do you say there, Irish?" Fast Eddie's eyes were opening and closing.

"You get some rest, pal. I'll come visit again."

"Don't wait too long, Devlin. We drop like ants under a magnifying glass in this place." His eyes closed. "One stretch there, last year I think, we lost some good women who had no reason to go."

"What do you mean?"

"What I mean is they came in one way and left on a gurney. This place sucks the life right out of people. I'm telling you, hang around too long you might go, too."

"One of them wasn't Ann Pearson, by chance?"

"Irish, I can't remember if I shit my pants five minutes ago, so I sure as hell don't remember names. All I know is what I saw."

"What did you see?"

"Same thing you're seeing right now, Devlin. Look around. How many nurses and doctors you seen since you been here? And how many of us? I saw fresh-faced women come in here to get back on their feet and end up dead, is what I saw."

"How many times did this happen?"

"Devlin boy, these questions; you writing a book or something? Besides, I'm older than Moses and not half as wise. Let me see… maybe three times I can remember."

"Three? Three different women?"

"If my feeble mind serves me, yes."

"You don't remember one named Ann Pearson?"

"They don't exactly put on a Sadie Hawkins dance around here every week for us to put names to faces, if you know what I mean. I do remember the last one came in, dark hair, nice smile, and went back to the hospital maybe a week later. Gosh, when was that?"

"Maybe last Spring? March?"

"Jesus, Mary, and Joseph. Another year stuck here? Couldn't tell you her name if you promised me one more go in the promised land with a wee young lass. Just couldn't tell you. But there was the one..." Fast Eddie snapped his fingers. "Yes, she liked to go to the dog track."

Ann Pearson.

Soon as he walked out of here, Devlin was going to call that tenacious hard-ass Max Daniels to track down the families of these two other women and see if it was true, if there was an ongoing pattern of neglect. That just might shine a little light on this case. The energy was boiling inside Devlin and already forming into a hard possibility: These people had crossed paths with the wrong plaintiff's attorney.

"Only way I know this, Irish, is I run my mouth with anyone who walks through that door. I can barely walk anymore, and I sure as hell can't do the old sideways jig. So talking is the only thing keeps me alive. Anyway, she's the one had a daughter, I think. But I could never forget her two friends came to visit here a lot, and they told me what happened."

"You don't remember her friends' names, do you?"

"Friends' names? Wait until you're my age, Irish. Some days you can't remember your own name. I'm afraid not. But I'll never forget their faces. There was a colored fellow, nice as could be, that one, and only had one arm. You don't forget something like that: Colored boy with one arm."

Devlin felt buoyed, a surging sense of purpose when he knew he was ready to take someone to the wall. "And the other?"

"The other? She was an old lady from New York who talked like the words coming out of her mouth were all hooked to a freight train."

Chapter Ten

"WELL, I AIN'T WEARING no stinking shirt and tie for no one," said Rick Dubrow, the still-unemployed welder who, unintentionally, loved testing his lawyer's patience and diplomacy. "Period. End of story." He crossed his arms and sat back.

"Hell, I don't care what I wear," said Lucy. "I'll wear a goddam clown nose and hang out the girls with bells on 'em if that's what you says gonna get us paid. How much you say again we'll get tomorrow?" She, too, had lost her job. But what she lacked in social diplomacy and employment status, she gained back as the only one of Devlin's three clients with at least one bare-bone standard of stability: an actual address. Her own struggles with alcohol and choosing abusive men were, at least, further afield in terms of admissibility.

Cocaine addict and eldest brother Bob was still AWOL. Yesterday, his siblings had narrowed his general whereabouts to a trailer cluster on the outskirts of the desert. They vowed to Devlin that they would return tonight, find Bob, keep him in lockdown, and ration out just enough cocaine to keep him from either slipping into a violent detox or disappearing altogether again. They even coined a new word for this delicate process: "stabilitilating." And they assured the lawyer that, in Rick's exact words, "We'll have that miserable bag of rooster droppings at tomorrow's settling-up hearing if it kills him and us. I mean, we won't kill no one *for real* kill 'em. Hell, you know what I mean, *lawyer*."

Devlin took a slow steady breath without changing his expression. That was a new one—just calling him "lawyer"—and he wondered again why he didn't just bounce them all out of here, right now, his patience winnowed down to zero. A few months back, Devlin had officially filed the wrongful death suit against Big City Auto Sales. Almost without exception, sixty days later the opposing side in any case would play the standard slow-down game by filing for an extension to answer. Another common defense strategy, which had occurred in this case, was to get a settlement call that was really just a lowball ploy to make the case go away. Given his clients' various challenges—personal, career, hygiene, and grammatical—Devlin was starting to wonder if he sided with the defense on this one: *Yes, please, make it go away!* If he didn't settle tomorrow, he was going to be stuck with these three for a long time. And asking a jury to hand large sums of money to this clan would be, in the vernacular of these same clients, dumb as shit. Amid the inane banter, the lawyer's mind drifted back to last year and meeting Lucy and Rick. He could pinpoint the timeframe because the meeting was shortly before Saigon officially fell. And unbeknown to Devlin around the same time, Ann Pearson was in her final days in the institution now in Devlin's crosshairs.

After visiting Mercy Care Center for the first time, Devlin's first phone call was Max Daniels. He put Daniels on the trail to find everything he could about the place and its corporate owner Flynn Enterprises. Then he called Ford Rockwell and told him about the two other possible victims during the same time span. Daniels hadn't been able to find any information yet about the deceased or their families. Rockwell, meanwhile, told Devlin he needed to find a good expert witness in the area of nursing home administration and health care. Devlin was working his network on that one, but hadn't found the right person yet. In 1976, he was discovering, few such people existed.

The second phone call was to Kay Pearson. Devlin called her work number from the pay phone at The Wellington, where he'd gone for lunch. Standing there in his tie-dyed T-shirt and shorts, he told her what he knew: that he was officially now her lawyer, and that he would call every week or so with an update. All along he'd thought Big City Auto Sales was his first big shot. Monetarily, that might still be true. But for sheer indignation and institutional arrogance, Mercy Care Center was now at the top of his hit list. He vowed to Kay Pearson that he would not rest until he'd exhausted every possibility of calling them on the carpet. Later, over Friday night beers, he told One-Armed Lucky the same thing.

The ensuing months had passed quickly. On March 20, Patty Hearst was convicted of bank robbery. Her attorney F. Lee Bailey failed to put across the defense strategy that Hearst had been brainwashed, coerced, and intimidated into joining her captors. Devlin usually followed such legal drama with keen interest, but he barely noticed this one. Nor did he notice, as both a music fan and an auto aficionado, The Ramones' self-titled debut or the rain-shortened result of the Indianapolis 500, the shortest in history, with Johnny Rutherford winning after just 102 laps. Long before filing any official lawsuit, Devlin's focus had already narrowed to not include much beyond the woman he'd never met: Ann Pearson.

In June, the hometown Phoenix Suns, after finishing the season with a ho-hum 42-40 record, shocked everyone by beating the defending NBA champion Golden State Warriors in the playoffs. In the NBA Finals, the Suns squared off against the Boston Celtics. But Devlin, again, missed most of the games, including Gar Heard's triple-overtime buzzer-beater in Game 5.

As a bookend to meeting the Dubrows, July opened with North and South Vietnam uniting to form the communist Socialist Republic of Vietnam. That's the way the geologic timeline of the law moved: In the same time span of accepting and building the case against Big City Auto Sales, the tectonic plates of world history were shifting around Devlin. The next day, Devlin was enraged with the Supreme Court's *Gregg v. Georgia* ruling that the death penalty was not inherently cruel or unusual and was, therefore, a constitutionally acceptable form of punishment. The decision and ensuing discussion put a pall on the normally jovial Friday night proceedings at AAA Bail Bonds. The weekend had culminated yesterday with the USA's bicentennial celebrations from coast to coast. Now it was Monday morning, and Devlin was listening to his clients squabble. A settlement tomorrow meant *vaya con dios*. He savored that thought.

However, Devlin wouldn't sell out the Dubrows with just any lowball figure the defense offered. The goal, instead, was scrape out something that would both appease his clients and satisfy Devlin's sense that he had served them well. In Devlin's mind, that meant a high target of $250,000, a landmark amount that would be, by far, his largest settlement to date (and one he'd already earmarked for the Ann Pearson case). More realistically, however, he would advise his clients to accept anything north of $150,000, maybe even $125,000 given the age of the deceased. His clients' overall stupidity induced headaches, but in terms of the case was irrelevant and inadmissible. Even so, he couldn't risk putting these people before a jury because that meant, well, they would be speaking, for starters. The purpose of today's meeting was Devlin's standard final briefing before any settlement conference. So it was time try to impart some vestige of decorum onto the people he had himself chosen as clients.

"When we meet with the opposing counsel tomorrow, I don't want anyone in the room except the two of you and your brother," he said with authority, snapping them out of their meandering diatribe. "That means no girlfriends, boyfriends, friends or cronies. Rick, fine, if you won't wear a shirt and tie then at least wear long pants and a collared shirt. No T-shirts, OK?"

Rick shrugged his shoulders. "I don't see why I got to change. I'm not the one killed Mom."

Devlin sighed. "First impressions speak volumes. The other side has never met you, so the first thing they'll be thinking tomorrow is, 'Will a jury like these people?' We don't want to give them any reason to think anything other than you are each wonderful, well-dressed, likable people."

"I understand. I got a shirt somewhere, I think, has a collar. But I ain't going out and buying—"

"Fine. Let's move on from this. What about Bob? He has to be here tomorrow for us to settle."

"Yeah, we'll go snatch him up tonight like we said," Lucy said.

"Besides," said Rick. "It's his loss if he don't come, right? That will just mean more money for us two?"

Devlin shook his head. "If he's not here tomorrow, we cannot settle this case. The defense will not settle a case piecemeal. We need all three named plaintiffs to be present."

"But you said we each got different cases, right?" Lucy said.

"No, you each have different *claims*, but it's one case against Big City Auto Sales. If Bob's not here tomorrow, then nothing happens. And let me speak to that point. We need to settle this case because, in terms of jury appeal, I have to say that's our best strategy. So let's not squander this chance tomorrow." The diplomatic dig was lost on the Dubrows.

"Fine," Rick said. "So what do we do tomorrow?"

"Yeah," Lucy added. "How's it work? We get the check during or right after? Because then I'm going to celebrate with my man who's getting a good meal and some hot action. You want to keep your man happy? Mama always said, 'Keep his stomach full and his balls drained.'"

Devlin sighed and let it go as he had a thousand times with this clan. "We will first meet in this room with the defense side and the mediator. He's a retired judge. Other than saying good morning, neither of you nor your brother will speak while we are in this room. The mediator will make some opening remarks and then each side will go into a different conference room. The mediator's job is to get agreement on a number that works for both sides. But the process can be like water torture. The first offer will be an insult, and we will reject it. From there, plan on being here all day. They'll make an offer, and we'll make a counter-offer. It will go back and forth like that all day long."

"Why they do that? Why not just settle up real quick and be done?" Lucy asked.

"It's a tedious diplomatic process born out of centuries of horse trading."

"Horse trading? That's funny," Lucy said, laughing.

"You think we'll settle up tomorrow?" Rick asked.

"We may or may not get to a number we like. You just never know how it will go."

"So what's our number?" Rick asked. "How much we shooting for? Aim high, right, lawyer?"

"Let's see how the process unfolds tomorrow. It's more about seeing where they start and going from there." In most cases Devlin's clients would be privy to their lawyer's planned moves and strategy. But giving these folks too much information was like handing a loaded pistol to a toddler.

The next morning, at precisely 9, there were eight people seated around the conference table in Devlin's office: The lawyer, his three clients, including a relatively sober-looking Bob Dubrow apparently bolstered by his "stabilitilating" process; two lawyers from Big City Auto Sales and a lawyer from their insurance company; and the retired judge-turned-mediator.

"There are no facts, only interpretations," the mediator said to open the settlement conference. "That's a quote from Nietzsche, and in the arena of law he is dead on. Both sides here today have a different version of the same story. Both sides must concurrently weigh the risk of going forward with their case against the benefits of settling today. There are risks and benefits to both, which both sides must carefully consider."

The mediator was David Nash, and Devlin was paying him some serious dough, $175 an hour, to be here. Nash was in his early 50s now, gray-haired with a sparse, white beard worn like Abraham Lincoln, and recently retired from the bench. Devlin had come through his courtroom during the run with Walsh, and Nash liked the kid's acumen and enthusiasm for the law. He'd already mediated several smaller cases for Devlin and through the process the two had developed a deep fondness for each other that neither would ever verbalize. Instead, it played out as a rapid-fire exchange of vulgar insults.

"Going forward means waiting another year or 18 months for a trial date. Going forward means assuming the costs for preparing the case for trial. There's also the wild card known as the jury. Most jurors have an innate instinct that usually comes to the fore upon opening statements. The rest of the trial, all of the evidence, is seen through the filter of how well the evidence squares with the original gut feeling inside each jury member. No matter how airtight, there isn't any case that can't be lost. Nor is there any case that can't be won. And then, even after a verdict, there is the appeals process that might further drag out final resolution for years."

He paused, looked around at each face, and then continued. "Likewise, there is a price to reaching resolution today. For the plaintiffs, there is the possibility of accepting an offer that is far less than a jury might award. For the defense, there is the possibility of paying an amount far more than a jury might award. This is the cost/benefit analysis each side must consider today."

Unbeknown to his clients, Devlin had already submitted a demand letter to the defense asking for $1 million. He could barely believe it himself, that he was asking for that much, but he knew the way the game worked: Start high and see if they called his bluff. The demand was split: $600,000 in the wrongful death of Claire Dubrow, or $200,000 to each of the decedent's children, plus a personal injury demand of $400,000 for Rick's back injuries and Lucy's two children.

After the judge spoke and the two sides exchanged a few more strained pleasantries, each group went into a different conference room. Devlin heard Rick Dubrow asking his brother if Nietzsche played for the Bears or Packers. Devlin left them to figure it out for themselves. Fifteen minutes later, the judge came into Devlin's office with the first offer. Devlin had intentionally sequestered himself in his office with the clients in the conference room. Normally they would be included in each visit from the mediator, but Devlin didn't want to spend an entire day listening to them bicker.

"All right, Devlin. Here it is. Ready?"

"Lay it on me, judge."

"Fifty grand."

"Total?"

"Total. Twenty five each for wrongful death and their injuries."

Devlin considered this. Offering $50,000 when he'd asked for $1 million was a flat-out, lowball insult. He was realistically hoping they would counter with something more serious; say, low $100s. Then if he hammered all day he might squeeze out close to that $250,000 mark. This was their message: *You have no case, Devlin, and we're ready to go to trial to prove it.* "What do you think, judge? They're fucking with me."

"Yeah. I'd say so."

"You think they're serious about settling?"

"I'm not sure. They're definitely probing you. How old was the deceased in this case?"

"Eighty two."

"I think they're going to try to make this case go away today, but they're going to wring you out in the process."

"Should we even counter? Or just reject it and tell them we'll only consider a serious offer?" Each passing year as a lawyer did change one's perspective, Devlin thought. Fifty grand was still a lot of money, but had lost its relative power of awe to the kid from Buffalo. Only six figures and up was going to do that now.

"That's one way to go. But you don't want to piss them off, either. You could go down to $750,000. Show them you're flexible and willing to move off your number, but that you, too, can play nickel-and-dime all day."

"All right. Let me go to the clients with this." Devlin grabbed his legal pad and stood.

"And Devlin?"

"Yeah?"

"Buy a decent fucking suit. You dress for shit."

Devlin shook his head. The suit was one of two, at $850 each, that he'd just had tailored. The judge was laughing.

"Yeah, and you can come shopping with me, judge. Let me go get your wheelchair and oxygen bottle, you ancient fucking fossil."

With that Devlin walked down the hall to the conference room. He told the Dubrow trio they'd receive an offer, that it was low as expected, and he was recommending they reject it.

"How much?" Lucy said.

"They offered $50,000."

"Oh hell no," said Bob, throwing his arms up as though such an offer was a personal affront. Homeless and jobless, twenty-four hours ago he was in a drug haze and knee-deep in cocaine-hungry women. Then Bob scoffed again as though the other side's lawyer had just urinated in his breakfast cereal.

"I agree," said Devlin. "We reject this and see what's next."

"Yeah," Lucy said. "Tell them to get serious." She, too, folded her arms.

It was time for Devlin to plant the seed. "Now, I don't know where we'll end up today, and if we don't get a number we like, I'm prepared to take this to trial." That last part was a small lie: a trial was out of the question. Devlin continued, "Now I've told you that trials are always risky. If we get something in the six-figure range, say $150,000, then I think you all need to seriously think about taking that offer. If we go to trial and lose, you get nothing. OK?" Devlin left before they had time to start arguing with him, and walked back to the awaiting judge.

"Well?"

Devlin scribbled on his legal pad and ripped off the page. "Go to them with this."

"Six hundred grand? You sure you want to move that much after their horseshit offer?"

"Judge, we have to settle this case today. I can't babysit those three idiots another year waiting for a trial date. They'll implode before we ever get to court."

"OK, Devlin. I'll see what I can do."

An hour later, the judge returned with the defense counter-offer. Devlin's willingness to negotiate seemed to have paid off: they were offering $70,000. A far cry from his demand of $1 million or even his target of $250,000, but they were now moving toward the arena, at least, of something he could start working on his clients to accept. He repeated the process, told his clients to reject it, and sent the judge back with a counter-offer of $525,000. He'd moved a lot the first time; now it was time for them to get serious.

Their counter: If Devlin was at $450,000, then they could be at $85,000. Devlin countered that if they were at $100,000, he could be at $450,000. The judge walked across the hall to deliver Devlin's latest. The defense didn't counter until after lunch.

"All right, Devlin. They went with what you offered: They're at $100,000 if you're at $450,000. Now here's the thing: They said that's as high as they're authorized to go today. The insurance guy said $100,000 is his check-writing limit without getting an override from corporate."

"That's horseshit. They send a guy to settle the case who can only go to $100,000 when our original demand was a million? They really don't think much of our case, do they?"

"Yeah, and from what you've told me, neither do you."

"Yeah, well... the case is decent; it's the clients who are idiots. But the other side doesn't know that."

There was no doubt in his mind that the dealership had blatantly committed fraud when they put the ratty Monte Carlo on the lot as new. Devlin's tire expert would assert that the rubber was shot, and Ford Rockwell would testify that Claire Dubrow died in the original impact from an axonal brain injury, not because she'd been thrown from the vehicle. And in depositions, Devlin was drawing out pure gold from the dealership's own employees. His case against Big City Auto Sales was as strong as any he'd ever had.

The defense, however, would assert that Claire Dubrow died as a result of not wearing her seat belt, which was documented in the autopsy report by a lack of any bruising across her chest and abdomen. They would further contend that her advanced age and various medical conditions were the real culprit. As icing on the cake, they would then throw up a cloud of obfuscation with various theories and possibilities about how the shoddy tires ended up on the Monte Carlo.

Ladies and gentlemen of the jury, has the plaintiff's side produced any evidence to document the condition of the tires before the sale? They have not. Has the plaintiff's side produced any evidence to refute the possibility that the clients themselves, for whatever reason, changed the tires after the sale? They have not. Has the plaintiff's side produced any evidence to refute the possibility that some third party, neither defendant nor plaintiff, switched out the tires after the sale? They have not.

But not even Devlin's clients were that dumb: Why would anyone change out tires on a new car within months of buying it? If anything, someone looking for some cash would sell the rims, but just the tires? It was a flimsy defense. And that's what raised Devlin's ire: Claire Dubrow was dead because of Big City Auto Sales. And he couldn't let them walk away from that reality for $100,000, which was their time-and-expense hit for taking the case through trial. Write a check and make the dead woman go away without all the hassle.

"Judge, tell them I guess we'll see them in court. And tell them to go fuck themselves."

"In those exact words, counselor, or do you want me to try to come up with something a little less vague?"

Devlin smiled.

"You sure about this, Devlin? A hundred grand is a helluva lot of money to leave on the table. You keep this thing going there's a good chance you get zilch. Plus you're stuck with those morons for God knows how long."

The judge had two damn good points there. But Devlin shook his head, because when he thought about Claire Dubrow, he also thought about Ann Pearson. He was the voice now for each, the only advocate who would stand up and try to wrench some measure of dignity and honor from an indifferent system. The obscene legal reality was that an elderly woman's life was, essentially, not worth a whole lot.

Claire Dubrow's collective being was being reduced to a one-line ledger item, just another automated check cut in that week's corporate accounting cycle. Devlin sighed because he knew that holding someone accountable was now his responsibility. So as he returned to the conference room and delivered this same news to his three hillbilly clients—that they were holding out for more—never was there a more apt description of the word "bittersweet."

Chapter Eleven

MERCY CARE CENTER (MCC) *is a seventy-six bed facility with twenty-four hour nursing care. Flynn Enterprises, a nursing home corporation based in Dallas, Texas, owns, controls, and manages MCC and more than seventy similar facilities throughout Arizona, Colorado, New Mexico, Texas, and Utah. Flynn Winston, an amiable and somewhat eccentric 63-year-old who claims to not own a single pair of socks, is the founder and sole owner of the company bearing his name. He's an Arizona native who based his corporation in Texas (he splits his time between Phoenix and Dallas) because of favorable incentives and tax laws, including no Texas state income tax.*

In the 1950s, Winston began buying land in and around the Phoenix area and throughout Arizona, and now controls large parcels in what he predicts will be one of the nation's biggest cities by the time his grandkids are coming of age at the turn of the century. Winston has locked up much of this land in trusts to pass on to his heirs. Before nursing homes, in the early 1960s, Flynn Enterprises was in the business of casting and machining industrial metal parts such as bolted fittings for huge polyethylene storage tanks in chemical facilities.

Flynn Winston is a long-time and key player in Arizona's conservative power structure. He was instrumental in getting Barry Goldwater on the presidential ticket in 1964 and was one of his biggest financial supporters during that campaign. He's also a lawyer himself who's steered his corporation through repeated litigious attacks related to his manufacturing operations. He is represented in all legal matters by Phoenix-based Bell &

Bauer, a tight shop with fifty-odd robot clones who routinely crush whoever and whatever gets in their way.

With a reputation throughout the western U.S., Bell & Bauer are the keepers of big business, big hospitals, and big government, and they guard those gates with every lawyer sleight-of-hand in the book: arcane precedents, endless filings, motions and well-timed causes for dismissal. Most of the cases against their clients are dropped, out of sheer attrition, or settled on Bell & Bauer terms. And when Bell & Bauer does enter the courtroom to litigate, it's like Ali and Frazier against your Hawaiian Champ. Perched at the apex of Bell & Bauer's holy and impenetrable hierarchy is Richard Bell II, heir to the throne and the bluest of the bluebloods his father's firm has to offer.

Soon after meeting Richard Bell II, he'll let you know of his track record in never losing a case brought against Flynn Enterprises. In every instance, he and his pack of associates got the case dismissed, or Bell & Bauer emerged victorious from the jury verdict.

UNBELIEVABLE. All of this was straight out of the report Max Daniels had created over the last two months. And for good measure, he'd even dug up some comic relief on Devlin himself with the *Hawaiian Champ* reference. Max Daniels, admittedly, was also a fan of detective novels and fancied himself a scribe. His report, therefore, read more like John D. MacDonald than staid cop-speak. Just as Lucky had guaranteed, this Daniels cat was top-shelf.

In January 1965, president Lyndon Johnson put forth "The Great Society" agenda. Among the provisions was what we now know as Medicare, which Congress passed in an amendment to the Social Security Act. Along with the relief millions of elderly people found, Medicare and its sibling Medicaid, also brought federal nursing home regulation.

Nursing homes, eager to open their doors to Medicare and Medicaid patients, now had to follow certain guidelines. In 1967, Congress authorized the first set of federal standards. The Health Care Finance Administration would be the enforcement arm of the United States Department of Health and Human Services.

But five years ago, by 1971, most nursing homes were still not in compliance with the federal standards. Rather than enforcing the already-established standards of care, some costly, Congress pushed through the "Miller Amendment" that created an alternative template: intermediate-care facilities. Under this classification, nursing home facilities would still qualify for Medicare and Medicaid reimbursement, but with fewer costly hurdles such as the number of skilled nursing staff required on site. Although the change was a welcome relief to people like Flynn Winston and other owners and operators of nursing homes, the act immediately lowered already-sagging standards of care. A year later, Congress tried to turn around the trend of declining care with one of the largest pieces of nursing-home reform legislation ever passed, Public Law 92-603, which changed the process of how Medicaid would be reimbursed. The problems, however, went unchecked, and provider fraud and poor care escalated throughout the country. In the legal arena, parallel to these changes, medical malpractice actions began to slowly gain ground in the last few years as cases started to become financially significant. Before that, medical law was relatively obscure, and grounded in the vernacular of forensic pathology.

Throughout this time, the manufacturing side of Flynn Enterprises continued to thrive in part due to lax regulatory standards. Prior to 1970, the whole business of monitoring pollution and air emissions was left to each individual state. With only a handful of air-quality regions even designated at the state level, not a single state had developed a full pollution-control program. Manufacturers could, for the most part, simply operate their businesses in order to maximize profits. It was not only common but acceptable practice to, for example, run a discharge pipe out the back of the plant, unfiltered, and pump all manner of effluent onto the ground. Any shrewd capitalist like Flynn Winston was doing exactly that.

However, things turned for Flynn Enterprises and many other manufacturers when, in 1970, Nixon formed the Environmental Protection Agency and passed the Clean Air Act. It was a domino effect of profit-eroding environmental awareness. Soon the EPA set national air-quality-standard levels, passed the Ocean Dumping Act and even banned the pesticide DDT, which Americans including Flynn Winston had been spraying for nearly three decades onto crops and around their homes and gardens to kill bugs. Winston comes from the "If it ain't broke, don't fix it" school and didn't see what all the fuss was about. Nonetheless, fearing that his business would eventually be choked off by federal and state regulators and their time-consuming inspections, Winston angrily liquidated his industrial concerns and began looking to parlay his seven-figure profit from the sale. Then he discovered a business with limitless demand: elderly care.

"We're all going in the box sooner or later" is Winston's worldview, and he even considered, and then decided against, using the phrase as the slogan for his new business.

Even more joyous: Unlike the chemical industry with all those pesky regulations and standards, nursing homes were virtually unencumbered. Flynn Winston toured a number of nursing homes, scheduled lunches with the owners, and learned everything he could about the industry. The guy does his homework. Amazingly, in spite of the new federal standards, regulatory examinations to oversee the care of the USA's elderly were sporadic at best and mostly non-existent. Flynn Enterprises had found a new cash cow that Winston planned to ride into his own twilight years.

"But whatever you do," he'd jokingly whisper to his lawyers and business associates as they began buying up the dilapidated facilities at bargain prices. "Don't ever put me in one of these places to die. I ever get that bad, just take me out behind the woodshed and put one in the back of my head."

Flynn Enterprises began by buying a handful of aged facilities in Texas. Other than a sign change, the buildings required little capital investment. Understandably, because he'd forged his shrewd acumen in heavy industry, he applied the same sensibility to his new venture. The aesthetics of a nursing home—fresh paint and manicured gardens surrounding the property, and framed art on the walls—were not going to increase profits, nor, he would argue, improve the level of care.

"You think someone in a coma cares what color the walls are? And their families? Hell no, they got bigger fish to fry, like, 'Is old Ed here going to see next Sunday?' Besides, if you had your granny in there wouldn't you want to see your money going to health machines and doctor stuff rather than to pay some gardener to mow grass the walking dead will never set foot on anyway?"

Flynn Winston's business philosophy is as ancient as Babylon: run each facility with rock-bottom fixed costs and a bare-bones staff. Reinvest all profits into buying more facilities. Winston got the ball rolling, set the template, and watched the money roll in from this business model. Before long, Winston was almost completely detached from the day-to-day details of running his multimillion-dollar empire.

Meanwhile, with barely enforced state board or federal compliance regulations, the quality and consistency of care varied widely from facility to facility. One consistency throughout Flynn Enterprises facilities has been poor morale among the underpaid employees. Fueling the employee grousing are low nurse-to-patient ratios and long hours with little incentive to perform beyond mediocrity. Those who try in earnest to reduce staff turnover and implement better systems of care are met from above with resounding disinterest, ever-shrinking budgets, and little encouragement to change anything. Eventually most of the good nurses and doctors drift away out of frustration and ethical concerns. What remains are not America's best and brightest caregivers, but rather those content to collect a bimonthly insult from Flynn Enterprises, but one with few strings attached: accountability, professional duty, or otherwise.

Subsequently, the medical records throughout the various facilities are often inaccurate, incomplete, or missing altogether. The monitoring and assessment of patients, their wounds, and aftercare is inconsistent at best and often cursory. Walls need holes patched and fresh paint. Burned-out light bulbs stay dark. Toilets run endlessly. Cracked windows stay cracked. Hot food comes cold, and cold food lukewarm. The buildings are drafty in winter and hot and muggy in the summer. No one—employees, patients, nor visitors—wants to spend time in any nursing home owned by Flynn Enterprises.

DEVLIN put down the pages. Daniels had obviously dug around and found some ex-employees willing to talk. Now Devlin had a litany of new questions firing through his mind, but at the core was a promising, and growing, possibility: Devlin's original intuition had been wrong. Maybe they did have a solid case against Flynn Enterprises. A big case with a big payoff potential. Even so, there was one seemingly insurmountable hurdle: A case against this client meant taking on Bell & Bauer, the most formidable of formidable opponents. And those smug stuffed shirts would love nothing more than to crush a gadfly like Devlin.

Chapter Twelve

"A WRONGFUL DEATH CASE against a nursing home?" the white-haired Avram Barak said. "You're as green as some things I've found at the back of my refrigerator. You can't be serious."

Devlin shifted positions. "I know there's not much precedent, but this is a case of criminal neglect. I want to pursue it like any medical malpractice suit."

Outside the August heat was stifling, at 109 degrees with thick humidity as the summer moisture swept up from the Gulf of Mexico. Nonetheless, Barak was wearing a tailored blue wool suit. He looked like a thin Santa Claus with his pure white beard trimmed neatly, and rosy cheeks. Barak had dedicated his life to medicine and helping others and, during the course of Devlin's homework, came up repeatedly as the most knowledgeable nursing home expert in the western U.S. Consequently, his expert witness fee, for trial preparation and testifying, was a ball-busting $190 an hour. And while Devlin and Barak had spoken several times by phone, wherein Barak had learned Devlin's mother was Jewish, this was their first meeting.

"Well, what med mal cases have you tried?"

"Well, none actually. I've done—"

"None. *Oy!* Do you know the term '*meshuggener*'?"

Devlin shook his head, but Barak went on without providing an answer. "Do you have any idea how difficult it is to build a medical malpractice case? And against a nursing home? In addition to all the medical pathology and terminology, geriatric medicine is even more complicated. There are a few of us alive in our 60s, 70s, 80s without a long and complex medical history, but not many. You also have to get up to speed on the regulatory issues, patient charts, and records, and then the administration side of budgeting and staffing ratios. Nursing homes are not hospitals. There is an enormity of assistance required in nursing home care, with the feeding and the dressing and bathing and moving these people. The court applies a much different standard of care to a hospital than a nursing home. You seem like a nice Jewish boy, but why would you want to waste your time on such things?"

"I know it's a tough case to build, let alone win, and I had my doubts, too. But my pathologist says—"

"Who is this pathologist?"

"Ford Rockwell. Over at the—"

"I know Ford Rockwell. OK, he is good. And what does he say?"

"He reviewed the deceased's autopsy report and charts and said the pressure ulcer she developed caused widespread sepsis that killed her."

"A *decubitus* ulcer."

Devlin nodded. Surrounding himself with good experts who know more than he did was going to be the linchpin in this type of case. Rockwell, and now, hopefully, Barak, fit the bill. To Barak's left, the entire wall from floor to ceiling was lined with books. Behind his desk was a credenza, and along the other wall, to his right, was a long row of scratched, dented filing cabinets in mismatched colors. Every square inch of space on the credenza and filing cabinets was covered with thick folders, stacks of paper, magazines, and several potted plants that were now dried sticks. The whole mass of stacked paper was at an odd and precarious tilt, as though an avalanche of reading material could be precipitated at any moment.

"And how old was your decedent in this case?"

"She was 76."

"Hmmm. Do you know how many of my nursing home patients had pressure sores?" Devlin could take a wild guess. Now 60 and semi-retired, Barak had spent the last twenty years owning and operating a nursing home for Jewish senior citizens and war veterans.

"All of them! Some of them had pressure sores on their pressure sores. When old people sit for any extended period, with their fragile skin like wet paper and their compromised immune functions, they get pressure sores. I sit for five minutes I get a pressure sore. I probably have one right now from since we began this *kibitz*. I'm sorry. An old woman with a pressure sore? You don't have a case."

"How did you alleviate those pressure sores in your patients?"

"You're a tenacious little sneak, aren't you? I tell you there is no case here and on you go with your questions."

Devlin smiled and offered only silence, his standard fallback.

"OK, I'll humor you because you're a good Jewish boy. To present and/or alleviate pressure sores, we'd move our patients. Roll them this way, roll them that way. Turn them over. Like a piece of fish you don't want too crispy on either side. I used to joke we needed to put them in one of those cement trucks with the big tub that constantly turns, so they'd always be moving."

"And what would happen to that piece of fish if you left it in the pan for, say, ten days without turning it once?"

"Ten days? You'll have gristle in your pan and nothing to *nosh*. Who leaves fish for ten days?"

"Mercy Care Center. Right downtown. About twenty minutes from here."

"You're trying to be clever. What happened is irrelevant unless you can prove it in court. Where's the liability? She was old and died right about when most of us are going to die. You'll never get a settlement or trial out of that."

"But if we could establish that liability would we have a case?"

"We? What I think you have is *dreck*, but you're going to push on with this regardless of what I tell you, aren't you?"

Devlin nodded. "But I'd need you to help me."

"Help you prepare a case you cannot win?"

"Yes."

"And you're willing to pay me my normal expert witness rate of $190 an hour to engage in this fruitless frivolity?"

"Yes."

"Even though I'm the same expert telling you there is no case here?"

"Crazy, huh. What was that you said...*meshuggener*?"

"Definitely *meshuggener.* You walk around with your head in the clouds. Your heart's in the right place, but still I almost feel guilty enough not to take your money."

"Almost?"

"Almost. Here's a legal pad. Let's get started. I'll bring you up to speed, but then we'll have to see about whether I'd ever testify on your behalf. I'm not going to be part of any courtroom folly. Not that you'll ever see a courtroom on this one."

"Do you want to hear the details of the case first?"

"I don't need details. You are the one who needs details. You need to understand what you're trying to do so that you can in turn educate me about your non-case. What a fun and profitable, for me at least, exercise this will be. Take this down: Your first prerequisite to be successful in this litigation is to prove that the actions taken by the provider were unreasonable in view of community expectations. What does this mean? It means you as the plaintiff's lawyer have the responsibility to prove the defendants violated their duty, that the plaintiff was in fact damaged, and that the breach of duty was the substantial impetus in causing the damages." Devlin made verbatim notes as Barak lectured.

"In medical malpractice the defendant's liability can be vicarious, which means Mercy Care Center is holding the bag for any schmuck employees in their employ. I got out of the nursing home business precisely because what I saw was disgusting. For most of these places now it's a cash-flow business that basically covers the land mortgage on which the building sits. It's not patient care, it's a long-term real estate play. The patients are not human beings who deserve our care and respect, they are annoying widgets that must be fed to realize profits. Near-term, these snake-oil charlatans can depreciate the building and assets. Then in fifteen or twenty years, they can cash out the land asset at appreciated values. So the best way to maximize profits is to cut staff, ignore patients, and keep costs as lean as possible. You think such disgraces cannot be happening in this great land of ours? Well, don't be fooled. *Se shtinkt.* Have you started writing the complaint?"

Devlin shook his head. He'd only just decided to take the case.

"My good boy, there's grass growing under your feet already. I suppose that means no 'Notice of Basis of Suit' nor any interrogatories either?" Barak could only shake his head at his woeful new charge. But secretly, which he'd never admit to Devlin, he liked the fire he saw in the kid. No way the kid was going to win this case, but he had the bullheaded drive and dedication to a cause it would take to become a successful lawyer.

Over the next months, Avram Barak walked Devlin through the labyrinth of medical case law, nursing home practices, and regulatory standards. They started with weekly sessions, in Barak's dark, messy office, that paper avalanche behind his desk always on the precipice but never surging forth. Around noon each Monday, Devlin would get a call at his office. With no greeting or salutation, Barak would say, "Why don't you bring me a sandwich. Pastrami on dark rye. Get one for yourself, too." An hour later arrived with Barak's lunch order. After each session, Devlin left with a full page of brain-twisting to-do's and a long reading list. The complex medical journals, textbooks, and Barak's research topics were a full-time job unto themselves. Simultaneously, Devlin was still deposing witnesses in the Big City Auto Sales case and racking up more ammunition. On top of these two big cases, Devlin still had thirty or so smaller cases in various stages. He was working seven days a week, fifteen hours at a stretch.

To ease the workload, Devlin was pushing a lot onto Nadia Flores. Her first mission was to go to Mercy Care Center and get Ann Pearson's complete medical records. The original charts Kay Pearson had given Devlin contained, as pointed out by Ford Rockwell, numerous gaps and omissions. Upon her request, Nadia Flores received a different set of records for Ann Pearson that was more complete, including added pages and handwritten notations. Devlin was suspicious that the records still weren't telling the whole story.

In preparation for the eventual suit, Devlin filed papers with the probate court appointing a third party to be a special administrator to Kay Pearson. Barak advised him to do so, which established an independent party to receive any eventual settlement in the case. This put the jurors at ease because they wouldn't just be handing a pile of dough to an ordinary citizen. Responsible jurors wanted to know that the money would be well-managed, properly dispensed, and responsibly spent.

At one session with his new Yiddish maven, as Devlin stepped into the dank office with the requisite sandwiches, Barak began lecturing with his back to his protégé: "We are building a causal link between Ann Pearson's death and Mercy Care Center, so we must document the track record of the nursing home. Your client, Kay Pearson, is obviously key. The jury must see her as a *shayner maidel*. You know this term?"

Devlin was looking for an open space to put down the sandwiches. "I think so. Basically we want the male jurors to love her like their mother, and the women to want to be her."

"Very good," Barak said, turning now and taking his sandwich. He never thanked Devlin for the weekly food deliveries, but he always paid for the lunch. Then he'd start eating and continue talking with a mouthful, "Do you plan to sue the doctors, too, from the nursing home and Phoenix Municipal? I think you should."

Devlin had been having a different intuition, which went against what every other lawyer and now his own expert was telling him. "I don't want to make the doctors the bad guys. I want to make them victims of the same faulty system."

Barak shook his head. "Too risky. Why would they go to bat for you? You're the ambulance chaser. Get used to doctors hating you and everything you do."

As much as he respected Barak, Devlin had a strong hunch on this one. "I'm not sure how yet. It's just a theory that might change during the depos."

Barak looked disappointed, as though his own son had just introduced a Catholic girlfriend. Barak changed the subject with, "Did your client hear back yet from HSD?"

Devlin nodded. At Barak's suggestion, one of the first things he did was ask Kay Pearson to write a formal complaint letter to the Arizona Health Services Department. It took three months to get this response, which Devlin handed to Barak:

Dear Miss Pearson,

The letter you sent the Arizona Health Services Department has been forwarded to the State Office of Long Term Elderly Care Licensure. In your letter, you expressed concerns about the care your mother, Ann Pearson, received while at Mercy Care Center from March 22, 1975, to April 1, 1975.

Although the violations you allege may have occurred, our investigation into the matter did not find sufficient evidence to substantiate any formal charges. We consider this matter resolved. Have a nice day.

"You believe these bureaucratic *schmucks*? They're whitewashing your client. You know what she needs to do?"

Devlin smiled. "I already had her go down there in person and demand an investigation. I told her not to leave until they agreed." Since her mother's death, Kay's keen intelligence and raw pain had coalesced into a focused drive for resolution. In her spare time, Kay Pearson had become unofficial paralegal to Devlin. She was happy to track down leads, make copies, run to the post office, and even knock heads with the drones at the Arizona Health Services Department.

"And?" Barak asked.

"They've grudgingly reopened the investigation into Kay Pearson's complaint."

"Nice work." Barak smiled. Even with the Catholic upbringing, maybe his wayward son was salvageable after all. He felt a strong urge to get up and embrace Devlin, but he stayed seated and continued chewing. If nothing else, this was going to be good fun.

BY the time Jimmy Carter defeated incumbent Gerald Ford to become the first candidate from the Deep South to win the U.S. presidency since the Civil War, Devlin had started writing the complaint against Mercy Care Center. Using all the records he, Max Daniels, Kay Pearson, and Nadia Flores had tracked down, Devlin drafted a voluminous and excruciatingly exact timeline of events from March 22, 1975, to April 1, 1975. He'd also written, and had Rockwell review, a detailed medical summary of Ann Pearson's health history.

With Barak's oversight, Devlin compiled a historical treatise on nursing homes, including the state and federal regulations under which they operated. In their weekly sessions, Barak began reviewing and marking up the Mercy Care

Center complaint draft. Before any edit, Barak would exclaim *oy vey*, roll his eyes to the heavens, and then scribble furiously. Praise, on the other hand, was evidenced only by Barak's silent nodding as he chewed on his sandwich. Devlin continuously fought the urge to step behind Barak's desk and right the precarious slant of books, magazines, and paper.

By December Devlin had scheduled a second settlement conference, for February, in the Big City Auto Sales case. He was killing the car dealership in depositions—he now had three former employees on record testifying that the dealership hadn't told them anything about the Monte Carlo's tainted history—and he was certain these damning revelations would nudge the defense out of the lowball stance.

In January, Devlin rang in 1977 by finishing the 104-page complaint against Flynn Enterprises and Phoenix Municipal Hospital. On behalf of Kay Pearson, he was suing for wrongful death, nursing home malpractice, and elder abuse. Devlin wasn't going directly after the hospital because the evidence was pointing squarely at the nursing home, but he named them as a defendant for two reasons. First, it would make it easier to depose hospital employees and get their needed documents with the hospital named in the suit. And secondly, his hope was that the two named defendants would start pointing fingers at each other. That could only bolster the plaintiff's case that something had gone horribly wrong during those ten days in 1975. The complaint asked for damages for Kay Pearson as the beneficiary, damages on behalf of the estate under the Arizona Elder Abuse Statute, and punitive damages.

In addition to the 100-plus pages detailing the claim, there were another 400 pages of supporting documents. Per protocol, Devlin noted the first round of depositions including the nursing home administrator and corporate representatives for Mercy Care Center. Devlin did not, against the vehement recommendation of Barak and several other lawyers, name the doctors in the suit. Devlin wanted to, instead, turn their testimony to the plaintiff's advantage, which would be a risky play. Nadia Flores delivered copies of the completed complaint to Rockwell and Barak for a final review at, of course, their respective hourly rates. Finally, with all the suggestions and edits noted, Nadia sat down, put a fresh ribbon in the typewriter, and spent several days tapping out the final version.

A week later Devlin had several copies of the finished, polished document. In early February, Nadia Flores hand-carried the document to the Maricopa County court complex and filed the suit. A week later, a package arrived at Bell & Bauer with a note to Richard Bell II that read, *"Enclosed please find a copy of the complaint in connection with the above-referenced lawsuit."*

Before the end of the month, Devlin filed his initial interrogatories and requests for various Mercy Care Center internal corporate documents. With these various missives, Devlin was trolling for any helpful evidence and, since that day at the nursing home, had now spent more than a year of his life digging to build the case against Flynn Enterprises. The response from Bell & Bauer, with its top client now the target of a potentially costly and damning lawsuit, was a resounding and protracted silence.

Chapter Thirteen

"BOY, YOU REALLY RATTLED 'EM, Devlin." Judge Nash smiled. "They're still at their last offer. Pitched a goddam tent on $100,000." He scratched his beard. "They must know you're a miserable lawyer."

"You got that right," Devlin said. "Who else would hire a geriatric mediator who can't even extract lunch money from these people?"

"Touché, counselor."

It was February, Round 2 in trying to settle with Big City Auto Sales. And the defense side had made it clear they weren't going around on this again: This was the "Last Chance Saloon" before playing it out at trial. Everyone had re-assembled at Devlin's downtown brick office: a lawyer each from the dealership and the insurance carrier, Judge Nash and Devlin, and Rick and Lucy Dubrow. Bob was allegedly on his way and was about to get, according to Rick, "thumb-fucked in both eyes until he feels like a rented mule." Devlin had been able to pass off Bob's absence as a traffic tie-up and suggested to the defense side that they start the proceedings. But if Bob didn't show, all bets were off on settling the case today. Eventually he ambled in and slumped in a chair with a bored look on his face, as though urgent and lucrative dealings elsewhere demanded his rare acumen and talents.

"I don't know, judge. Just to demonstrate good faith I think they should have come up from where we ended in the first go-around. I don't know how to play this."

"Here's an idea: take the hundred grand. To celebrate you can go buy yourself a Pez dispenser shaped like a cock and then do what you do best."

Devlin laughed. The old judge, he had to admit, still had it.

The judge's face turned more serious. "Devlin, come on, you're not going to do any better at trial. Not with those clients. Would you hand those three a bag of money if you were on the jury? You go to trial, and you get nothing. How much you got in costs?"

Devlin had spent the previous evening reviewing those exact figures: the Monte Carlo and the expert to examine the tires, the growing tab for videotaping all the depositions, and tracking down witnesses across the state. He was surprised to see he'd already sunk $11,000.

"Eleven grand? Jesus Christ, Devlin. Take the hundred grand just so you can cover your expenses and be done with it." Hearing the number over and over, $100,000, was like being strapped to a jukebox stuck on a bad Buddy Holly song: flat-out painful. Included in Devlin's expenses, which he didn't tell the judge, was $1,900 in loans to Rick Dubrow, who had just called again last week asking for another $500. Devlin had to turn him down. His client ended the call by saying, *Lawyer, what kind of greedy cat don't help out his own?*

"I've got to settle this case today," Devlin said. "But I'm not going to completely roll over. How about we go to them with $150,000?"

Judge Nash studied his notepad and chewed on his pen. "If you're serious about wrapping this up, let's go to them with one-thirty five. Not as a number to negotiate from, but to settle right now: $135,000, and we're done." It was a far cry from the original demand of $1 million. But it was still a big settlement, would cover the lawyer's expenses, and clear the case from his docket.

"Fine," he said. "Do it. And don't take any crap from those corporate tools."

Judge Nash left Devlin's office and returned 10 minutes later. He was shaking his head. "They have no fear, Devlin. He's ready to go to trial. He's not even throwing you a bone anymore."

"How much?"

"Hundred grand."

"No," Devlin said. Buddy Holly again. Now the ego was flaring up: The defense was holding three of a kind and had called Devlin's bluff. Take it or leave it. They knew he had a strong case, but walking away from a guaranteed six figures was always a risky play.

"You got to give them credit, Devlin; they're determined to grind this one out."

"Did they bring a bigger checkbook this time?"

"Probably. But this case is probably worth a hundred grand, and that's why they're sitting on their number. I'd guess they have check-writing authority up to $150,000 at the absolute most."

"Well, they're going to have to up it from where we are. Tell them $125,000. Not as a negotiating point. That's our bottom settlement figure."

"Didn't we just do that at $135,000?"

Devlin just shrugged his shoulders.

"OK," the judge said, shaking his head. "I'll tell them whatever you want me to tell them. Mind if I slip in there what a worthless litigator you are?"

"You should worry less about me, old man, and more about whether those bad dentures are going to fall out."

Judge Nash stood up, laughed and said, "The sum total of your legal prowess could be written on a single square of toilet tissue I'd use—"

"Get the hell out of my office, old man, and go do your job before I can you." Both the lawyer and retired judge were laughing as Nash walked out.

By lunch, after four hours with the defense team ensconced in a conference room across the hall from Devlin's office, the two sides had made no progress. The defense refused to move above $100,000 in the back-and-forth plays.

"You know what I think, Devlin. I told you to settle last time at $100,000. The pot's still on the table. Take the money and cut these clients loose. Then you can go concentrate on your nursing home case because, God love you, you're going to need all the time you can get on that worthless pursuit."

It gnawed at Devlin. Maybe if he rolled the dice and went to trial, he might squeeze out a verdict in the $500,000 range. Claire Dubrow's life and memory were worth at least that much, and Devlin was optimistic about his chances of getting a jury to agree. But sometimes, no matter how good the case was, there came a point when there wasn't any more juice a lawyer could wring out.

Knowing when to throw down his cards and take a small stack of chips was an imperfect art, another one of the nebulous tenets they didn't teach at law school.

"Devlin, I can see the wheels spinning. For Christ sake, there's smoke coming out your ears. Don't do it. Following the dictates of your ego, whether in a mediation, a courtroom, or in the sack with a hot broad, is a dangerous master to serve. Look, the goal is to win the case, not particular points with clients, the opposing side, judge, or witnesses. And from your view, a six-figure settlement is a win. Don't piss away a win trying to prove you've got the biggest one here."

Devlin took a deep breath and laughed. "For a senile old man, sometimes you actually say something worthwhile. I'll see if I can convince these three to take the hundred grand."

Devlin had already done the calculations a hundred times: After deducting his expenses and fee, the Dubrows would have to split just under $60,000. Not quite $20,000 each. Judge Nash was right: All things considered and the long odds of going to trial, a six-figure settlement was a victory.

And yet, as he stood outside the conference room door, Devlin felt a deep sadness. A victory on paper, perhaps, but not the final chapter he'd hoped to write for Claire Dubrow. Straight out of Nash's mouth and accurate as hell, this would always be a particularly tough one to swallow: Rule #4—The goal is to win the case, not particular points with clients, the opposing side, judge, or witnesses.

Chapter Fourteen

TWO MONTHS LATER, Devlin still hadn't heard from Richard Bell, or anyone at Bell & Bauer, about the Pearson case. His brilliant suit against their client had not even merited the courtesy of a response. He continued to call and leave messages, and continued to get stonewalled. Finally, days before the sixty-day response deadline for Flynn Enterprises, Richard Bell phoned and apologized profusely. Supposedly he'd been out of state deposing witnesses and just hadn't had time to draft a response that matched the eloquence and thoughtfulness demonstrated in the complaint itself.

Devlin, of course, knew it was a crock of shit, and that the last-minute call for mercy had probably been in play from day one. But at least Bell was inviting Devlin in for what he termed "an informal settlement probe." In other words, Bell gave the lawsuit no credence and was only interested in ferreting out the smallest number necessary to get rid of this gnat of a lawyer.

Three days later, Devlin drove the Porsche with the windows down as the first whispers of summer heat descended upon the desert. It was May now, and the high would be creeping close to 100 degrees by late afternoon. In thirty days, Devlin and everyone else in Phoenix would be sealed in air-conditioned bubbles until the heat broke again around Halloween.

Bell & Bauer occupied the top two floors of a high-rise on Central Avenue. Devlin headed north from his downtown office and passed the famed building where he'd taken the bar review course, with The Wellington on the bottom floor and the Playboy Club at the top. *Jesus Christ,* he thought. *Where have seven years gone?* Devlin down shifted, found Bell & Bauer's building, and parked in the garage. Here he was, at last, riding the elevator into the legal stratosphere. Welcome to the Big Leagues, kid.

Whoever finished out the place must have razed several small countries just to appoint the foyer in exotic hardwood, all of it oiled to a sheen reflecting awe and fear in the faces of Bell & Bauer's clients and opponents alike. The receptionist, too, looked to have been plucked not from the Phoenix typing pool, but rather from some higher order of European Super Secretary. She was elegant and lithe with large, green eyes, and spoke with an indistinguishable accent. Everything about the place was precision-refined.

As Devlin sat waiting in deep-buttery-leather comfort, however, he was unfazed by the show of power. He might have been awe-struck the first time around, but he'd sat in ten carbon copies of this place with similar players high up on the arrogance totem pole. If anything, he felt a surge of confidence and energy that, after almost seven years, he'd finally slipped a sharp burr under the saddle of the big establishment. Now it was Richard Bell's turn to squirm.

Then the door opened, a door that probably claimed eighty-seven cherry trees, and another stunning Euro-broad appeared: olive-skinned and wrapped in a perfectly tailored blouse and skirt that flaunted the line between professional and curve-hugging tightness. She smiled at Devlin and said, "Mr. Bell will see you now."

Yes, Devlin thought, the almighty ruler was now summoning the supplicant. From the décor to the hired help to the prevailing ambience, Bell & Bauer ran with the efficiency and emotional warmth of a German dental practice.

"I'm Devlin," he said to her as they walked down carpet so thick each step left a footprint. No response. "Or Connor," he said. As they walked, Devlin took in more of the same standard power décor: dark wood, dark leather, and towering shelves lined with crisp statute books.

"Nice digs. You worked here long?"

She smiled. "Would you like something to drink? Coffee, tea, ice water?"

"Only if you're having something." She laughed. He smiled and said, "Good. I was starting to think that was against the rules here. What's your name?"

She was tall, probably six feet in her heels, and had the legs to match. The legs, in fact, were stunning. She had her jet-black hair pulled back into a tight bun. She paused, ever so slightly, before saying, "I'm Devon."

"Devon. I like that. French?" Devon had a slight accent as well. *Where did they get these women?*

"Well, here we are, Mr. Devlin." She motioned toward the office door.

"Yes. Here we are."

"Mr. Bell will see you now."

"I'm sure he will. And will you be joining us, Miss Devon?"

She laughed again. "Would you like something to drink?"

"You must pick that up by being around lawyers all day."

"Excuse me?"

"Every time I ask a question, you answer me with a question. Be careful; you're starting to think like them."

"And you, right?" she said.

"See. There you go again. Me? Nah. Practicing law is just a means to an end. But these guys? Definitely lawyers. You see my point?"

She smiled again, a simple, seductive glance that might launch any number of good, decent men into war on her behalf. "Is there anything I can do?"

There was a list so long, he thought, too lengthy to even begin. He just smiled.

"Mr. Devlin. Is that you?" A voice, presumably that of Richard Bell, boomed from within the office large enough to hold all three of Devlin's cars and the fourth he'd been eyeing. First the delayed response to the lawsuit and now this poorly timed interruption as Devlin tried to make time with the office stunner: Bell had a knack for inserting monkey wrenches.

"Nice to meet you," she said.

"Yes. Likewise. We'll talk some more later."

She smiled, paused, and then said, "We'll see about that."

"Hey, we're making progress. At least it wasn't a question."

Minutes after meeting Richard Bell for the first time, Devlin sat on an expansive black leather sofa. Bell sat opposite, with a thick coffee table between them, in a high-backed chair. This appeared to indeed be, as promised, an "informal settlement probe": no associates, no sign of the actual complaint Devlin had spent a year preparing, no paperwork or stenographer. Bell didn't even have a legal pad or No. 2 pencil. Devlin could imagine just how many other would-be assailants had faced a similar opening salvo by Richard Bell, which included a tedious round of lawyer small talk. Although he was enjoying his bottle of imported and ice-cold water, Devlin had no interest in tap dancing all afternoon with Dickie Bell.

"So when might you be responding to our discovery requests? We're ready to go with the depos." Although there was no official *We*, Devlin had unconsciously used the plural pronoun to include his client and modest assemblage: Avram Barak, Max Daniels, Ford Rockwell, and Nadia Flores. And Kay Pearson as client and unofficial paralegal.

"All in good time, Mr. Devlin."

"With all due respect, my time's worth money, and you've already burned up a lot of it by making us wait so long. If we don't start seeing some action we're ready to go down the hardball route, including a motion for our fees and sanctions."

"Mr. Devlin, my good man, I invited you here in the spirit of compromise, and that is what I'm prepared to do today."

"OK. What does that mean?"

"That means that my client, Flynn Enterprises, has granted me check-writing authority in the aforementioned matters. Rather than jumping ahead to divisive talk of motions and sanctions, perhaps we can reach an agreement right now to avoid any unpleasantness. No one wins if we continue down the path of litigation. Wouldn't you agree?"

"Guess it depends on whom you ask. My client, for example, might disagree with that stance, since she needlessly lost her mother."

"Of course, and that is why we are here. Your client has suffered a terrible loss. So foremost, I know that Mr. Flynn Winston, along with myself and everyone here at Bell & Bauer, would like to extend our deepest condolences."

"Thank you for your concern." A sharpened and oiled chainsaw couldn't cut through the malicious subtext filling the space between the two savvy pros.

"To that end, we are prepared to settle this matter today and thus avoid putting your client through any further pain. What she most needs now is resolution." Richard Bell was like some sort of unflappable robot lawyer. He was as sharp as they came, but his overall look—a Western-cut suit, cowboy boots, and a thin, Charles Bronson mustache—didn't match his erudite diction. What Devlin saw was *Death Wish*; what he heard was Ivy League aristocracy.

"Now on that point, Richard, I couldn't agree more. *Resolution.* How do you propose we arrive at such a mutually beneficial plateau?" He might be a blue-collar kid who liked to get drunk the night before big law exams, but Devlin, too, could adopt the Queen's English.

Bell sniffled and, unconsciously, wiped his forefinger under his nose. "My client is hopeful that you can give us some guidance in terms of what might reasonably bring closure to your client in this matter." Then he did it again: the quick sniffle and finger to the nose. Bell might be a great lawyer, but he'd make a terrible poker player. Inside of two minutes, Devlin had already read his tell. And whether he was actually authorized to settle or not, Bell was now fishing for a number to gauge his opponent's confidence. Clever move. But not so fast there, pal.

"What are your thoughts, Richard, as far as settlement?"

"Whatever it is that would bring closure for your client."

Being a lawyer was at times, Devlin had learned, a lot like being a stubborn child again: *You go first. No,* you *go first. No, I'm not going until you go. He started it, judge. Did not:* he *started it.*

"And that's all we're looking for, Richard. Of course I'll have to go back to her with any potential amount before I can authorize a settlement."

"My belief is that the quicker we settle this matter, today even, the sooner your bereaved client can move through her grief process. How might we do that?"

Devlin shook his head. They must send defense lawyers and car salesmen to the same "Let's make a deal" academy. "I'm not going to give you a number out of the blue. You tell me what you're thinking, and I'll take it back to my client."

"Unfortunately I am not authorized to extend settlement amounts, only to approve the plaintiff's demand up to a certain threshold. Is there a number you have in mind?"

Authorized to extend settlement amounts. The guy even *spoke* in contract language. He probably wished he could wear a barrister's wig all day. A random image flashed into Devlin's mind: Bell sitting on the toilet at home in his barrister's wig reading a magazine. "I filed this lawsuit months ago and, to date, still do not have any kind of official response from this esteemed law firm that bears your family surname. We've made our case, and now the burden's on you to tell us where you stand. Give me your best number, and I will take it under advisement."

Bell sniffed his finger again. He clearly wasn't flustered, just annoyed that the ambulance chaser hadn't rolled over already. Bell was used to getting what he wanted, and Devlin hadn't in any way tipped his hand. "OK. First of all, off the record..." Bell shifted in his seat and looked around his own office just to make sure no one had crept in undetected and set up sensitive recording devices and video cameras. Only then did he continue: "Your case has no merit whatsoever. None. My associates found so little precedent in this arena that our first response to this frivolous piece of fantastic fictional fantasy will be to write a compelling motion for dismissal."

Devlin wasn't really listening. All he could think was, the guy could alliterate like a motherfucker. Off the cuff, or did he compose that prior?

"... That, we suspect, will be the end of your pseudo-case. Come now, suing a nursing home for wrongful death? Med mal cases are difficult enough to get through, but we both know this is beyond preposterous."

"It may be, but we're confident the judge will side with us on at least letting our little 'pseudo-case' go forward into discovery. But for now, here we sit. So what's your number?" *No, you go first.*

"Let me put this forth as a rather unorthodox method of settling a case. I talked to Mr. Winston personally, and he authorized me to make this offer on the contingency that you either accept or deny it before leaving."

"Take it or leave it, huh? I'm guessing you're not the president of the local chapter of the 'Win-Win Club,' huh?"

Bell smiled, but continued to ignore Devlin and plowed ahead with his canned precise vernacular. "Given the complete lack of credibility or substantiation in any element of your claims against Flynn Enterprises, it is an exceedingly generous offer indeed."

"*Exceedingly generous?* Wow, I can barely wait to hear it myself."

"Do we have an understanding?"

"I guess. You're going to throw out a lowball number, and then I have to decide on the spot, without consulting my client, if we'll take it? Is that about right, counselor?"

"The offer I'm making is a fixed settlement position not subject to negotiation. So when I state the figure, I'm not looking for you to make a counter-offer and thus send us down the road of mediation. This is not a mediation."

"No, of course not. God forbid we actually mediate. What did you call it, an 'informal settlement probe'? I'm not so sure I'd call all this 'informal,' but I'm certain this next part is where I get the probe. Please be gentle; it's my first time."

Nothing. No smile. No chuckle. Somewhere inside this guy there had to be a faint pulse of a sense of humor, but Devlin hadn't found it.

"You are also informed that should you decline this offer, we will not re-extend the offer at some future point. After today Bell & Bauer will use the full weight of our client's considerable financial and community resources to get this case dismissed. Mark my words, Mr. Devlin, this case will never see a courtroom in Maricopa County. Nor will you ever receive a nickel in settlement from our client if you walk away from today's offer. I've never lost a case, and I will, excuse my language, kick your ass up and down the street in this one."

"I've got to give it to you, Richard, but I've never had so much build-up to hear one number in my life. My palms are actually sweating from all this suspense."

He let out a deep sigh. "Are you ready to hear the figure?"

Devlin looked around, half expecting to see one of the Euro-babes emerge from the shadows with a snare drum and start a soft roll to heighten the drama even more. Devlin inched to the edge of his chair and motioned with both hands. "Lay it on me, Richard."

"And remember, should you accept, we will draw up the paperwork immediately and have you sign before leaving."

"Richard, for God's sake, I can see why it takes you two months to return a phone call. Just say the number before your head explodes."

"To settle this case today, as a measure of our condolences to your client and to alleviate her suffering, our one-time, fixed-settlement position is $25,000."

Devlin pushed himself back into the deep leather sofa and smoothed his pants. Without looking up he said, "Would you say that number one more time, please?" When he heard the number again, he had several internal reactions, none of which he expressed outwardly in any way. The first was laughter, followed quickly by disbelief, and then, slowly, fuming anger. Devlin repeated her name to himself: *Ann Pearson*. This was worse than the boys from Big City Auto Sales, trying to close the books on another dead woman with an amount Flynn Winston could pull from a shoebox under his bed.

Devlin smiled at Richard Bell, stood up and smoothed his tie. A thousand vicious verbal jabs flashed through his mind, but Devlin held back. The practice of law, with its time-honored tradition of civility and protocol, had long since replaced lopping off each other's heads with broadswords. And besides, he'd save the disemboweling for the courtroom stage, Act III.

Chapter Fifteen

ALMOST A MONTH after the meeting with Richard Bell, Devlin finally received an answer to the complaint against Flynn Enterprises. It was the standard boilerplate response that took fifteen pages of legalese to say: *We deny everything and blame everyone else for anything that might have (allegedly) happened.* Then there was the long laundry list of every conceivable type of objection to each discovery request. The lawyers at Bell & Bauer refused to produce any corporate documents and had filed numerous protective-order motions to keep the company's records sealed. Further, they refused to produce any names for the depositions, pending their long-winded motion for dismissal based on ... *the decedent's advanced age, various co-morbidities and Mercy Care Center's diligent conformity to numerous state and federal regulations.* The Bell & Bauer troops had dug in their position.

"Can they do that?" Lucky asked, wiping sweat from his brow in the June heat. Rain or shine, hot or cold, Friday night at AAA Bail Bonds was a sacred tradition. Devlin had stripped off his suit jacket, tie, and dress shirt and now sat in his soaked T-shirt. The space between the two buildings was well over 100 degrees and was only made tolerable, barely, by the cold beer bubbles and early evening shade.

"Yes and no. It's sort of like in football. Can a defensive end punch the quarterback in the throat under the pile? No, not technically, but if the referee doesn't see?"

"Has the referee seen?"

"Not yet. Eventually we'll write a Motion to Compel asking the judge to make them respond. They're really grinding me out on this one, Lucky, unlike any case I've ever seen."

"Who's the attorney?"

"Richard Bell."

"Bell & Bauer," Lucky said, taking a drink of beer. "Heard of the firm, the *Killer B's*, but they don't do much criminal, my neck of the woods."

Devlin nodded. "I'm up against the Killer B's. That's fucking genius."

"How you like your chances?"

"They're a tough bunch, I'll tell you that. I'll bet Bell has six associates cranking out motions as we speak. They know how to work the process of law."

"So that don't answer my question. Can you win this thing? For Annie?"

Devlin let out a sigh. "Jesus Christ, sometimes you get so buried in the legal morass you forget why you took the case in the first place. Something's up for sure. We've got two different versions of Ann's medical charts, and in parts there's big gaps with no entries."

"No shit?"

"Yeah, like forty-eight hours. Nothing."

"That don't sound good for them."

"On the other side, our case is tough. With all due respect, she was pushing eighty with a long history of health problems. Even if she was neglected, it's tough to separate the existing health issues from whatever the nursing home staff did or didn't do."

"So we're looking at long odds," Lucky said.

Devlin nodded. "I've spent almost a year and a half on this case, and so far I haven't even scared them enough to give me the names of their people to depose. I don't know..." Devlin's voice trailed off.

"You hang in there, Big-Time. They wouldn't be throwing up so many roadblocks if they ain't at least a little scared."

"Yeah. I'm sure I'm keeping Richard Bell up late at night." He pictured Bell again in his curly, white barrister's wig, brushing his teeth and getting ready for bed, then banging his old lady from behind while she did a crossword puzzle.

"Hey, come on now, you're Big-Time. Never know what Bell's thinking. And the jury's going to love you. They'll see you're for real."

Jury. The thought of this case going before an actual jury seemed like some vague dream Devlin couldn't quite see forming. "We've got a long way to go before we start thinking about a jury. They're trying to get the case dismissed."

"They assign a judge yet?"

"Bennett. I don't know him. You?"

"I do know Samuel Bennett. Judge Sammy. His kid got in a scrape a few years ago, and we actually bonded out the little snot. I went and sat in on a few proceedings in Judge Sammy's court. From what I saw, that's about as good a draw as you could get. He's straight-up fair, real patient, and I'd say if anything he leans toward the plaintiff's side, sort of a man for the people. You done good there, Big-Time." If nothing else, Lucky's take on the judge went in the ledger as one of the few marks in the asset column.

The next week, Devlin filed for a Rule 16 pretrial conference. At that hearing, Judge Bennett would set a trial date and establish various discovery deadlines. It would probably be another two or three months before they would get a hearing on the judge's calendar. In August, David Nash, the mediator Devlin used on the Big City Auto Sales case, scheduled an early mediation with Bell & Bauer at their offices. It was the same week the cops nabbed David Berkowitz, the Son of Sam, back east after his year-long murderous spree in New York City.

This time, when Devlin stepped into the conference room with Kay Pearson, there were five other lawyers in suits lined up on either side of Richard Bell. Bell had on a similar Western-cut cowboy suit, the same shiny cowboy boots, and the same cheesy moustache. True to Bell's word, the "informal settlement" probe days were long gone. This had the uneasy look and feel of a full-on rumble, switchblades glistening. Devlin didn't waste any time.

"Good morning, Richard. When are we going to get our discovery responses? Maybe I could just take them with me today?"

Several of the associates chuckled. Bell smiled. "Good morning to you, too, Mr. Devlin. I was under the impression that this was a settlement mediation and not a time to get into legal wrangling before your client. A successful mediation will render our response and any further action wholly unnecessary." The guy might look like a cowboy on his way to church, but he spoke like he was lecturing at Harvard Law. It was an unsettling juxtaposition.

"Gentleman," said Devlin. "My client, Miss Kay Pearson." They all stood and shook her hand across the conference table. The scene was, on both sides, a picture of tight-lipped pleasantries.

"Now how about it, Richard? We need to start with our depos."

"Well," he flipped through his calendar and then turned to one of the associates. "When will the Willingham trial conclude?"

Willingham? No question, the client list at Bell & Bauer was culled from the ethereal realms of blueblood aristocracy.

"Probably late September."

"When can we provide Mr. Devlin our disclosure?"

"October."

"There you have it, Mr. Devlin. We are in the throes of trial preparation, but my associate has assured me we can respond to your request by October. Bear with us a bit longer?"

"Fine."

Devlin and Kay sat alone on the other side of the conference table. Judge Nash gave a variation of the same opening remarks he'd said prior to the first Big City Auto Sales settlement mediation, and then one of the Bell & Bauer associates led Devlin and Kay to their conference room. Once the door was closed, Devlin spoke freely to his client.

"Don't get your hopes up today, Kay. I don't think they are in earnest in wanting to settle this case."

"I'm just so tired of dealing with this. All I want is someone to admit they're wrong for what they did to mom and to accept responsibility. I want changes made so this never happens again to another family. Is that so hard?"

"Well, it is and it isn't. In the legal arena, the currency of getting to that admission is, unfortunately, this less-than-perfect process. To get their attention, I've asked for $1.5 million in the wrongful death of your mother."

"One and a half million! Oh my goodness. That's unbelievable. Are you sure? That would make me at least feel like they'd been held accountable. That's enough to hurt them, right?"

"That's the idea, but as I said, don't get your hopes up. They are going to offer far less, and when they do we'll just decline and keep moving ahead, OK?"

She nodded. "OK. Thank you."

And when the retired judge came back with their offer—the same $25,000 Bell had originally offered Devlin at the "informal settlement probe"—Devlin just shook his head and said, "We're not even going to dignify that with an actual response. Instead, when you go back in, give him this. Devlin wrote on a legal pad and handed the page to Nash, who read it aloud: *"The plaintiff's demand for $1.5 million is a fixed-settlement position not subject to negotiation, and is good for today only."* The mediator shrugged his shoulders, confused.

Devlin smiled and said, "Inside joke. He'll get it."

Meanwhile, unlike Flynn Enterprises, the other named defendant in the suit was cooperating on all fronts. Phoenix Municipal Hospital was being represented by Smith, Hawley & White, a capable firm with ten associates. Jeffrey Redmond was a savvy defense lawyer who'd been practicing just a few years longer than Devlin. But unlike Devlin, Redmond had always worked under the safety and security of a stable firm, and his worldview and approach to law mirrored that conservative nature. Redmond was simply more comfortable sitting inside the castles of big business and big government and deflecting the arrows of people like Devlin. Without completely giving away his case, Devlin had met with Redmond over dinner and posited his opinion that the hospital staff had discharged Ann Pearson in a weakened but relatively stable condition and, when she returned ten days later, had done everything right in trying to save her life. That opinion, according to Ford Rockwell, was substantiated in the detailed hospital charts.

Redmond, of course, appreciated Devlin's cooperative approach. But Redmond never fully trusted plaintiff's attorneys, and especially not ones who had named his client in a lawsuit. Their mutual positions, therefore, created a professional interplay tinged with warm smiles and prudent distrust. Unlike Bell & Bauer, the hospital didn't seem to have any trouble locating their documents and employees, and, as requested in the lawsuit, produced Ann Pearson's medical charts and a list of employees for deposition. Devlin immediately deposed the six nurses who had attended to Ann Pearson in any capacity, as well as the primary care doctor, Wayne Michaels, and the doctor who performed the eleventh-hour surgery, Dr. Jeremy Sanford. First up was Dr. Michaels, the hospital's primary witness, who was nervous, since he'd been deposed in several other malpractice cases.

Depositions, Devlin had decided in law school, were the legal equivalent of getting a root canal. With the tape recorder running, harsh lights glaring, and voyeuristic lawyers wide-eyed around the table, the person being deposed gets fitted into the cruel chair and then probed for several hours with the cold, sharp instruments of direct examination. It's uncomfortable at best and, at its worst, can be flat-out excruciating. If there was a suspicious or embarrassing tender spot, a good lawyer would find and jab the area without mercy. For those reasons, Devlin always had empathy for those under this microscope. And he extended this empathy to both sides—whether it was his own witness, who might need constant reassurances, or the opponent's witness, who was just another human being who wanted to be anywhere other than a deposition.

With that mindset, depositions were not a time to try to destroy people or their credibility. Depositions were not the place to wheel out the cold stainless-steel table lined with razor-sharp cross-examination tools. Nor were depositions the time or place for Devlin to expose his case theories and trial strategy. Rather than uncomfortable inquisition, Devlin approached the person being deposed with the air of a curious acquaintance. The goal: exhaust every possibility of what that person was willing to tell. Sure, there were times to go heavy and take a few shots at a witness if an opening presented itself, but for the most part it was a civil conversation to draw out the witness' memory, knowledge, and opinions. Devlin's approach was that, in the end, a lawsuit was simply a process to try to definitively answer the question both sides were asking: *What really happened?*

Jeffrey Redmond smiled and said, "I trust, Mr. Devlin, that you will be nothing but erudite?"

"I don't think my sexual orientation is relevant here," Devlin said.

The friendly repartee was lost on the doctor, but made both lawyers laugh aloud. Devlin was going against conventional wisdom in not naming the doctors in his suit. Now he was bucking trends again: He wanted to videotape the depositions. Few lawyers bothered with the expense, the hassle of setting up the bulky and cumbersome equipment, and the court-order paperwork required to videotape depositions. Of course Bell & Bauer had objected to videotaping any depositions in this case, but they had objected to everything short of the grade of paper on which Nadia Flores typed the complaint and the ink density of her typewriter ribbon. And even his own expert, Avram Barak, didn't like the idea, because even the best and brightest witness can look like a *schlub* on camera. Devlin, however, knew the power of the jury seeing all the unspoken gestures, the telling signs that never showed up on the deposition tape or transcript. A quick roll of the eyes, a head shake, tears welling up in the eyes of the witness being deposed.

Devlin led both doctors through Ann Pearson's two stays at the hospital before and after the ten days at the nursing home. He documented their medical opinions, methodology, charting procedures, and beliefs about what might have led to Ann Pearson's rapid decline. Throughout, Redmond objected less and less as he saw that Devlin was sticking to the script he'd alluded to at their dinner meeting.

Depositions were the heart of Rule #2: *Never be surprised—Surprise is death.* After exhausting every possible detail, fact, recollection, and possibility that he could possibly cover, Devlin was satisfied. Neither doctor had documented anything other than what Devlin had wanted to establish going in: On March 22, 1975, Phoenix Municipal Hospital sent a patient on the upswing to Mercy Care Center. When that patient returned to Phoenix Municipal Hospital on April 1, 1975, something was horribly wrong. The hospital staff did their best to save Ann Pearson, but the damage had already been done in that ten-day period.

In late September, the Porsche 928 debuted at the Geneva Auto Convention. Uncustomary, however, was that this key development in the auto world escaped

Devlin's gaze. After several unsuccessful attempts to schedule depositions of various Mercy Care nurses who had attended to Ann Pearson, and increasingly direct letters to Richard Bell, the defense lawyer finally called, apologized profusely, and asked for another extension until mid-November. Devlin grudgingly agreed.

Meanwhile, Max Daniels was making progress in spite of Bell & Bauer's stonewalling. He'd dug up at least one key name: Fay Fancher was a nurse, the unit manager during Ann Pearson's brief stay at Mercy Care Center, and had been fired from the facility for as-yet-unknown reasons. Daniels had dug around and tracked her to a similar facility in California where she was now working. He was still trying to find her home address and phone number. He was also working a lead that there were at least two other nurses who had worked at Mercy Care Center during Ann Pearson's stay who had both quit or been fired. No one was talking, and he didn't have names yet. It was good enough for Devlin. He immediately sent Bell & Bauer notices of deposition on Fay Fancher and the two departed nurses. To share the good news, Devlin called Richard Bell, whom he'd nicknamed "Sniff" because of his odd habit with his nose and index finger. After being on hold for several minutes, Bell answered.

"We know about the two departed nurses. We're wondering why they quit, or got fired, or resigned, oddly, shortly after Ann Pearson's death? Anything you'd like to share with me, Mr. Bell?"

No response. Then Bell said, "Mr. Devlin, I'm currently with clients, if you'll excuse me." Devlin, like all lawyers, used the same lie all the time. It was a little gamesmanship trick that always worked. Like stealing signs in baseball, it wasn't really cheating if everyone did it.

"You can't keep hiding from this case. Eventually the court's going to order you to produce these witnesses. If I were you, Richard, I'd go scramble some of those associates of yours into action. I'd have them get letters out to every ex-nurse, ex-doctor, and ex-janitor who was in the employ of Mercy Care Center between March 1 and April 30, 1975. If you don't get to them before we depose them, who knows what might slip out under oath. And anytime you'd like to schedule another informal settlement probe, my door's always open to you."

"Good day, Mr. Devlin."

Two weeks later, Devlin received a letter from Bell stating that, unfortunately, Mercy Care Center was unable to locate any departed employees except Fay Fancher, but that they were filing an objection to deposing her because they still had not named their witnesses. They were also filing a protective order against deposing Rupert Styles, the nursing home administrator. Not surprisingly, the gang over at Bell & Bauer was always able to dig up some novel legal concept as a foundation for each maneuver.

This was the breaking point for Devlin. The day after three members of Lynyrd Skynyrd died in a plane crash, Devlin began hand-writing and revising a motion outlining the plodding of Bell & Bauer since he'd filed the complaint. In the language of the court: *Plaintiff presents this Motion to Compel Discovery*.

Devlin wrote that the disclosure from Bell & Bauer was now almost six months late, that the defendants were making excuses, withholding documents, and putting up endless roadblocks in starting any depositions. Devlin asked the court to order responses to all outstanding discovery requests, and asked for attorney fees and costs for all the wasted time in tracking the defendants. Devlin spent far too long writing and revising a simple motion, but he wanted it just right to move the judge to action.

Finally, Nadia Flores typed up the motion and drove the original copy down to the courthouse herself. At 4:30 on the day before Thanksgiving, she filed the motion with the clerk of the court. Then she drove a copy to Bell & Bauer and dropped it off with the stunning, raven-haired receptionist. As had become custom in this case, the response from Bell & Bauer was, again, more resounding silence.

Chapter Sixteen

IN THE WEE HOURS of December 14, *Saturday Night Fever* went up on the movie-house marquee. Devlin drove past in the Porsche and saw the guy on a ladder putting up the last red "R." At that moment, the realization hit Devlin: He hadn't seen a film all year. Not one. Not Clint Eastwood in *The Enforcer*, not *A Star Is Born* or *Close Encounters of the Third Kind*. And he only knew the titles of what he'd missed because friendly conversations eventually turned to who had seen this and that. His friends urged him to go to *Smokey and the Bandit* if only because Burt Reynolds drove the latest generation of the same TransAm Devlin owned. But the lawyer never did make it, and, six months after it hit theaters, Devlin was one of the remaining six hundred people in the country—among agoraphobics, severely mentally ill patients, and elderly shut-ins—who hadn't seen *Star Wars*.

The year had opened with great promise: In February he settled Big City Auto Sales and filed the complaint against Flynn Enterprises. A banner month. But the action in Ann Pearson's case had been stalled ever since and, with two weeks left in 1977, Devlin didn't have much to show for the year. Still no word yet from Sniff and the stonewall gang over at Bell & Bauer. Limited disclosure. Little on all the outstanding discovery requests. Even with the big case consuming most of his time, his pipeline of smaller cases still had 40 files, mostly of the blue car/ red car variety. Getting Jill a $5,000 settlement because Jack blew a red light wasn't exactly righting society's great wrongs. And that's the fire that burned in this lawyer: a seminal victory in a landmark case. That's why all his energy was going into deciphering the medical vagaries of Ann Pearson's health history. Once discovery began in earnest, he'd be deposing fifty witnesses, at last count.

Then, on the last business day of the year, Friday, December 30, Devlin received a package at his office: those at Bell & Bauer had finally spoken. Nothing, of course, happened over at the gulag by chance, so Devlin wasn't surprised that afternoon—and into the evening back at the Scottsdale condo, a fitful night of sleep, and a bright morning—that in the disclosure statement the Bell & Bauer associates had penned yet another example of their firm's obstreperous stand.

Sniff and the Bell & Bauer charges still weren't giving up any names or addresses of witnesses. No names of "persons with knowledge" for the depositions. No names of any personnel who treated Ann Pearson except Fay Fancher, but that's only because Max Daniels had already found her. No incident reports, quality assurance reports, written memoranda, or any other reports related to Ann Pearson's care. Bell & Bauer had hoisted the drawbridge and had Flynn Winston and his corporation safely ensconced behind four-foot-thick castle walls of legal maneuvering.

Devlin glanced up when the phone rang. A workout buddy.

"What, d'you fucking die? Let's go pump some iron."

From his couch, Devlin could look out the triple French Doors to the golf course beyond the low fence. It was a sun-drenched, 68-degree Saturday in the desert. Unbelievably, Richard Bell had taken almost a year to write and send his disclosure. It was time to fire back with a quick motion.

"Nah, I've got a bunch of work stuff."

"C'mon, it's Saturday."

To Devlin, that distinction no longer existed. "It's quieter here on weekends than at the office."

"Devlin, it's fucking New Year's Eve."

"I'll catch up with you guys later," he said, but his mind was elsewhere.

"No, get on your gym clothes and get your ass out the door."

"Not now. Thanks." They said goodbye, and Devlin hung up the phone. There was an ever-so-brief flash of remorse for passing up some air and movement. But then just as quickly he focused his attention back to his legal pad. He mumbled aloud what he'd written so far:

... in direct defiance of the court's order in this matter, defendant continues to frustrate discovery with repeated refusal to disclose requested documents, medical charts, and standard corporate financial statements for Flynn Enterprises. As set forth in the previous motion, plaintiff has not been able to take a single deposition; plaintiff has not received the names of the nurses who attended plaintiff's decedent; and defendant's responses to written discovery are inadequate, with frivolous objections raised. And now, despite knowing about this claim for almost a year, defendant claims that many key documents cannot be found. In order for this case to be prepared under the schedule imposed by the court, plaintiff asks that a number of discovery issues be ruled on..."

And on and on he wrote for six pages. When he finished the other motion for sanctions, Devlin looked at the clock: It was now 9:30 p.m. He realized, for the first time, that his hand was cramping up from all the writing. Half an hour later, he'd showered, put on slacks and a nice plaid jacket and was rolling out of the garage in the Porsche. By 10:30, he was still nursing his first beer at The Wellington, which was packed to the gills as 1978 drew nigh. Then he saw her.

The overall effect—the low lighting and smoky ambience, Walter Murphy's "A Fifth of Beethoven" from the *Saturday Night Fever* soundtrack, and her hair that had been unleashed and now fell to her shoulders in sultry bunches—was eye-popping. As she fought her way through the crowd, Devlin positioned himself in her path.

"Miss Devon. I told you we'd talk more later."

"Have we met?"

He could tell by her smile it was a ploy. "Always with the questions. At least you're predictable."

"Oh, I would say I'm anything but. You must not be a very good lawyer."

"So you do remember me."

Without breaking eye contact, she shrugged her shoulders. "Should you even be talking to me?"

"What do you mean?" he asked, but he knew exactly what she meant.

"You're suing my employer's biggest client."

"You seem to be in the know."

"Someone has to type all those motions and briefs. And if there's one thing we do at Bell & Bauer, it's type a lot of motions and briefs. Isn't this a conflict of interest?"

"Two people having a drink together? Not at all, as long as we don't discuss the case."

"We're not having a drink together. I bought this drink." They were being jostled back and forth by the crowd, and had to yell to hear each other. The room started to thump with "You Should Be Dancing" by the Bee Gees.

"Well, you heard the man," Devlin said. "Shall we?"

She smiled. "You avoided my question. Aren't you crossing the line here, counselor?"

"You have so many lines I'd like to cross that I don't even know where to begin."

"OK, then. If we are having a drink together, then I'll take another martini. Extra olives."

For the next hour and a half the two huddled in a corner. She was sharp, had a keen interest in the law, and asked a lot of insightful questions. Devlin obliged and was careful to avoid anything remotely connected to the case. The conversation was easy, the laughter abundant. To ring in the New Year, amid a full round of shouts, gusto, and champagne spray, Devlin leaned in and kissed his adversary's receptionist. It was a sensual moment, a lingering lip-lock that left him weak in the knees.

He pulled back and took her in, and in her smile he could see them back at the Scottsdale condo and half undressed before getting out of the Porsche. The lawyer could see this goddess ripping at his shirt and scattering bouncing buttons into the import's dark crevices. Then in his bedroom, where she'd pull her dress over her long, elegant form and stand there in full glory, nothing but black lace and dangerously high heels. He'd already crossed the line with the kiss, and that's where he drew a new line. God Almighty, it was tempting as all hell, but too close to home. He just couldn't do it. And Devlin knew if he didn't break this trance, say his goodbyes, and walk away in the next three to five seconds, he'd be powerless to resist.

Chapter Seventeen

A MONTH AFTER THE BIG TEMPTATION with Devon McCoy, by early February, little had transpired in the Ann Pearson case. Devlin was surprised and heartened by Kay Pearson's level of interest and involvement in the tedious legal trivia. She insisted on driving downtown to see Devlin every week for updates. And every week now, all he could do was repeat to Kay what he'd said the previous week: *We've filed a second Motion to Compel, and prepared and filed a brief for the upcoming pre-trial conference, and the defense side isn't going to do anything until there's another mandate from the court. We're still waiting to hear from the Health Services Department regarding the investigation. A negative report could really boost our case.*

That was all he could tell her. He didn't have much to delegate to her, either, but he assured her once the depositions started she could attend all of those if she wanted. She was a tireless supporter of her cause and the case. It was the daily morning phone call with her mother that Kay missed the most. About half of their visits would end with Kay crying and Devlin trying to comfort her.

On February 6, Kay Pearson was seated at Devlin's side for the pre-trial conference. Richard Bell had only brought two associates for this one. Jeffrey Redmond sat on the defense side, alone, behind the attorneys from Bell & Bauer. Devlin's strategy seemed to be working: the co-defendants' lawyers were not speaking to each other. Besides the judge's bailiff, clerk, and court reporter, the only other person in the room was One-Armed Lucky, who was seated directly behind Devlin and Kay Pearson. When the bailiff shouted, "All rise," Devlin's heart sank when he saw the judge striding up to the bench.

"Be seated."

Something wasn't right. It was not Judge Bennett, but a much older judge with a face wrinkled into an angry grimace, one Devlin could not place. But there was something about that face that was making Devlin's stomach turn. Like a panicked paralegal rifling files for a lost document, Devlin's brain churned away to place the judge and case from a list of hundreds. Even when the judge read from his notes he sounded angry: "Superior Court of the state of Arizona is now in session. Case number PB1977-002736. The estate of Ann Pearson, by and through Davis Leonard, special administrator; and on behalf of natural child Kay Pearson, plaintiffs, versus Flynn Enterprises, a Texas corporation doing business as Mercy Care Center, and Phoenix Municipal Hospital. Who now appears before this court?"

As the defense lawyers introduced themselves, Devlin's mind raced to identify the judge. Even as he introduced himself and the hearing began, Devlin allocated a portion of his brain to keep searching for an answer.

"From the plaintiffs, I have read a brief and two previous motions to compel in these matters. I have noted Judge Bennett's previous order to the defendants to produce the requested discovery within seven days, but before we get to all that squabbling, where are we with a settlement mediation in this case?"

Glances back and forth across the aisle.

"Don't everyone speak at once," the judge growled. "Start with you." He pointed at Devlin.

"Your honor, we have attempted to settle this case on two previous occasions, and in both instances the defendants did not appear to be in earnest in their—"

"I didn't ask for your editorial stance. So you've tried to settle twice? OK. You now." He pointed at the defense table.

"Yes, your honor," Richard Bell said. "We have made two offers of settlement, and on both occasions the plaintiffs left the mediation without providing even a counter-offer."

"That true, counselor? No counter-offer, no give-and-take?" The judge glared down at Devlin.

"Your honor, in all fairness, both offers by the defense were the same amount, and in the first instance I was told that it was a take-it-or-leave-it offer and that the named defendant was not interested—"

"Again with the editorial sidebars. I'm going to have to keep my eye on you, counselor. OK, so bottom line here is two attempts, no settlement. I'm going to order a mediation settlement in this case to be completed within the next 60 days, and I want both sides to stay there and get this thing done. It is my position that every civil case can be settled to the mutual satisfaction of both parties. The good citizens of Maricopa County have better things to do than sitting on a jury and listening to you lawyers. Understood?"

The four lawyers nodded in unison.

"Now, where are we with the discovery? I know the plaintiffs have concerns. What about the defense?"

"Your honor," Richard Bell began, "if I may, defendants in this case find this lawsuit frivolous and unsubstantiated in any way, and we would ask the court to rule on that motion as a solution to, as you stated, wasting the time of the good citizens of Maricopa County."

"That's an excellent idea, counselor," the judge grumbled. Devlin's heart sank, and he felt Kay Pearson grab his hand. Three years since Ann Pearson had died, and one grumpy judge could throw everything out the window right now. That was one of the flaws in the system: Judges had enormous power, with little accountability or oversight. One bad case of hemorrhoids on the bench and Devlin's case went away. Devlin took a deep breath. He could feel Sniff looking his way, with his smug arrogance shouting, *I told you from the start you would never get a nickel from Flynn Enterprises, you pathetic ambulance chaser.* Devlin had to at least try to save the sinking ship.

"Your honor, if I may, the plaintiffs vehemently disagree with Mr. Bell's Motion for Dismissal and contention that—"

"Keep your pants on, counselor. I've read the complaint and don't need you to review it for me. I'm quite literate and capable in that department, thank you."

This had the feeling of a railroad job. Had that sneaky bastard Sniff somehow used his political might to recuse Judge Bennett and insert Mr. Personality here? Kay Pearson's grip was turning Devlin's hand white. Then, as the old curmudgeon rifled some papers, it hit Devlin square. No wonder he couldn't place the face, because it had been almost eight years since Devlin had appeared before this judge during his disastrous first case. Hundreds of reasonable and qualified Superior Court judges in this county, and Devlin gets this guy again. The realization was cutting Devlin down at the knees, and he had to grab the table for support. It was highly unlikely, given the endless stream of lawyers over the years, that the judge would ever recognize or remember Devlin's opening volley. And Devlin certainly wouldn't do anything to help the old judge recall the catastrophe.

"The court will now rule on the aforementioned motions, starting with the defendant's Motion for Dismissal." Without looking up or breaking his rhythm, the judge said, "Motion denied. The court finds, by the absolute narrowest of margins, a reasonable presentation of the alleged facts by plaintiffs to merit going forward. On the Motion to Compel Discovery filed by plaintiffs—"

"Excuse me, your honor," Richard Bell said. Blindsided by this unfortunate news, Old Sniff was now the one scrambling. The Irish kid would savor this tap dance: "We would ask the court to reconsider its ruling—"

"Counselor, if there is one thing I will not tolerate in my courtroom, it's being interrupted. I read your motion, and now I've ruled on your motion. If there's some part of that you don't understand, I'm sure one of your capable associates there can explain everything to you later."

How quickly the winds can shift in the courtroom! Without question, seeing Sniff get a proper beat-down was the high moment in this case. Then, just like that, the gales shifted hard left again.

"And you," the judge boomed, turning his gaze to Devlin. "I'm allowing this case you've concocted to go forward, but rest assured you are hanging by a thread. You are making serious allegations against a respected name in elderly care on behalf of a very compromised decedent. I will not stand for frivolity, legal shenanigans, and money-grubbing in this courtroom."

A heavy silence settled onto the courtroom. Jeffrey Redmond had not uttered a word. The good news was that the judge was not in Bell's back pocket as Devlin had feared. The bad news: With the burden of proof on the plaintiffs, the impatient old judge would likely favor the defense.

"Now, if *I* may," the judge said mockingly, "defendants are hereby ordered to produce all outstanding discovery requests within sixty days. Now beyond that ruling, I can see this is going to be contentious, and my docket is filling fast with several long trials. I implore both sides to keep moving forward toward resolution."

Devlin started to say something, but knew not to push it. Giving them two more months, after all the time they'd already burned up, was a slap in the face. Now Bell & Bauer could simply kill sixty more days sitting on their disclosure and turn it over at the court-mediated settlement conference. The judge was, effectively, sending Devlin into the mediation without giving him the chance to bolster his case. So if the judge and Bell & Bauer weren't going to play fair, Devlin had to dig harder and uncover something in the next two months to rattle the other side. Devlin was going to depose nurse Fay Fancher no matter how loudly Bell screamed. And, of course, it was time to get Max Daniels on the trail to find the two departed nurses.

Chapter Eighteen

FAY FANCHER, A REGISTERED NURSE at Mercy Care Center, loved the overtime pay. As a single mom, the only way she could make her bills was by working sixteen hours a day, five days a week. Luckily, Mercy Care Center didn't have any policies that limited her hours and, therefore, her earning potential. Some months she picked up extra shifts and worked fifteen days straight with no break. She was always tired, often grumpy, but showed up every day and did just enough to keep her job. Barely. As the charge nurse, she oversaw the nursing staff during each shift she worked. She supervised and helped coordinate patient care, interfaced with the doctors, dispensed medication, and managed the charting and medical records.

From her position of authority, and because she was always exhausted, Fancher liked to sequester herself in the administration office and issue care instructions to the nurses from her chair. She always had a cup of coffee at her side and a cigarette smoldering in the ashtray as she ostensibly worked through the stack of patient charts. Her job was to make sure that all the nurse and doctor notes were properly recorded, chronologically, with no gaps or omissions.

But Fancher worked hard to become a registered nurse, not some administrative secretary, so she hated the endless bother of handling, checking, and filing charts. Instead, she became a masterful procrastinator. During most shifts the charts sat untouched while she retreated into her beloved science fiction novels, usually Isaac Asimov, and burned her way through a pack of smokes each shift. On a good week, she could plow through three books and then, in a flurry of gritty focus, go over all the charts in one sitting. She was proud of her ability to simultaneously do the job asked of her, earn a (so-so) paycheck, and read more books than anyone she knew.

"Let's back up for a minute," said Devlin. He'd been carefully picking away at her in this deposition for three straight hours, and she was getting cranky. Now he'd finally elicited some testimony that corroborated what Devlin himself had seen at Mercy Care Center: The facility was in shambles, with poor charting procedures and shoddy management oversight. She'd just admitted as much.

Meanwhile, Bell and his two associates, quite frankly, seemed more interested in the view from Bell's panoramic conference room windows. The sun-scorched mountains looked oddly close under the cloudless sky. There was a tranquil beauty to the austerity and bleakness of this corner of the world, the Sonoran Desert, which stretched west into California and south into Mexico. But this appreciation was lost on the savvy defense lawyers who, at the moment, were thinking about other to-dos in other cases. They knew Devlin was scratching around for crumbs, and that the credibility of one disgruntled ex-employee was marginal, especially one who'd been fired for the poor performance she was admitting here.

For Devlin, stepping off the elevator earlier and seeing the ever-cordial and stunning Devon McCoy made him both question and celebrate his New Year's Eve decision to turn and walk away. There would forever be a strong measure of regret on passing, along with an equal sense that he'd made the prudent choice. Devlin began a series of questions to establish that Fay was the registry nurse on duty on March 22, 1975, when Ann Pearson arrived.

"And did you note anything peculiar when she arrived?"

"I barely saw her before nurse Kelman did the initial assessment."

"Nurse Kelman?"

"Debbie Kelman. Nurse Debbie Kelman." Devlin smiled at Bell; he was guessing that was one of the two departed nurses, and now he had a name. Bell shrugged as though Devlin had found a random nickel on the floor. Indeed, Bell's brain was barely engaged—*Keep the lousy nickel. Find another nineteen, and you're up a whole dollar. Oh boy!*

"And what of note, if anything, was found during the initial assessment of Ann Pearson?"

"Objection, hearsay." Bell was actually still staring at something in the distance.

"She just said she didn't do the assessment. She doesn't have to answer any questions about an intake she didn't do." Then, to the nurse Bell said, "Don't answer any more questions."

"Mr. Bell, we both know that in her capacity as registry nurse she, too, was responsible for anything her staff wrote in the chart. I'm just asking her to recollect what one of her staff members wrote in the chart."

Bell shook his head. "My objection stands. She can't testify on behalf of someone else."

Devlin knew it was just a standard lawyer roadblock. But he did have a new name and enough testimony to cast doubt on the overall operation of Mercy Care Center. Let the deposition end with Bell thinking he'd won again. Finding this Debbie Kelman was key, and now that she was out in the open, Bell couldn't stop Devlin any longer on that front. After the deposition, Devlin and Kay Pearson walked to the elevator. Just before the doors closed, Devlin gave Devon McCoy a quick wink.

That night Devlin dialed the number for Max Daniels and gave him the name: Debbie Kelman. Devlin hung up and stared at the papers stacked and scattered all around. With midnight looming, the March night was windy and unseasonably warm. Devlin thought about Devon McCoy and imagined her dark silhouette moving from behind the floor-to-ceiling drapes fluttering in the light breeze. Just the thought of her sent a warm jolt through his body. He'd never met anyone like her: so raw, so mysterious, so lithe and elusive. And dangerous. She was the forbidden fruit, impossible to deny. The breeze rifled the drapes again, and she was gone.

Chapter Nineteen

ON APRIL 10, THE DISCOVERY DEADLINE mandated by Judge Elmore Stearns, Bell & Bauer delivered their response. The courier arrived at Devlin's brick office just before 5 in the afternoon, of course, as another reminder to Devlin as to who was puppeteer. Nadia Flores brought in the box and set it on Devlin's desk. Previously, the mediation ordered by Judge Stearns had done little: Bell & Bauer bumped their settlement figure to $35,000, which was more insult than serious attempt at resolution. After four hours without any movement upward, Devlin left.

The box from Bell & Bauer, fourteen months after the complaint was filed, finally contained some actual answers: names of corporate employees Devlin could begin deposing, and some of the requested documents. There were, of course, still numerous objections to turning over financial and internal records from Flynn Enterprises, and no cooperation in making Flynn Winston available for deposition. Of note among the documents was, finally, Ann Pearson's 80-page medical chart. First up: Devlin would scour every handwritten note and entry and compare the record, line by line, to the chart they already had. Then he'd have Ford Rockwell do the same so they could compare notes. It wasn't all here, but at least Judge Stearns had knocked loose some information. The phone rang.

"You ready to nail those bastards from Bell & Bauer?"

Devlin knew the voice: Max Daniels never was one for salutations and pleasantries. He called when he had something important to say, good or bad, and when he had something important to say he didn't waste valuable time jawing about the weather.

"You got something?"

"I do. What say you: Wanna help me play detective?"

"Now?"

"Tomorrow night. Around midnight."

"Midnight?" Everyone, Devlin thought, should have a Max Daniels in his life. He knew he'd never get a Christmas card from Max Daniels, but this cat had his back.

"Sure. What are we doing?"

"Not over the phone. I just want some back-up to pin this thing down."

"All right. I'm in. Just tell me where."

The next night, around 11:30 p.m., Devlin met Max Daniels at the Third Street office. Daniels rolled up in his cherry-red 1964 Chevelle that gleamed even at night. The black top was up. Devlin was leaning against his Porsche.

"Get in," Daniels yelled. Devlin slid into the tan leather interior that felt as buttery and blissful as Richard Bell's office couch, the historic site of the "informal settlement probe."

Daniels smiled and said, "You're going to fucking love this, pal."

"You going to tell me what's up, or just surprise me?"

Daniels, with his crew cut and angular jaw, looked menacing in the shadows. He said nothing.

"OK, fine," Devlin said. "Surprise me."

They drove west on Interstate 10 and were quickly surrounded by the inky blackness of the desert. No moon in sight. Twenty minutes later, Daniels exited the freeway and parked at a truck-stop diner with a billboard: "*Truckers Food Shower*." The fluorescent lights made the Chevelle hood appear sickeningly orange. The lawyer looked around and laughed.

"Seek the unconventional," Devlin said aloud.

"What?"

"Nothing. Something a friend told me." It was, in fact, Avram Barak who had independently instructed the lawyer to go where other lawyers may not. This place in the middle of the night certainly fit *Rule #5—Seek the unconventional.*

Inside, the diner was about half full. There was a jukebox in the corner, and someone had selected "Too Much, Too Little, Too Late" by Johnny Mathis and Deniece Willams. The music didn't suddenly stop when the duo stepped inside, but many glances fell upon the two. "Hopefully not the soundtrack to this case," Devlin said. He was still in his suit, and his hair, while combed, was longer than anyone else's, including the waitresses. Max Daniels smiled, but he was already moving toward a booth in the corner. They both slid onto the cracked red vinyl. The song switched over to "Baby Come Back" by Player.

"So why are we here?" he asked Daniels.

"Her." Daniels was nodding to the approaching waitress.

"You boys want coffee?" she asked, holding up the pot.

"Sure," Devlin said.

"You're Debbie Kelman," Max Daniels said.

She stopped pouring and looked at Daniels. "Depends who's asking. You cops or something?"

Daniels shook his head. "He'd like to talk to you." She glanced at the lawyer.

"Yeah? About what? The special's *huevos rancheros*, but I wouldn't eat it. Any other questions, doll? Because I'm about to go off shift."

Devlin smiled. Daniels had timed their visit perfectly. "I'm a lawyer, and I'd like to talk to you about one of my cases."

"A lawyer? Good. It's about time, because I haven't seen a nickel of child support from that bastard. You here with some good news, I hope? Hold on, I'll be right back."

Devlin shrugged his shoulders. "At least she's willing to talk."

"Yeah, about her split-tooth old man. But is she a whistle-blower? I don't know."

"Why'd you do it this way?" Devlin asked. "Why not just give me her name and where she works?"

"When I found her here I came in to confirm everything. She just struck me as the type who would respond better to two of us sitting here in person.

Plus it would be hard to reach her by phone in this place. I couldn't find a home number."

"Good work," he said as Debbie Kelman approached.

"Look, I just got sat two tables late, stupid son-of-a-bitch boss. Anyway, I can't really talk now. You have some money for me or not?"

"I'm not here about that," Devlin said.

"Well, what the hell kind of lawyer are you anyway? I didn't do anything wrong, did I?"

"I'm a plaintiff's lawyer."

"A what?"

"I'm representing a client in a wrongful death case against Mercy Care Center. Ring any bells?"

She smiled. "You mean the shithole? You want to talk to me about being a nurse?"

Devlin nodded.

"Doll, that goes back three careers and several good-looking truckers. Being a nurse. No one's asked me about that for years."

"The time period I'm interested in is while you were working there between March and August of 1975."

"Seventy-five?" She laughed. "This look like the face of a woman who has time to keep track of what happened three years ago? I tried to push that place out of my mind anyway. Look, I gotta go take this order."

"But you would be willing to talk to me? When you have more time?"

She paused and smiled again. "So wait. Does this mean you're against them?" Devlin nodded. She leaned closer. "I'd love to talk to you about that place, bunch of sons of bitches. Anytime, sugar. You know where to find me."

Max Daniels nodded and took a sip of coffee. "There you go, counselor. Ex-nurse number one. She might have a line on the other one, too."

Devlin nodded. He hadn't touched the coffee. He pulled out a $20 bill to leave for the two cups and tip. "You thinking what I'm thinking?" he asked.

Daniels narrowed his eyes. "Maybe so. Too easy?"

"Too easy," Devlin said, nodding. Disgruntled ex-employees rarely translated into great witnesses from the plaintiff's side. Whatever help they brought forth was always tinged and offset with questions of their motives and thus, their entire credibility. Any defense lawyer three months out of law school would be able to discredit a disgruntled ex-employee. Richard Bell would probably be able to turn her into a deviant witch who practiced the dark arts and commanded a platoon of evil flying monkeys.

"Her boss at this diner is a son of a bitch and so was everyone at Mercy Care Center. It's a great find, buddy, but we'll have to keep digging." Devlin knew Daniels was right.

First thing the next morning, Devlin called Sniff and got him at his office. "Richard Bell, it's Devlin. How are you, pal?"

"I'm well. I trust you received our discovery response?"

"Oh yes, thank you for that. But that's not why I'm calling."

"Oh?"

"I just wanted to let you know I'm ready to schedule the Debbie Kelman deposition. Anytime this week or next, you just name it. I assume you'll want to do it at your office like the other one?"

"I think we've already told you that she is no longer with the company and that we have no idea as to her whereabouts. Scheduling a deposition is, literally, an impossibility at this particular juncture."

"Well, actually, I have some good news on that front." Bell didn't respond. "I just spoke with her last night, and she's very eager to come in and tell us all about her experiences. Very nice lady."

"I will, unfortunately, have to object to this deposition on numerous grounds."

"Well, you go ahead and object, and meanwhile let's move forward with the deposition anyway, which is what Judge Stearns would want. If you win your motion, we'll throw it out."

Silence. Bell had probably figured Devlin would eventually dig up all the ex-employees, but was perhaps surprised at how quickly his opponent had unearthed one of the skeletons he wanted to keep buried.

"OK," Devlin said. "I'll take that as a 'yes.' Grab a pen, and I'll tell you where you can find her. She's completely out of nursing now. You believe that?" Then he lied to Richard Bell. "My PI has also found the other nurse, too, so you might as well get her in and prepared. We could do them back-to-back, which might be easier for you, schedule-wise."

If Bell didn't call the bluff, he would serve up the nurse for Devlin without Max Daniels having to track her down. If Bell pushed for a name, Devlin would slough it off until Daniels found her. But apparently Bell wasn't sure what to think about this upstart who was proving crafty. So it was with a grudging respect that he didn't call the bluff and instead only said, "I'll be in touch with you."

Devlin hung up and smiled. He called Nadia Flores into his office. "I finally got one up on this guy, Nadia. And now I've got his wheels spinning."

"Sir, I have no earthly idea what you're talking about," she said. "Should I get my notepad?"

Devlin shook his head and waved it off with, "Never mind."

The intricacies of practicing law—the terminology and subtle maneuvers and moment-to-moment shifting dramas—were usually lost on anyone other than the lawyer immersed in the case. Devlin savored it another moment and then moved on to the next phone call.

TWO weeks later, Devlin and Kay Pearson stepped off the elevator at Bell & Bauer and walked to Devon McCoy's desk. She looked particularly alluring in a beige blouse and brown jacket that highlighted her form. The three exchanged pleasantries. When Devlin and Kay Pearson entered the conference room, Debbie Kelman was already seated at the head of the long table. Along the opposite side, to her left, were Richard Bell, three of his associates, and Jeffrey Redmond from Smith, Hawley & White, the firm representing Phoenix Municipal Hospital. Devlin had repeatedly asked Kay Pearson if she really wanted to sit through four hours of tedious questions. There was no way, she said, she would miss a single minute.

The first hour of most depositions was even more boring than the next three. Devlin went down the long list of questions to establish Kelman's name, educational background, detailed career history, and how she came to be at Mercy Care Center in March of 1975. Five lawyers on the other side of the table, and not a single objection. By the second hour, however, Devlin started getting into the heart of his questioning about the policies, procedures, and inner workings of Mercy Care Center. On cue, Bell noted objections to almost every question Devlin asked. But nonetheless, Bell was powerless to suppress the story that began to emerge.

Fay Fancher's privileged status and hands-off approach created resentment among many of the other nurses, but not Debbie Kelman, an LPN who loved the autonomy of having a disinterested supervisor. She could do, or not do, just about whatever she wanted on any given shift, because she knew Fancher's system and that she wouldn't check the patient charts for a week. Kelman took that leeway and created her own sub-system for charting that better fit her work style and energy levels.

She chose the overnight shift, 6 p.m. to 6 a.m., because she knew that shift had the fewest admissions and discharges and, therefore, the least amount of attendant paperwork. Kelman could make her rounds without picking up a chart (she made mental notes on each patient) and then sit undisturbed in the patient ward for hours. She liked to needlepoint all night while the patients slept and Fancher read her stupid books and smoked in the office. Then, around 5 a.m., Kelman would go back through the charts and make her care notes from memory, which Fancher never once questioned.

So Kelman was not happy when she arrived for her shift, twenty-five minutes late on March 22, 1975, to find she had a new admission: Ann Pearson. Kelman noted the black man waiting with this new patient. Not only short and colored, the guy only had one arm, and that sort of thing sticks around in your mind. Kelman took the chart from Fancher, who was holding a copy of *The Gods Themselves* by Asimov and a lit cigarette, and wheeled Ann Pearson back to her bed.

By then, Ann Pearson was tired, didn't feel like talking and just wanted to go to sleep. That suited Kelman, because she pretty much felt the same on all those fronts. She helped Ann into bed, brought her a glass of water and did a thorough assessment of her condition, making detailed notes on her chart. Then, an hour after arriving at Mercy Care Center, Ann Pearson was sleeping soundly. Kelman was digging in her bag for her needlepoint project. And Fay Fancher was back in the office, behind her cluttered desk, wonderfully immersed in her book in the thick haze of cigarette smoke.

"Let's back up for a minute," Devlin said. "You just testified that you normally made mental notes as you examined a patient and then only later wrote on the patient's chart. Is that about right?"

"I knew she was hurting, is why I made notes right then."

"Objection, non-responsive," Devlin said for the record. "Miss Kelman, my question was—"

"I remember the question. Yes, that's usually how I did it, but not how I did it that time."

"OK. Fair enough. And how long had you worked at Mercy Care Center?"

"Like I said, about thirteen months."

"Just over one year." Devlin had won the battle with Bell over videotaping this deposition, and at the head of the table sat the technician behind a phalanx of bulky equipment. The camera was catching every eye roll, angry head shake, and heavy sigh emitted by Debbie Kelman. "And now it is your testimony that after following your procedure of making mental notes first and writing on a patient's chart six, seven, ten hours later, that on March 22, 1975, you spontaneously changed this procedure when you saw Ann Pearson?"

"Object as to form," Bell said, who had explained to Kelman that his objections were for the record only and, unlike in court where a judge would rule on each objection, she should simply answer the questions after any objections.

"That's what I'm saying. She looked sick. Real sick."

Devlin spent the next fifteen minutes documenting what "real sick" meant to Debbie Kelman, who explained that Ann Pearson had a huge, oozing sore on her backside upon admission.

"So just to clarify, on March 22, 1975, you changed your normal procedure by assessing Ann Pearson immediately and then noting on her chart this huge oozing sore on her backside. Is that correct?" Devlin watched Kay Pearson wince and close her eyes whenever they discussed her mother's physical condition.

"Yes."

"And then one hour after arriving with this huge, oozing sore, Ann Pearson was sleeping soundly, you were doing needlepoint and Fay Fancher was in her office reading?"

"Objection, hearsay," Bell said. "She can't testify as to what other people were doing outside of her view."

Devlin restated the question: "It is your testimony that one hour after arriving with this huge, oozing sore, Ann Pearson was sleeping soundly and you were doing needlepoint?"

"I'd say that's about right."

Devlin glanced at his watch: They were about three hours into the deposition. This was a good time to back off. Devlin had Dr. Wayne Michaels' deposition testimony that he discharged Ann Pearson in stable condition thirty minutes before she arrived at the nursing home. Now he had a nurse, he suspected, who was flat-out lying about Ann Pearson's condition upon admission. Devlin suspected Kelman wanted to take shots at Mercy Care Center for getting fired, but she also wanted to cover her own ass in the process.

Devlin didn't want to tip his hand in any way to Bell and his lackeys. So as a countermeasure, he went down a new line of questioning just to take another hour out of his opponents' day and, hopefully, dilute any suspicion that Devlin had exposed anything useful. He hammered hard on policies and procedures, patient charting practices, internal management structure, and corporate oversight of the facility. He finished with a question he knew the defense would use at trial to discredit her. Better, Devlin thought, to get it out there now: "Miss Kelman, you are no longer employed by Mercy Care Center and currently not under subpoena to give this testimony. Why are you coming forward voluntarily with this information today?"

"That's easy. The fact that I... this has always bothered me, and I just don't... I don't like seeing people neglected. I don't like abuse, and I don't like nurses who allow that to happen. And the way they run Mercy Care Center, such as demanding we do this and that, just means the people don't get treated the way they should. I care what happens to those people, I guess is what I'm trying to say. I cannot be a part of that, which is why I left and got out of nursing altogether."

Devlin would have to cover that one in a minute, but first: "You care about your patients?" Always present tense.

"Absolutely. That's why I'm here today. I don't want to be like those people who killed that poor woman when I did everything I could to alert them to her condition."

Perfect. Now back to that other point: Devlin had to get on record that Debbie Kelman did not leave voluntarily, but rather she was fired. He then had to walk her through the details that led up to that firing and separate those facts from her ability and credibility as a nurse.

"HOW did we do?" Kay asked as Devlin helped her into the Porsche. The April sky was cloudless, and the sun was beaming down in glorious brilliance.

"We did well. Her testimony is exposing the multitude of problems within Mercy Care Center. The downside is that she was fired and maybe not all that credible."

"But just because she was fired doesn't mean that what they did to my mother was OK."

"I know. I know. But a jury's going to consider her motivation for coming forward, and whether or not that affects her credibility. But we're OK. We need to find that other nurse. We need the same testimony from someone with more credibility."

There was another looming concern that Devlin didn't want to get into with his client: Who was lying about Ann Pearson's condition on March 22? It was either the caregivers at Mercy Care Center or those at Phoenix Municipal Hospital. The hospital staff was claiming she left in stable condition, and the nursing home side was saying she arrived with a horribly infected sore. Both stories couldn't be true. Against the prevailing wisdom, Devlin had pinned his strategy on going after the nursing home. But if the defense could create the possibility that it was, in fact, the hospital staff that was to blame, then his entire case fell apart. Devlin needed Max Daniels to find the other nurse.

Chapter Twenty

"YOU WERE RIGHT," said Ford Rockwell, sipping Grape Nehi in his crisp lab coat that looked like he'd ironed and starched it five minutes ago. "Three Times A Lady" by The Commodores was playing at low volume on his desk radio.

"I take it that's good news," said Devlin. "I could use some."

It was a June Tuesday with a predicted high of 116 degrees. Ford Rockwell's swamp cooler was already straining to keep pace; sweat trickled down Devlin's face and neck. Growing up in Buffalo, New York and then putting down a stake in Phoenix was like moving from Nome, Alaska to the surface of Mars. But, oddly, Devlin's mind and body acclimated to the searing heat. Temperatures once considered heat waves back home—90s—were balmy respites; temperatures once unbearable—110-plus—were wholly tolerable and barely an annoyance.

Yesterday, Devlin had heard that serial killer David Berkowitz, "Son of Sam," got twenty-five years to life. Then, a few minutes before 5 p.m., Richard Bell called to say that, unfortunately, Flynn Winston was unavoidably detained in Dallas and would not be able to make it for today's scheduled deposition. Ava Quinn, the corporate administrator for Flynn Enterprises, was also unable to make the trip.

"Let me show you," Rockwell said. "OK, the first chart you gave me, the one they gave to Kay Pearson, it's thirty pages. Then the second one they sent as part of the discovery request had grown to fifty pages. Nothing too alarming there. Medical charts, they'll say, are often in different departments and with different agencies and when collected, can grow in size. But now this third version they sent is about seventy-five pages. Just like you, I went through all three versions. Now on the two subsequent versions, there are new handwritten entries."

"Right. I saw that," Devlin said. "But again, they'll contend charts are updated and finalized, etcetera, etcetera."

"Mmm," Rockwell said, nodding. "But how will they explain this?" He showed Devlin versions #2 and #3. "There's a forty-eight-hour window here with no record whatsoever. Nothing. She was only there ten days, and they don't have any care records for a full two of those days?"

Devlin smiled. He had discovered the same discrepancy, but he wanted his expert to independently confirm what the lawyer suspected.

"Two days with no records?" Devlin said. "That's unexplainable."

"And not the easiest thing to figure out. If the defense has good faith in what their client is telling them, which I'm sure they do, then this may not trip any red flags over there, which means..."

"I can sit on this and spring it at the trial. This alone could sink them."

"Perhaps. But don't forget your deceased was a frail and aged woman with various co-morbidities. Even if you nail them on this issue... you just never know. The jury might say, 'Yeah, the nursing home dropped the ball, but they did the best they could and she was going in the box soon anyway. Here's twenty-five grand for any outstanding medical bills and final expenses.'"

"You've got a lousy way of sharing good news, Rockwell."

"It is good news, Devlin. Just trying to earn my keep. No surprises, right?" The music changed to Nick Gilder singing "Hot Child In The City."

"That's it: *Never be surprised—surprise is death*." But what Devlin was really pondering was how and when to bring up the purple-mouth issue caused by Grape Nehi.

The summer of 1978, three years now after Ann Pearson's death, passed with little movement on the case. Devlin's mind flashed back, fresh from law school eight years ago, to his exalted images of days bathed in some sort of noble glow cast by a powerful and humane intention. But the tedious wrangling and pedantic march of the law had all but squeezed out the fresh-faced activism and naïve Irish immigrant ideals of his youth. Devlin was not, in fact, carrying the tired and the poor to safety on his back. The huddled masses still yearned to breathe free. For every client he helped, there were 10,000 cases that never crossed his desk. Devlin had not lifted his lamp beside the golden door. And even for Ann Pearson, there was no way he could guarantee any sort of triumph that would stamp out the pain.

In September, with Richard Bell canceling deposition after deposition, Menachem Begin and Anwar Sadat sat down at Camp David, Maryland, and began the peace process. The day they signed their peace agreement, September 17, Devlin called and left Richard Bell a message with his secretary: "Please tell him that if the Jews and Arabs can break bread, there's certainly hope for us in this case. Tell him this is a friendly last chance to schedule all open depositions before we file another Motion to Compel with the court. Call me."

No news, in the case of Bell & Bauer, was usually bad news, and they were able to uphold their stand of deafening silence right through the end of the year. With 1979 closing in, Devlin had spent almost three years on the case with no end in sight. He'd earmarked what he got from the Big City Auto Sales settlement for this case and had already used that up, about $25,000, videotaping depositions, getting counsel from Ford Rockwell and Avram Barak, and paying Max Daniels to track down ex-nurses. Devlin had conflicting patient charts with a forty-eight-hour gap in patient care, but no one yet to establish what might have transpired.

As often happened in the whirlwind of juggling so many cases, the months ticked by quickly to December. Devlin's final volley of the year in case number PB1977-002736, the estate of Ann Pearson versus Flynn Enterprises, was to write that Motion to Compel. In some places scathing, the document he had promised three months back included a request for fees and sanctions.

Devlin detailed all the instances of Bell & Bauer objections to disclosing documents and information on their client's corporate and regional business practices. He wrote that the defense routinely cancelled depositions, and when they did allow them to go forward, were obstreperous throughout. He detailed their schemes to preclude information because it was privileged when all they had to do was redact the names.

Devlin wrote until his hand ached about how Bell & Bauer objected to any questioning of witnesses as to how finances were handled by Flynn Enterprises and Mercy Care Center, and their assertion that plaintiffs had not demonstrated this was a punitive damages case. It took Devlin and Nadia Flores another three days of fine-tuning, typing, and retyping drafts until the motion was ready. One changed word or typo on a page meant Nadia had to retype the entire page: Devlin wanted it perfect *sans* corrective white blobs.

Finally, on the last business day of the year, Friday, December 29, Devlin drove the Porsche downtown and filed the motion with the clerk of the court. Two days later, Devlin planned to head out around 9 p.m. for New Year's Eve to meet friends at The Wellington. But instead, exhausted from working three weeks straight without a day off, he fell asleep on his couch at 7 p.m. and didn't awake until after 2 a.m. As he came to, groggy, he sat up, rubbed his face and saw the time. Then it took his sleepy brain a good ten seconds to pull it all together. And then he realized, of course, that it was 1979.

Chapter Twenty-One

ON JANUARY 4 OF THE NEW YEAR, the State of Ohio agreed to pay $675,000 to the families of the four dead and nine injured in the Kent State University shootings. Lawyers for the parents and wounded students had been trying for years to bring civil suits against Ohio's governor, the university president, and the National Guard officers who'd fired shots into the crowd. The courts, however, dismissed the actions by citing "sovereign immunity." The U.S. Supreme Court opened the door for the plaintiffs by ruling that sovereign immunity was not absolute, but qualified, and the parents and students brought the suit.

Devlin had read the newspaper accounts with great interest. It had taken five years, but the State of Ohio was writing the settlement check, with a good chunk of it going to Dean Kahler, a young man paralyzed in the shootings. The process of personal-injury law, though not perfect, had garnered some measure of resolution for the families by demanding accountability and, in the form of hard currency, responsibility. It put into perspective Devlin's long battle with Mercy Care Center, bolstered his spirit, and became good fodder the following night.

"Hell, you just getting started, Big-Time," One-Armed Lucky said, leaning against the brick wall at AAA Bail Bonds. It was only 4 p.m., but the gap between the buildings was cast in long shadows. "How we doing, anyway?"

It was a fair question with no simple answer. Devlin scratched above his ear and took a long drink of cold beer.

"That good, huh?" Lucky laughed and shook his head. "Annie would be fed up with this whole process. She never had time for this kind of monkey business. Know what I'm saying?" From Lucky's battered radio, Devlin could hear "Night Fever" by the Bee Gees, a song you couldn't avoid hearing at least twelve times a day. As soon as the song started, Devlin wanted to kick the radio down Madison Street.

"We're hanging in there," Devlin finally said, though he wasn't even sure himself what he meant. Beyond the case not being dismissed outright, Bell & Bauer seemed to be winning the highbrow battle of hide-and-seek. And until the court ruled otherwise, Richard Bell was going to keep things on lockdown.

"Just between you, me, and the wall," Devlin said, "I wonder if I got in too deep on this one. My experts have given me stacks of books on pathology and geriatric medicine and nursing home administration. I start after dinner every night and read until I fall asleep some time after midnight. Then I wake up in a cold sweat three hours later trying to collate those ten days she spent at the nursing home, the medical chain of events that led to your dear friend's death. At that point, my mind's spinning and no way I'm falling back asleep. So I'll pick up another book or her medical charts and start reading them again. The best depo we have is from a nurse who got fired, so her credibility's about as good as the retread flunkies you bond out every day. And everyone's telling me even if we win—which they're quick to point out will be nigh on impossible—my end of the settlement probably won't even cover my expenses. So how we doing? You tell me."

Lucky nodded and picked at the label on his bottle. "I known this old salty defense lawyer who used to chew up prosecutors in this real quiet, calm way. He never let nothing rattle him, and just kept plugging along on his cases. Prosecution could have the damn Pope lined up as their star witness, and it wouldn't bother 'ole Larry. I remember one time he said he always knew the longer he worked a case, the easier it got, because he could start eliminating theories and possibilities and strategies. Then at some point whatever's left is the case you got, and that's what you go with, win or lose."

162

"Makes sense," Devlin said, nodding. "And it'd be nice if 'ole Larry could help me schedule some actual depositions to narrow the possibilities."

"Yeah, back from the grave. You remind me of that old bastard, Big-Time. He was probably Irish, too, same bulldog approach and weren't afraid of nothing. You doing the same thing. Just keep on truckin'. You hang around long enough you always got a chance to win."

Devlin took it in, pondering, but he wouldn't realize the full genius of Lucky's reminiscing until he got an excited phone call from Kay Pearson. Since Lucky's prophetic words that Friday, this was the first big movement in the case. This time when Kay called for her weekly update, she was breathless with excitement.

"Slow down, Kay. What is it?"

"I got the response. Finally. They answered my letter."

Devlin had fifty-plus cases he was working on top of the Ann Pearson case, which had grown to fifteen or so boxes crammed with notes, medical documents, motions, briefs, all the correspondence to and from Bell & Bauer, and deposition transcripts. So he had no idea what she was talking about. "What letter?"

"From the state."

Devlin was almost embarrassed that he still wasn't following his client, on a case he'd been working for three years. "I'm sorry, Kay. From whom did you receive a letter?"

"The Arizona Health Services Department. About investigating Mercy Care Center."

With that, the data popped to the fore of Devlin's brain. No wonder he couldn't remember: Kay Pearson sent the letter more than two years ago. "Well, it's about time. What are they saying?"

"It's long. Like ten pages. It's something called a 'Field Trip Report.'"

"OK, that's good. That means they actually went and investigated."

"I don't understand all this technical jargon, but, here, let me read you the end. Let me see... *Based on the available documentation... worsening and increase in size of the pressure sores on the resident's bilateral buttocks and right heel...* more medical stuff. OK, here, last sentence: *The facility in question failed to provide sufficient assessments of the patient's physical status in order for her to attain optimal physical well-being, and this allegation is substantiated."*

"Kay, that's wonderful news. I'll need to see that full report immediately."

This allegation is substantiated. There it was: third-party corroboration of Debbie Kelman's deposition testimony, and this time the source was the state of Arizona. No way Bell & Bauer could dodge this little bombshell: Now their client was in violation of state law.

"I'm on my way," Kay said. "May I come now?"

"Yes. Absolutely. I'll wait for you here at my office."

Devlin pulled out his notepad and scribbled Lucky's previous insight, which he incorporated and crafted as *Rule #6—As you move through the case, the issues become smaller and smaller.* Indeed, now the game was narrowing. With the state flagging Mercy Care Center with one or more health violations, Bell & Bauer would be forced to open the information vault they'd sealed from day one. All the internal documents and financial records and cancelled depositions were now fair game.

On February 1, officials released convicted bank robber Patty Hearst from prison after President Carter commuted her sentence. Devlin saw the story in the newspaper, but he missed, as did most Americans, the small blurb about an obscure leader in the Middle East. The Ayatollah Ruhollah Khomeini, after nearly fifteen years of exile, returned to Tehran, Iran. Ten days later, Khomeini seized power. On April 1, Iran's government became an Islamic republic by a ninety-eight percent vote, which officially overthrew the Shah.

Later in the month, following an extended absence from the bench due to a bout with pneumonia, Judge Elmore Stearns delivered Devlin a long-awaited victory. In a three-page court order, Judge Stearns dressed down Bell & Bauer on every point Devlin had been making in his repeated Motions to Compel. On paper, at least, the kid had made some headway in gaining the judge's respect. Stearns' court order was some of the most beautiful prose Devlin's eyes had seen since reading Dostoevsky at Notre Dame:

Court Orders dated April 25, 1979

Following plaintiffs' Motion for Sanctions and to Further Compel Discovery, and other discovery issues, the following orders are hereby entered:

1.Within seven days, defendants shall produce to plaintiffs all payroll records for staff that were on the unit or units that provided care to Ann Pearson from March 22, 1975, to April 1, 1975.

2.Within seven days, defendants shall produce to plaintiffs the budget variance analysis documents located at Flynn Enterprises in Dallas, Texas.

3. Defendants shall schedule and facilitate completion of the following depositions within the next 90 days: Flynn Winston, CEO Flynn Enterprises; Rupert Styles, administrator; Ava Quinn, corporate administrator; and Maggie Strahan, unit director.

4. Defendants are solely responsible for all travel expenses related to depositions, between Dallas and Phoenix, including deponents, defense counsel and associates, and plaintiff, plaintiff's counsel and plaintiff's associates up to (4) persons total per trip. For any deposition not completed within the court-ordered time period, defendants will pay the court a sanction of $500 per day until said deposition is completed.

5. If any of the above items are not produced in a timely matter, an award of attorneys' fees and a sanction of $5,000 will be entered against defendants as punishment and in order to mitigate the burden of the expense of having to move to compel production of documents that should already have been produced.

6. Notwithstanding the court's previous admonition to reach a settlement in this case, trial date for this case is hereby set as November 5, 1979.

It was a resounding knockout. The only disappointment was that the judge had let Bell & Bauer off with a hand-slap by not imposing any sanctions. To that end, Richard Bell was no doubt claiming victory because he'd effectively stonewalled his adversary for more than two years without official penalty. Now he'd huddle his sleep-deprived associates to celebrate how well they'd deployed the legal tools at their disposal. Then they'd strategize this next phase, and Bell would send them off to begin preparing in earnest for the upcoming depositions: *Battle positions, young charges, the plaintiffs are about to breach the castle walls!* Meanwhile, Devlin, too, spent the morning rallying his own troops. From the Scottsdale condo, he called Kay first and told her the good news. There was a pause on the other end of the line.

"Kay?" Then he heard her crying. When she collected herself, she said, "It's just been so hard without Mom. And this is all taking so long. I had no idea it would take this long. I just want them to stand up in public and look me in the eye and say they were wrong. I want them to apologize and fix things so this never happens to someone else."

"I know," he said. But he knew that even if they won a settlement or jury verdict, the defendant would never admit even the slightest fault or wrongdoing. Contrition and apology were not the way of the legal system. Mostly because any admission of guilt would negate any possibility of appeal, but also because such an acknowledgment would be like chumming the waters for other plaintiff's attorneys. One faint whiff of blood, and Flynn Enterprises would be engulfed in a feeding frenzy. Devlin felt a twinge of anger and sadness that, even in victory, the law would fall well short of giving his client the resolution she deserved.

"So when you say we finally have a trial date, it just all hit me: Maybe by year's end this will all be over. That would be so wonderful. I know you can do it."

"I will do everything in my power to make that happen," he said. But what he was really thinking was that even with a victory in court, the litigation would drag on as Richard Bell filed the requisite appeal.

"Thank you, Mr. Devlin. Thank you, thank you. And let me know when for the next deposition. I will be there for every minute of every one." He'd never seen such a dedicated client.

"Your mother would be proud of you, Kay."

Next he called Ford Rockwell and Avram Barak and ended up leaving messages with secretaries. Devlin wanted to make sure they blocked out their calendars for a possible November trial. Plus he needed to talk deposition strategy in unraveling the corporate doings of Flynn Enterprises. Then, on day seven of Judge Stearns' deadline, shortly before 5 p.m., thirteen banker's boxes arrived at Devlin's office containing, ostensibly, the missing documents he'd been requesting since Carter took office. At first he thought it was a mistake, that he'd received a delivery intended for someone else. The missing documents he requested would take up two, maybe three boxes.

But as he thumbed through the first box of files, however, he realized that Bell & Bauer were simply up to their old tricks. *Thirteen boxes?* Choosing that number was not a coincidence: it was bad-luck voodoo wrapped in the letter of the law. Bell & Bauer weren't going to suddenly be transparent and forthcoming just because some Superior Court judge issued a little court order. So instead of just providing what the judge had ordered, Sniff and his cronies sent over what Devlin requested and then intermingled those documents with reams of nothingness. Enough to fill thirteen boxes. The suits at Bell & Bauer knew Devlin couldn't officially protest to the court until he at least went through every page in every box and cross-checked each document against what he had requested. Nor would the court sanction Bell & Bauer for being overly cooperative. Devlin immediately called Richard Bell.

"Richard, it's Devlin."

"Mr. Devlin, hello. Listen, I'm just about to go into a meeting. Can we make this brief?"

"Hey, I just wanted to thank you. We received the documents and everything looks great." There was a slight pause. Richard Bell didn't think the young lawyer was that dumb, but he couldn't be certain. More likely, he decided, Devlin was simply returning the gamesmanship in stride. Bell was impressed with the kid's deft moves.

"Excellent," Bell said. "Thank you once again for your infinite patience. Anything we can do to facilitate the process."

"Great. Actually there is: How we doing on getting those depositions scheduled?"

"My associates assure me they are diligently pursuing that per the court order, and we will meet our deadline."

Fucking lawyers, Devlin thought, separating himself from his own profession. On the first day of law school they should strap every would-be lawyer to a chair and tattoo "Human Being" on the back of both hands. Maybe then they'd remember, throughout their careers, how to relate to people minus the ego and never-ending lawyer-speak. Lawyer or not, Devlin liked to keep things simple.

"OK, but let's not string this out right to the end. Ninety days was the maximum, but is there any reason we can't just get them going?"

"I assure you, Mr. Devlin, we are doing everything in our power to get those scheduled stat. Mr. Winston is a busy man. He's actually currently out of the country."

"That's convenient. When will he be in the country?"

"Well, I would prefer not to get into the scheduling details and travel logistics at this moment."

"You're right. How about the others? They out of the country, too? Come to think of it, since you're picking up the travel tab, let's just depose everyone overseas. Ahh, springtime in Paris... magical. We could sip espresso and eat fresh croissants at a café on the Champs Elysees." Not even a chuckle.

"My clients are actually waiting for me in the conference room. Let me get back to you with some possible dates, OK?" There probably wasn't a client within ten miles of Richard Bell's office right now.

"I won't hold my breath, Richard."

"No; I would trust that you wouldn't."

Devlin hung up and stared at the stack of boxes in his office. That was, unfortunately, the next order of business. But they'd never all fit into the Porsche; he'd have Nadia Flores arrange delivery to his condo, where he would begin the tedious process of sorting through each page. He flipped through his calendar: seven months until the trial. He had a case built mostly on conjecture. The missing nurse was still out there; Richard Bell hadn't volunteered her name and Max Daniels hadn't turned up anything yet. Everything was riding on the upcoming depositions. Unless Devlin started drawing out the testimony to corroborate his theories, he had no chance of settling, much less winning a trial.

Later that night at home, Devlin picked up the first box. It was easy to see what Bell & Bauer had done. If the judge ordered Mercy Care Center payroll records from March 22, 1975, to April 1, 1975, Devlin received six months' worth of payroll records. And, of course, it wasn't chronological, so he had to sift through everything to pull out what he needed. He had to dial Max Daniels' phone number three times that evening before getting an answer.

"I've got a list of names of everyone who was working at Mercy Care Center when Ann Pearson was there."

"Which means our nurse should be in there," Daniels said.

"You got it."

"I can't believe I haven't been able to find her," Daniels said. "Obviously I started with Mercy Care Center, but none of those zombies are talking. None of the patients there can remember names back that far. I even had my guy at the phone company dump the records on outgoing calls from Mercy Care Center from that time—you'll see that as 'research fees' on my invoice—and I followed up every goddam one of those numbers. Nothing."

"I didn't hear what you just said."

Daniels paused. "Right. Sorry. I followed up with our friend Debbie Kelman and tried to get her to give up the name, but she said she didn't want to pull anybody into this that didn't come forward on their own."

"Noble of her. Did you try to fuck her? She might have told you then."

"I never mix business with pleasure. Unless, of course, she's got tits like Bo Derek. So I got another guy at the county tax office who pulled their W2's—"

"I'm not hearing this, either," Devlin said. He knew Daniels was good at finding information, but it was best if he didn't know the inner workings of his methods.

"Anyway, their records are shoddy, so that was no help. I went down to the courthouse and checked the county records to see if she bought a house. Nothing. I asked around at other nursing homes to see if someone new used to work at Mercy Care Center."

"Well let's try this list and see if she turns up." Devlin read the list of the twenty-six names he'd gleaned from the payroll records. He saw all the names of the key people he'd come to know in the case: Rupert Styles, Debbie Kelman, and Fay Fancher.

"You'll have to cross off the janitors, cooks, dishwashers, and administrators. Hopefully what you have left includes our nurse."

"All right. I'm on it."

"Thanks, pal."

Hours later, Devlin was dozing off as he plodded through box #3. Surrounded by financial records from Flynn Enterprises, he'd been drifting in and out of sleep for a few minutes. He looked at the clock: almost 2:30 a.m. Then he fell asleep again and saw a shadowy image of Devon McCoy emerge from the bedroom. She was in a short skirt with black boots that went up to her knees. She was carrying a manila envelope she dropped on the table. *A little going-away present*, she said. *Your whole case is in this envelope. You're going to win this case.* Then she moved away from the table. When she got to Devlin, she pushed the stacks of papers from the couch to the floor. Somehow, in one fluid motion, she was straddling and kissing him with a hunger demanding something beyond what his body could give her.

Chapter Twenty-Two

TWO WEEKS LATER, Devlin had made it through all thirteen boxes. He worked methodically each night, after dinner and basketball, and sometimes was still reading when the morning glow first cracked across the manicured fairway outside the French Doors. Surprisingly, Bell & Bauer had actually sent Devlin everything he'd requested. Finally, Richard Bell phoned to say he had scheduled the depositions of CEO Flynn Winston and Ava Quinn, corporate administrator for Flynn Enterprises, for June 15. As usual, with the July deadline from Judge Stearns looming, Bell had arranged one day, a Friday, for two depositions, and suggested deposing Flynn Winston in the morning and Ava Quinn after lunch. And everything would take place at the Flynn Enterprises corporate building in Dallas.

"I don't like it. *Se shtinkt.*" Avram Barak chewed a bite from the sandwich Devlin had brought him and then talked with his mouth full. "He scheduled two depos on one day to try to squeeze you for time. And by doing it on a Friday, you won't be able to carry over to the next day. He'll make sure they're both booked with other things that weekend." Barak nodded at his own words. Devlin had scheduled the meeting, at Barak's rate of $190 per hour, to discuss deposition strategy. He also needed some guidance on navigating the financial and administrative side of running a nursing home. Devlin was thinking about Rule #4. "One thing I try to do is remind myself that the goal is to win the case, not particular points with the client, opposing side, judge, or a witness."

"You read that out of a first-year law book?"

"No, but if I can do both depos in one day and get what I need, then I don't need to press them on how they're scheduled."

Avram shrugged. "Maybe. But the only thing I would add is that if you're into the first one and it looks like you'll need more time to properly elicit what you need, then don't feel pressured in any way. They'll just have to make the other person available on another day."

Devlin liked it. He would go along with Bell's ground rules, but only as long it wasn't interfering with his case. Barak had a small radio playing "With A Little Luck" by Paul McCartney and Wings. "You trying to tell me something with this music?"

"I told you from day one: *Meshuggener* as the day is long. So, yes, the song is apropos."

Devlin spent three full days preparing with the Jewish maven, including Barak's scheduled deposition with Richard Bell. They talked endlessly about possible defense strategies: how the nurses and doctors at Mercy Care Center were consistent in their care of Ann Pearson. It was, in fact, her advanced age, severe cardiac condition, malnutrition, and anemia that killed her, not neglect of care. Further, Mercy Care Center had no part in decisions made by others at Phoenix Municipal Hospital, and could not be expected to be held accountable for those actions. And it was hospital staff who chose to discharge Ann Pearson so quickly, after only three days, to a different facility. The defense would additionally contend that Mercy Care Center was a stable facility with high standards of care that, notwithstanding the recent violation, passed numerous inspections by federal and state agencies. This preparation with Devlin's expert witness added another $5,000 to the running total on the case. With Max Daniels and Ford Rockwell simultaneously running their own meters, Devlin was now $20,000 in the red with the trial still six months away. By then, Devlin would need a $100,000 settlement just to break even on a case he'd been working on for almost four years.

At the end of the third day with Barak, Devlin was exhausted. He and Barak had scoured the financial records of Flynn Enterprises going back ten years. They reviewed charting procedures, staffing ratios, and budget variance data on every revenue and expense that went through Mercy Care Center. It was an enormous amount of information to process and collate into depositions that would be capped at four hours each. Devlin smiled. "You know, for an old Jew, you're pretty fucking smart."

"Damn right, kid. Win or lose, I'm the one getting $190 an hour to babysit you."

The song on the radio changed to "If I Can't Have You" by Yvonne Elliman.

On June 14, Devlin, Kay Pearson, Nadia Flores, and One-Armed Lucky flew to Dallas courtesy of Bell & Bauer. Kay Pearson was determined to come, but Devlin didn't need Nadia and certainly not Lucky. But the judge had said "up to four people," and so four people it was. The next day, Deposition Day, was a cloudy, hot, humid affair. Devlin stepped from the hotel lobby into the oppressive Texas morning. Across the street, emblazoned on the side of an old brick building, was: *Welcome to the Republic of Texas. Land of the Free.*

"Fucking Texans," Devlin muttered, shaking his head as the other three emerged from the hotel. Thirty minutes later, the four arrived at Flynn Enterprises, a modest five-floor building in an industrial area that smelled like burning rubber and something sour Devlin couldn't place. Then he saw the sign on an adjacent building: *Peterson Pickle Company*. The four waited in the lobby for fifteen minutes before Richard Bell appeared with two of his associates. Amid the flurry of introductions, Devlin caught Bell suspiciously eyeing One-Armed Lucky, who was decked out in a pinstripe suit that looked more pimp than lawyer. Devlin simply said, "This is Mr. Lucky, one of my associates."

Just after the introductions, Jeffrey Redmond arrived. Although the hospital wasn't directly involved in these depositions, his firm Smith, Hawley & White wanted him present at every turn of the case. So the group of eight went through the same introductions again. Then they followed Bell onto the elevator and rode to the top floor of Flynn Enterprises. It looked more blue-collar than corporate, more industrial than polished. There was no marble foyer, no cherry or other fine woods, or any other appointments that belied the purpose there. Inside Flynn Enterprises, it still looked like 1960, when the company was casting and machining industrial metal parts for polyethylene storage tanks. And Devlin got the sense that it didn't particularly matter— bolted fittings or old people on respirators—to the secretaries and men in suits behind ugly metal desks. They were wringing out a paycheck either way.

"This place stinks," Devlin said as they squeezed down the narrow hallway. "Literally."

"Yes, I'm sure you saw the pickle factory next door," Bell said. "You won't even notice the smell after five minutes."

"That's what my old lady says during sex," Lucky said, nudging Devlin. Devlin wanted to reprimand his friend, but couldn't help laughing when he saw the look on Bell's face. Bell led the group down a long hallway to a large conference room that, per Judge Stearns' orders, was already equipped with video equipment and a technician, who sat next to the court reporter. There were also two more associates in suits and a thin, attractive woman who was smoking a cigarette. Devlin pegged her immediately: Ava Quinn, corporate administrator. The way they'd kept her hidden for two years, Devlin felt like he was finally meeting a Hollywood starlet who'd been living in recluse after her halcyon days. Once again, Bell went through all the introductions for the group that now numbered thirteen. Devlin had never experienced anything like this. In most cases there were three people in the room for a deposition: the person being deposed and a lawyer on each side. Devlin wondered if Bell might squeeze in a few more to really make it a party.

Devlin scanned the room: He still hadn't met Flynn Winston. Lucky glanced around the room and thought about how many dollars all these lawyers were burning up just standing around drinking coffee. Kay Pearson huddled close to her lawyer and squeezed his hand for comfort. Nadia Flores was as unimpressed with Texas as Devlin, and thinking about the stacks of paperwork she'd left behind just to be on this boondoggle. Finally everyone was seated, with Ava Quinn, still puffing away, taking the spot of the deponent at the head of the table. Devlin narrowed his gaze at Richard Bell.

"Mr. Devlin, I do have to apologize. I know we talked about you deposing Mr. Winston first, but he was unavoidably detained at an out-of-town meeting last night and will be returning to Dallas mid-morning."

"Don't take it personally, Richard, but he always seems to be as far away from you as possible." Several laughs, including two of Bell's associates.

"Yes," Bell said. "He is quite busy. If it's acceptable, my proposition is that we just reverse the order we discussed, proceed now with Miss Quinn, and then continue after lunch with Mr. Winston."

True or not, things had devolved to the point that Devlin didn't believe a word that came out of Richard Bell's mouth. Every move, it seemed, was calculated to gain any possible advantage, however insignificant. Bell knew Devlin would be prepared with his questions in a certain order, so why not flip-flop the day's order, throw Devlin off his game ever so slightly. Bell lost nothing and, perhaps, gained that tiny advantage. If nothing else, it would be a fun and irritating little jab at his opponent. *Ha! Got you again, Irish.* If there was one thing Devlin despised more than arrogant lawyers, it was arrogant lawyers who weaseled on you throughout a case like a rat in the corner working a stale carrot. But Devlin played his hand like a pro holding nothing but a pair of threes. "That's perfectly fine," Devlin said, smiling. "I'm sure Miss Quinn is eager to have this behind her."

"That would be an understatement," she said, laughing nervously.

"We all set, Carl?" Devlin said, turning to the video technician and using his name, a little detail nine out of ten lawyers wouldn't remember from a few minutes ago because all they ever thought about was (1) themselves; (2) their precious cases; and (3) themselves.

"Miss Quinn, being deposed is like going to the dentist: No one really likes it, but it's usually not as bad as we think it's going to be. Just be yourself, and we'll have you out of here before lunch." She nodded and smiled. Richard Bell nodded almost imperceptibly, acceding that he'd never thought to do that at a deposition. This kid was smooth.

Devlin, before diving into the thick notebook he and Avram Barak had prepared, looked at One-Armed Lucky and Kay Pearson and took a long, slow breath. All lawsuits were by nature time-consuming, tedious, and painful. In wrongful death cases like this one, someone had lost a loved one. The very process of litigation meant years reliving that death and all its attendant details, which warped the timing and natural grief cycle for the people involved. As the case dragged on, it was easy for lawyers on both sides to become the very symbol of agony and suffering.

Since he'd taken this case, day by day, Devlin felt the pressing burden of trying to end the litigation as soon as possible, on terms favorable to his client, so Kay Pearson could cross the line into resolution and healing. That's why Devlin was here on a Friday, 1,000 miles from home, in this smoky shithole of a conference room that smelled like Bell's jockstrap after two hours of racquetball, in the thick and sickening humidity of this Godforsaken dust-blown state.

Then he closed his eyes ever so briefly and remembered that day he visited Mercy Care Center. He called up the longing looks and wide-eyed desperation he saw, the conversation with Fast Eddie, whom he'd he gone to visit several times as promised. He said her name in his mind: *Ann Pearson*. If he didn't take this brief pause to connect to these human elements of *why*, it was too easy to just be another bad lawyer cliché with his expensive suit and self-import and endless questions in search of a big payday.

"For the record, would you please state your name and spell it?"

And so began the tedious march of establishing who she was, her job title, work experience, and history, and all the other minutiae necessary in building his foundation. His strategy: establish a corporate environment, per documented policies and procedures, that fostered abuse and neglect in its various nursing home facilities. That would include endless details about how they ran their business, their planning processes and strategies, and overall corporate philosophy. Fifteen minutes into it, most in the room were fighting to keep their eyes open. Nadia Flores and One-Armed Lucky, especially, would have rather been just about anywhere else. Bell's eager charges didn't even seem particularly interested in the captivating details of Ava Quinn's long, dry corporate career. It wasn't until after the first break that Devlin got into a line of questioning that got everyone's attention.

"Now your involvement with Ann Pearson, as I understand it, was that some time after she had been discharged from Mercy Care Center on April 1, 1975, you were called in by Rupert Styles, the facility administrator in Phoenix, to review the chart and determine whether or not there were any concerns you had as the regional clinical director. Is that correct?"

"I visited our Phoenix facility regularly, so I don't know that I went there just to review a chart."

"But you do recall reviewing the chart while there?"

"I do."

"And according to Rupert Styles' report, you thought the charting of Ann Pearson was good. Is that correct?"

"This was four years ago. I remember reviewing the chart. I don't recall exactly what I told Rupert Styles that day."

"Who owns Flynn Enterprises?" he asked, switching gears on her.

"The company? That would be Flynn Winston."

"Flynn Winston. One man owns Flynn Enterprises. Correct?"

"That is correct."

"He's the sole shareholder as far as you know?"

"As far as I know, yes."

"Would it be fair to say that Flynn Winston is the one person in this company who not only runs the entirety of the company, but is the final word on anything and everything relative to this company?"

"Yes, that's fair."

"I still haven't met him. He's always traveling somewhere. I'm beginning to think he might actually be a ghost. Have you seen him lately?"

She looked around as though he might have sneaked into the room. "Actually I haven't, no."

"Is he coming today?"

"Objection," Bell said, shaking his head.

Devlin continued without missing a beat: "OK, have you talked to Flynn Winston about this lawsuit and the allegations we are making against Mercy Care Center?"

"I have not."

"Is it your testimony that Flynn Winston would know about any serious problems at Mercy Care Center?"

"I would have to say it depends."

"Well, specifically, he would have to know about the recent citation by the Arizona Health Services Department?"

"Yes."

"How many times during 1975 did Flynn Winston visit Mercy Care Center, meet with the executive director, meet with the director of nursing, and talk to the staff he has entrusted with the care of so many elderly people?"

"Objection. Relevance and hearsay. She can't be expected to testify as to the whereabouts of Flynn Winston four years ago. You can go ahead and answer."

"I don't think Mr. Winston ever personally went there."

"Let's move on to a different area. Why do we have three versions of Ann Pearson's chart?"

She visibly shifted in her seat. "I think you're asking me to make an assumption."

"No, I'm asking you, Miss Quinn, why we have three versions of Ann Pearson's chart?"

"First of all, I can tell you… well, there could be several reasons for that."

"Are you speculating now?"

"Yes, I would be."

"Let me rephrase. We have received, on different occasions from different people, three distinct versions of Ann Pearson's medical chart, which strikes me as odd. Can you clear that up for me?"

"What's the question?" She lit another cigarette and took a deep pull. The room was already smokier than The Wellington at last call, but no one noticed the fog.

"Let me repeat it: Why are there three different charts, in varying lengths, for the same patient?"

"I don't know about different charts."

"Is it standard operating procedure at Flynn Enterprises to have three different charts floating around for the same patient?"

"Objection. Asked and answered. Go ahead, Miss Quinn."

"No, it is not."

Devlin asked again. "Then why do we have three here?"

"Same objection." Bell nodded at her again.

"Well, one thing is that after she was discharged, the records from other departments would filter in and be added. That's pretty normal for any patient."

"How long would that take, for everything to filter back in?"

"I'd say ninety days."

"OK, ninety days. Fair enough. Was it also OK for someone to go back into that chart after discharge and kind of clean it up, add things like doctor names, patient names? Was that OK?"

"That's a medical records action, and the process of putting together a medical record—adding a physician's name, medical record number, or room number—does not alter the content of the clinical information in the chart. It just simply puts the patient's name, the doctor's name, formal stuff like that."

"OK. Fair enough. What I want to know is that after that ninety-day time period we discussed, is it OK for someone to go back into a chart, even if it's something as simple as adding a doctor's name as you mentioned, when the company is facing legal liability?"

"Well, is it, you know, optimal timing? Probably not."

"Is it acceptable?" he asked.

"Yes."

"My client sued Flynn Enterprises in February 1977. So it is your testimony that it is acceptable under Flynn Enterprises policies to make changes to a subpoenaed chart almost two years after the patient was discharged?"

"Objection. Beyond scope. She's not corporate counsel. She can't testify as to company legal policies." Bell nodded at her. Now she was sitting cross-armed, puffing away, all of which was being captured on video. "Well, I don't think that's how I put it together, but I guess that's what I said."

"You guess?"

She sighed. "Like I said, it's not optimal. As long as it did not alter the content of the clinical information and the medical records."

Devlin couldn't have asked her to say it more clearly even if he'd scripted it himself. He had more for this witness, a lot more, but he would save that for the trial.

"Just one more time, to make sure we're clear: It is your testimony that it's OK for Mercy Care Center, after their documents have been subpoenaed, to go back in and make changes and alterations? Is that OK under Flynn Enterprises policy?"

"I don't know about the specific policy or what it states. I personally would not find that acceptable. Except for what I said about changes that don't affect the integrity of the patient care record."

Later, for lunch, Bell had sandwiches brought in and put the plaintiffs in a corner office.

"Damn, Big-Time, that is some straight-up, boring-ass shit. Sure ain't like Perry Mason. That all you do all day, one boring question after another? How you stay awake through all that?"

Everyone laughed. "I'd have to agree," Nadia said.

"How'd we do with her?" Kay asked.

"Do you mind?" Devlin said, motioning to the others. He wouldn't discuss her case in front of them unless she gave the go-ahead.

"No, no, not at all."

Devlin lowered his voice. "She laid my foundation perfectly for going into the charting issues. I'll do more with that at the trial. I don't want her attorneys to know what I think I've figured out about them changing those charts. I don't even know if they know."

Richard Bell opened the door. "Mr. Devlin. May I speak with you?"

Devlin finished chewing and wiped his mouth with a napkin. He shook his head and stood up because he knew what was coming. In the hallway, Richard Bell, in almost a whisper, said, "I'm terribly sorry. Mr. Winston called. He is still in Austin on business and has to stay over through the weekend. I'm afraid we'll have to re-schedule his deposition."

Devlin nodded. "How far's Austin?"

"Excuse me?"

"How far is Austin from here? If we drive?"

"Why does that matter?"

"Because if he can't be here, then we'll just go to him."

"I'm afraid that's not possible. He's involved in a business acquisition down there. He's with clients. If he had four hours to do a deposition he would just come back to Dallas."

"Why did you let him schedule a business acquisition meeting when he knew he had a deposition we've been waiting two years to do?"

"It's not a question of me *letting* Mr. Winston do or not do anything. He pretty much does what he wants, when he wants. This was a last-minute meeting he scheduled without my knowledge. I'm truly sorry."

"Look, Richard, I don't want to be a hard-ass, but this is bullshit and we both know it." Richard Bell, ever the lawyer, acknowledged no such thing. Not even a nod of the head.

"All right," Devlin said. "Here's how we're going to do this. You've got two weeks until Judge Stearns' deadline to get this scheduled, along with the others. And I'm not coming back to Texas again."

"I'm sorry, Mr. Devlin, but with Mr. Winston's schedule it will be all but impossible for him to do the deposition anywhere but here."

"I have the utmost confidence that you'll figure it out. And if there's a problem, I'm sure Judge Stearns will be more than happy to help you." The judge's last ruling was tipped in Devlin's favor, but the lawyer still had a clawing notion the judge didn't particularly like him. He threw it out to Bell as leverage, but inside he hoped they'd get this sorted out without having to go before the judge again.

"Well, I guess we'll be in touch," Bell said, offering his hand.

Devlin shook Bell's hand. "Yes we will."

Chapter Twenty-Three

MAX DANIELS WHEELED the cherry-red Chevelle into the dim parking lot at Phoenix Municipal Hospital. It was past midnight, but the 110-degree June heat was roiling up from the pavement in relentless waves. Daniels drove with the top down and let the hot wind blast the sweat off his face. But as soon as he stopped, within seconds the perspiration beaded up and dripped from his face and neck. It angered him that he hadn't been able to find the second nurse. Then he got a brainstorm: Perhaps, like discovering car keys in a front pocket after turning the house upside down, he'd find her working right here at one of the named defendants. Right under his nose this entire time. He'd checked the nursing homes, but not the hospitals, simply because there were seventeen hospitals and clinics throughout metropolitan Phoenix. All he had was a random list of names of who had worked at Mercy Care Center four years ago. It was a long shot and would take a while to ask around at all these places, but after all this time, and a nice chunk of Devlin's money, he was out of leads.

Daniels had called Devlin's office earlier and gotten the names of the two Phoenix Municipal Hospital doctors Devlin had already deposed in the lawsuit: Wayne Michaels, Ann Pearson's primary care doctor, and Jeffrey Singer, the doctor who attempted to save her life with the eleventh-hour surgery. He'd also called the hospital, and both were scheduled to be here now. It made sense to Daniels to start with them under the guise of working on the case. But since the doctors' employer was being sued by Devlin, they weren't going to volunteer anything if they knew who had put Daniels on the clock. Time for a little subterfuge.

Daniels prided himself on his independent station in life. His thirty acres south of Phoenix were surrounded by a thick citrus grove of orange and lemon trees, and out of earshot of most human activity. He worked when he needed to work and never had to take assignments he didn't want, because his nose for real estate deals kept him flush. He'd had romances here and there, but at 45, still hadn't completely settled on the notion of a wife and perhaps, someday, a kid or two. These were decisions, he decided, he'd readdress when he turned 50.

Being independent, to Max Daniels, also meant he was free to dress however he chose, which usually meant black shoes, black pants, and a white, short-sleeved, button-down shirt. Max Daniels liked to keep things simple. But for this gig, against all he believed in, Max Daniels had donned his best dark suit and a tie. His long-sleeved white shirt was already soaked through, so pulling on the jacket was especially painful. But, checking himself in the rear-view, he looked like any good lawyer. A sweaty one, anyway.

After a few minutes inside, Daniels found the floor where Wayne Michaels was working, and then the doctor himself. "Dr. Michaels, if I could have a moment of your time?"

The doctor continued down the hallway. "And you are?"

"One of the lawyers working on our case."

"Our case? What case?"

"The lawsuit against us and Mercy Care Center."

"I'm busy right now. What do you need?"

"Well, Mr. Redmond and I are having some difficulty locating one of our witnesses. We're looking for a nurse employed by Mercy Care Center during the time of the incident with Ann Pearson. I'm hopeful you could put me in touch with someone in your personnel department who might be able to help us locate her."

"Does she work here now?"

"That we don't know." Daniels was annoyed that they were still walking down hallways.

"You don't know? What's the nurse's name?"

"We don't exactly know that either."

The doctor stopped and looked at Daniels. "Shouldn't the lawyers for Mercy Care Center be telling you this if it was their employee?"

"Absolutely, Dr. Michaels. But, unfortunately, they have been most uncooperative."

"Do you normally visit your clients, unannounced, at midnight?"

"Not normally, sir."

"Unannounced, or at midnight?"

"Both. But with this case, we've been working around the clock."

The doctor eyed Daniels suspiciously. "What'd you say your name was again?"

"Me? Oh, I'm nobody. I'm just an associate with the same firm as Jeffrey Redmond: Smith, Hawley & White. The ones defending you and the hospital in this case."

The doctor considered this answer and resumed his brisk walk. "Look, go back to the nurse's station, and she can tell you whom to contact in personnel. They might be able to help you find your nurse."

"Thank you, sir. That's very helpful."

Daniels tried to retrace their route back to the nurse's station, but was lost after so many turns. Finally he found it and got a contact name from the nurse, who said the personnel manager worked eight to five, and then added, "But it's really more like nine to three with a two-hour lunch, if you know what I mean." Then she winked at Max Daniels.

TWO weeks after the Ava Quinn deposition, on Friday, June 29, Richard Bell finally called Devlin.

"Just when I was beginning to think it was over between us, Richard."

"Pardon me?"

"Never mind. You know we're about out of time on these depositions. I hope you have your checkbook nearby."

"Mr. Devlin, I would be most grateful if you would grant me a brief continuance to get these scheduled."

"Richard—"

"Please. Hear me out."

Devlin leaned back in his chair. *This should be good*, he thought. "You're not getting out your probe again, are you?"

"Pardon?"

"Never mind. Go ahead."

"Thank you. I know we've had plenty of time to get these scheduled."

"Yes, ninety days to be exact. No, make that *several years*."

"Precisely. My own client, however, has been difficult to pin down and unwilling to be deposed. We've spent considerable time convincing him he doesn't really have a choice."

"And this is my problem *how?*" Devlin thought about using what Max Daniels had said about his two-drawer filing cabinet and telling Bell he never looked in the drawer marked "Your Shit." But, really, why gloat? First the judge's court order and now this little "alms for the poor" soliloquy by Richard Bell. There was a subtle and palpable shift in the momentum of this case and, for now, Devlin was pulling strings. But he certainly wasn't making plans to establish a base camp on this dangerous plateau. Litigation was a hulking, capricious beast that could be soothed in one moment and strike a fatal blow in the next quick second.

"Truly, I am appealing to your gentlemanly nature in asking for this favor. Grant me this continuance, sixty days, and I will—"

"Sixty days? Richard, you've had years! Another sixty days would push us into late summer, with a November trial date."

"I understand completely. We've just had a particularly big case drop into our laps, which has scrambled our resources somewhat. My associates are working—"

"Richard, I appreciate what it means to be busy. I have sixty-plus cases myself right now." It was more like forty or so, but Devlin padded it for dramatic effect. "But c'mon, how hard is it to schedule some depositions? Two of your obsequious little minions should be able to knock that out in a day or two at the most."

"Any leeway you could grant us would be most appreciated."

Devlin took a deep sigh. He quickly ran through the pros and cons of doing something he truly didn't have to do. But what bubbled up was Nash and *Rule #4—The goal is to win the case, not particular points with the client, opposing side, judge, or a witness.* He could be both flexible and firm without trying to crush the guy on this one point that, ultimately, wouldn't matter.

"All right. In the spirit of compromise, I'll give you another fifteen days without mentioning this to the judge."

"With all due respect, how about forty-five days?"

"With all due respect, that'll be a cold day in hell."

"Thirty days?"

"Too long," Devlin said.

"Twenty-five?"

"Richard, this isn't a car auction. If I give you another twenty-five days you'll call me in twenty-four and ask for two more weeks. I've got to keep you on a short leash now." *What the fuck, but did you really just tell Richard Bell II you've got him on a leash?* This was getting good.

"Understood. Thirty days, then?"

"Keep going," Devlin said. "You're getting warmer."

"Twenty-one days."

"Warmer."

Silence.

Devlin took a deep breath. "Fine. I want everything scheduled in the next seven days, with all these outstanding depos completed in the next twenty-one."

"Fair enough. I will draft a Motion for Continuance stating our agreement on these terms."

"Now hold on," Devlin said. "Before you run off and rally the troops and start cranking out motions by the truckload, we're going to do this off the record, a handshake deal between you and me."

"Handshake?"

"Yeah, ever hear of it? It's what people did before lawyers."

"I don't understand."

Ahh, the sweet irony! "Richard, you're going to have an aneurism if you don't lighten up a little bit. I'm just saying, do what you say you're going to do, and the court is never the wiser. But if you miss this private deadline, the axe falls and I'm go straight to the judge to invoke his original order. At that point you'd be at the mercy of the court's deadline, which at $500 a day ought to get your attention."

"I don't know if I'm comfortable with that arrangement."

"I don't know that I care how comfortable you are."

"Yes, but Mr. Devlin—"

"Look, before you make another eloquent speech, think of it this way: You get the extra time you need, and I keep some leverage if you don't honor our agreement. There's no need to go to the trouble and expense of writing and filing motions when we already have a standing court order from the judge. Everything we do in life doesn't have to be in a formal motion filed with the court."

"I prefer to have everything be part of the official record."

Jesus. Was everything in this guy's life part of the official record? Devlin pictured a court reporter sitting in the corner of Bell's bedroom while he's pumping his wife:

MR. BELL: Ooh baby, that feels good.

MRS. BELL: Are you almost done?

MR. BELL: Tell me you like it, baby.

MRS. BELL: How much longer? I have clothes to fold.

Devlin chuckled to himself and said, "One thing I learned early is that my word is worth more than a thousand pages stamped by a notary. Just do what you say, and we won't have any problems."

"OK."

"In the meantime, my witnesses and experts are all ready to be deposed by you. We need to get those scheduled, too." It was a lie of semantics: Devlin's witnesses and experts were all certainly available, but aside from Avram Barak, none of them were ready to go into a deposition. Not Kay Pearson. Not Ford Rockwell. For each, Devlin would spend a day or two going over possible questions and addressing the subtleties of faring well in a deposition.

The two lawyers said goodbye and Devlin hung up. He'd done the right thing, he thought, without giving anything away. But still… he couldn't shake the nagging feeling, even with the looming threat of Judge Stearns' sanctions against Bell & Bauer, that he'd somehow just been played again by that sneaky bastard Richard Bell.

Chapter Twenty-Four

SIX DAYS LATER, Richard Bell called Devlin and left a message with Nadia: He had everything scheduled for the week of July 16, which would just meet their handshake deadline of Friday, July 20. Bell scheduled the deposition for Rupert Styles, administrator, who would be at Bell & Bauer on Wednesday. And on Friday in Dallas, the big fish himself: CEO Flynn Winston. When Devlin read the message, he shook his head. He'd given Bell an inch, and the guy was taking a mile by making Devlin fly to Dallas again. He thought about standing firm on making Winston come to Phoenix, but he decided to let it go: Rule #4, stay focused on the big prize. And with Bell paying the travel tab, Devlin couldn't really make much of a fuss with the judge. At least, after two-plus years, the key depositions were finally scheduled.

Max Daniels, meanwhile, was perfecting his lawyer act as he worked through the list of hospitals and clinics. The personnel manager he'd followed up with later at Phoenix Municipal had found Daniels intriguing and attractive, and she was overly cooperative without ever asking to see a subpoena. She made Max Daniels coffee, let him behind her desk, and helped him search employee files for the missing nurse. It was easy to pull any nurse applications submitted after July 1, 1975, and check each applicant's employment history.

The process was a little uncomfortable at first as he looked through the paperwork, because she kept inching her chair closer and closer, and he could feel her leering eyes. He would then make some excuse to get up and re-establish the distance between the chairs upon his return. The personnel manager was plain and dressed herself down, but Daniels, too, was intrigued at what lay beneath the mousy facade. It was tempting as all hell. However, he was already operating undercover and didn't want to further complicate things. Foremost in his mind, he couldn't put Devlin's case at risk in any way. Ultimately, he ascertained that none of the nurses Phoenix Municipal had hired had ever worked previously at Mercy Care Center. That was one dead end tied off.

Daniels had repeated the procedure at three more hospitals and two clinics with no hits. He wasn't too surprised at how willing the personnel people were to open their files without a subpoena or any compelling reason to do so other than being asked. The gates to the medical malpractice arena were just beginning to open, so doctors and hospitals getting sued was the exception and not the rule. Many practicing doctors enjoyed long careers without being sued even once. And when they and the hospitals that employed them did become a target, a firm like Bell & Bauer made the problem go away with relative ease and little cost. All of which, of course, made Daniels' job easier.

If the mystery witness were still in Phoenix and still in nursing, Daniels knew it was just a matter of time now before he found her. The clock was ticking: He had to find her well before the trial started in less than four months. Devlin would need time to both convince her to testify and then prepare her to do so.

On Monday, July 16, Rupert Styles arrived at Devlin's brick building for his deposition. The temperature, just before 9 a.m., was 107 degrees. Even so, Styles was wearing a suit per Richard Bell's instructions yesterday. Bell led the way to the building with Styles and two associates, and everyone was eager to get into the air-conditioned confines. Nadia Flores showed them to the conference room where the video technician, court reporter, Devlin, and Kay Pearson were already seated.

Rupert Styles was pale and was wearing a suit jacket that was a size too big for his slender frame. His first deposition, Devlin knew, just from shaking his hand and watching his eyes. Styles, as a licensed nursing home administrator, would help support Devlin's theory that Mercy Care Center was rife with procedural problems that negatively impacted patient care. Devlin had briefed Kay Pearson on his strategy and told her not to expect too many fireworks. What he anticipated was four hours of eliciting dry testimony about administrative protocol and operational procedures. After several minutes of awkward small talk among the divergent participants, everyone took their seats around the table. With nods from the video technician and court reporter, Devlin began.

"Good morning," Devlin said. "Tell us your name, please."

"Look," Styles said, shaking his head. "I just gotta say for the record I hate you, I hate those lawyers right there who supposedly are on my side—"

"Mr. Styles," Richard Bell said. "I would have to object."

"You're objecting to your own witness?" Devlin said.

"I'm well aware of whose witness he is, Mr. Devlin. Mr. Styles, as we discussed?"

"I got a right to say what's on my mind."

Devlin turned to Bell. This was going to be fun. "I would have to concur."

"Fine," Bell said. "Say your piece and please be brief."

"I want this on the record that I'm only here because the law says I have to be here, but I just want everyone in this room to know I hate all lawyers because all you do is twist things around to suit your needs and fatten up your bank accounts. All y'all. It ain't right. I work hard and do my best to help people in my job, and all y'all just trying to bring me down and get rich in the process."

"Thank you for being so forthcoming," Devlin said. "I appreciate your passion, your sense of duty, and your commitment to your patients."

"Is there a question in there somewhere?" Bell asked, obviously irritated that his own witness had already opened doors Bell wanted to keep shut.

Devlin repeated his opening: "Just for the record, please tell us your name."

Styles nodded, buoyed that Devlin had simply validated what his own lawyer refused to during their all-day preparation session yesterday. This Devlin cat, Styles thought, was a sleazy lawyer, too, but at least he pretended to listen. After walking Styles through the necessary details, Devlin skipped what he'd planned and went to the heart of what he wanted from Styles. Devlin sensed that he could turn Styles' opening diatribe into a positive.

"As you've already demonstrated, Mr. Styles, you're obviously a man of belief and passion. Is that about right?"

"Yeah, I'd say so."

"Do you recall having a concern about the adequacy of skin care at your facility?"

"Form and foundation," Bell said.

"Yeah, I knew there was an issue with that." The kid from Buffalo, the one who absorbed the hard side of the human condition in blue-collar bars and dingy bowling alleys, was turning a subtle move. It was like Styles was Devlin's witness now, with Bell trying to minimize the damage by his own client.

"And what was the problem," Devlin asked, "as you perceived it?"

"Form and foundation," Bell said.

"It was just one of those things I know we were looking at, you know, ways to improve."

"Do you recall what you did to implement some kind of system of skin care?"

"I can tell you what we should have done."

"Yes, what should you have done?"

"Well, for starters, educate the nursing staff on the basics of skin care, nutrition, and turning the patient."

"And encourage them to follow those parameters?"

"Absolutely."

"And was that a continuing issue that you addressed during your employ there?"

"Form," Bell said.

"I only worked there six months, but... I don't know. It's hard to even remember, but I know we had in-service on it and things like that."

"In your résumé that we discussed earlier, you stated that upon your arrival at this new job the facility was in a state of meltdown. What did you mean by that?"

"I mean, the only way I can answer that is that there was a new administrator and director of nurses, and no sense of working as a team. We had to try to get things turned around that way."

"Did this meltdown extend to patient care?"

"Form."

"Maybe not directly, no, but then again I'd say you can't have a meltdown that doesn't affect everything in the facility."

A day later, Devlin had similar success deposing Maggie Strahan, unit director. During each deposition, Devlin was eliciting testimony to support his theory that poor care devolved into neglect, and that's what killed Ann Pearson. The administrative staff was key in establishing the lax environment and poor procedures within Mercy Care Center. That would be the heart of the case along with the conflicting and incomplete medical records, including the forty-eight-hour gap with no patient record for Ann Pearson.

On Thursday, Devlin was up at 4 a.m. to begin preparing for the Flynn Winston deposition the next day in Dallas. He also had to spend a few hours trying to get a handle on all the open to-do's on the case. First up were all the depositions he still needed to take: the EMTs who transported Ann Pearson from the dog track to the hospital, and seven more nurses, doctors, and radiologists from Phoenix Municipal who participated in Ann Pearson's medical care from March 19, 1975, to March 22, 1975. Then he had a registered dietitian to depose, to explain the nutritional assessment process, the physiology, and the interconnection between nutrition, hydration, and pressure-sore development and healing.

He'd also discovered that Bell & Bauer hadn't included several documents and charts in the thirteen boxes they sent over. They had, however, sent the weekly and monthly skin reports and summaries, their quality indicator reports to Medicare, and the photographs of Ann Pearson's wound. Devlin didn't even bother calling Richard Bell this time. Instead, he'd already started drafting a supplement to his original Motion to Compel. Additionally, at Avram Barak's suggestion, Devlin was compiling several charts of his own that would become trial exhibits. He was creating timelines to show, day by day and hour by hour, the development of Ann Pearson's decubitus ulcer and how that corresponded to the nurses on duty, their notes, and how often they were repositioning her.

Finally, Devlin needed to write and file a motion asking for punitive damages. The compensatory, or actual, damages in the case were a given. He would be trying to recover, on behalf of Kay Pearson, monies for medical bills and other expenses incurred by his client. Including punitive damages in the case, which were intended as a broader punishment against the defendant and a deterrent to similar actions in the future, was at the discretion of Judge Stearns.

In Devlin's motion, he would have to convince Judge Stearns that Mercy Care Center had acted with malice, fraud, wanton or willful activity, or a gross disregard for the rights of others. This was the task everyone around him was saying would be nearly impossible. In all likelihood, the court would rule that punitive damages, typically not covered by the defendant's insurance, would be excessive punishment. The problem, for Devlin, was sparse precedent and few Arizona case statutes to cite as grounds for establishing punitive damages. Just as he'd been warned from the outset.

Devlin looked at the boxes and stacks of paperwork and took a deep breath. He grabbed a legal pad and started on the motion: *Plaintiff moves for a preliminary ruling that there appears to be sufficient evidence to allow plaintiff to proceed with discovery on the financial status of Flynn Enterprises for purposes of punitive damages...*

Devlin didn't get up from his chair, except to go the bathroom, for the next six hours. Just after noon, with his hand cramping up, he flipped back through what he had written: twenty-five pages that would condense down to fifteen or so when Nadia Flores typed everything. After a quick sandwich, Devlin started preparing for Flynn Winston's deposition and didn't finish until it was dark. He hadn't set foot outside all day, and the only other humans he saw were the occasional golfers playing through beyond his doors. At 11 p.m., still working, Devlin was startled by the phone. When he answered, Devlin heard the voice of his nemesis.

"Mr. Devlin, I am so sorry to bother you at home at this late hour."

"You have no earthly idea how disappointed I am to hear your voice, Richard."

Devlin was wondering how he got his home phone number, which he never gave out.

"I am going to begin by apologizing profusely for what I'm about to say."

"Don't tell me you're canceling the depo again."

"I'm afraid that's why I'm calling. Mr. Winston is in New York on family business with an ill relative who has, unfortunately, taken a turn for the worse."

Devlin would bet his last nickel that, at this very moment, Flynn Winston was sipping single-malt at his palatial Dallas home. "I'm sorry to hear that, Richard."

"Thank you for being understanding. As you might imagine, this is completely out of my hands and beyond anything I could have foreseen."

"I do understand."

"Thank you for being so gracious, Mr. Devlin. I owe you one."

Devlin looked at the paperwork in which he'd buried himself for an entire day. His vision was blurry and his hand ached from writing motions. "Well, I'm not really going to be that gracious."

"Pardon me?"

"We had a deal, Richard. Handshake. Remember that discussion? You broke the deal."

"Counselor, in the spirit of compromise, this is beyond my control. I had everything scheduled as we agreed, we've completed three of the four, and now this last-minute hiccup. I'm sure we can reschedule for next week."

"That would be great. Next week's good for me. But you still broke our agreement. I'm afraid I'm going to have to go to the judge on this one, Richard."

"Now I think you're being underhanded."

"Let's not get into a pissing match about being underhanded, Richard. From day one on this case you've been grinding me down."

"Are you sure, Mr. Devlin, that this is the path you want to choose?"

What the hell is that supposed to mean? The fear crept back into Devlin's mind, that Bell might know something Devlin had missed. "Richard, for the record, you're the one that missed the judge's deadline. I think I've been nothing but fair with you."

Silence.

Devlin continued, "OK, well, as long as you called to get the party started, I'm also filing a supplement to my original Motion to Compel because you still haven't turned over some documents. I'll just roll these latest happenings into that one, and we'll let Judge Stearns rule on everything. He's reading my motion on punitive damages."

Richard Bell laughed aloud. "You'll never get punitive damages in this case, Devlin. Get serious."

"I guess that's for the judge to decide."

"You're only going to piss off Stearns with a motion like that."

"Well, we'll be even then, because I'm intrigued to see what he does when he finds out you missed his deadline by a month." That was enough to shut up 'ole Sniff. The two lawyers said goodbye, each equally emboldened by the exchange.

THAT same month NASA's Skylab caused weeks of hubbub as it sped back toward Earth. The two lawyers and their respective teams, however, would have only noticed if the orb re-entered the Earth's atmosphere and hit, instead of the Australian bush, the Maricopa County court complex.

In early August, Devlin filed the two motions that had taken longer than anticipated to finish, polish, and type. Meanwhile, in his dealings with Richard Bell, things had gone from grudgingly civil to downright frosty. The only time Devlin and Bell spoke was during the ongoing depositions. On that front, Avram Barak and Ford Rockwell (minus the purple mouth after Devlin's diplomacy proved fruitful) were both stellar as Bell and five associates tag-teamed them repeatedly.

Devlin's experts were earning every bit of the combined $365 an hour Devlin was forking out for their time. With weekly meetings with each to prepare for trial—along with Max Daniels' ongoing search for the nurse— Devlin's tab on this case, since June, had almost doubled to $38,000. A six-figure settlement of $100,000 would only leave, after expenses, about $20,000 for Devlin. Amortized hourly over the four years he'd spent on the case, he'd do better waiting tables.

Over the next weeks, everywhere Devlin went he couldn't escape two songs getting endless airplay: "Grease," by Frankie Valli and "My Sharona" by a new group called The Knack that struck Devlin as a third-rate Beatles rip-off. But nonetheless, change was afoot. Disco's pop-music lifeline had been shorter than that of the litigation timeline in the Ann Pearson case. With disco dying on the vine, Devlin couldn't believe it was almost 1980.

ON September 26, 1979, just five weeks before the trial, Judge Stearns held a pre-trial hearing to rule on all outstanding motions. Unlike most of the judges Devlin had spent his career appearing before, Judge Stearns was now in the Old Courthouse building. In contrast to most of the drab, windowless courtrooms throughout the nearby complex—the ones in which he'd cut his legal teeth under Walsh's hard glare—this courtroom in a stand-alone building had high ceilings, large windows filled with natural light, and, overall, a grand ambience that imbued a sense of finally being on the main stage, the legal equivalent of Shakespeare's Globe Theater.

"Regarding plaintiff's supplement on the previous Motion to Compel..." Judge Stearns removed his glasses and looked at no one in particular. "Did I not make myself clear on these matters in my previous court order?" Neither Bell nor Devlin knew where Stearns was directing his inquiry. "Counselors?"

"Your honor, if I may," Devlin said, standing. Kay Pearson was not in the courtroom, nor were any other spectators. Bell brought along his requisite two associates. Jeffrey Redmond was seated behind Bell.

"Not you," he said. "You." Judge Stearns was pointing his glasses at Richard Bell. Devlin slid back to his seat as Bell arose.

"Your honor—"

"Didn't they teach you at law school that when the judge asks a question you should answer it?"

"Yes, your honor," Richard Bell said, searching for an out.

"Well, did I, or did I not, make myself clear regarding these outstanding discovery requests from the plaintiff?" He had, effectively, boxed Bell into a corner from which there was no good answer. While Devlin enjoyed the moment, he was also tense and poised for a similar treatment as soon as the judge finished whittling down Bell.

"You did, your honor. If I may—"

"No, you may not. If there's one thing I hate it's repeating myself in my courtroom on matters on which I've already spent time and taxpayer money writing eloquent court orders. Let me make this as emphatic as possible, counselor. If we have to address this issue of the plaintiff's discovery requests again, I will move to have you in contempt, and I will levy a sanction of $15,000 against your firm that will be payable before the close of business if, and when, that day ever comes. You have seven business days to uphold my previous court order and provide Mr. Devlin everything he outlined in this supplement."

"Yes, your honor."

"Good. Your understanding of that scenario is synchronous because it is parallel to the sanction of $10,000 I'm imposing today for your blatant disregard of my previous court order and your ongoing behavior related to these most reasonable discovery requests. Are we clear on that and the payment terms thereof?"

"Your honor, we will messenger a $10,000 check payable to Mr. Devlin before the close of business today."

"Excellent. I think we're making headway now. Also, counselor, I don't know why your firm keeps sending me Motions to Dismiss when I've already denied previous such attempts."

"Your honor, in light of new evidence obtained during depositions—"

"Save it for the trial, which apparently is a road down which the two of you are recklessly barreling at dangerous speeds. Motions to Dismiss by defendant are denied, and if I see another one of those from your firm regarding this case you will not like what happens next. Are we clear?"

"Yes, your honor. Of course."

So far, so good. Devlin was cleaning up.

"Now, on this matter of the decedent's alleged gambling activities. I've considered the motions before me from both the defendant and plaintiff. I'm not inclined to hear any further clarification on the matter. The court finds that the decedent's alleged gambling activities and associations thereof are not relevant in this case because those activities, in the court's estimation, would not necessarily negatively impact the decedent's health in any way, which is at the heart of this case. However, if the plaintiffs open this door during direct or cross-examination, I'm going to allow the defendants to respond in kind. But for now, the decedent's gambling and any associations arising out of that social activity are not admissible." It was almost too good to be true. Devlin braced for the most important ruling of his career.

"Let's see," the judge continued, "I have before me plaintiff's Motion for Determination of Prima Facie Case for Punitive Damages." He put his glasses back on and peered down at Devlin, who swallowed back a lump in his throat. Devlin could only think, *Here it comes. Please let it be good.*

"Excellent motion, counselor. You present your case for allowing punitive damages very well. However, I'm inclined to side with the defendant on this matter simply because opening the door to unreasonable jury verdicts seems to be a dangerous precedent. There have already been several medical malpractice cases in which juries have awarded punitive damages well beyond the scope of reasonable and equitable punishment, and I don't want to help fuel a bonfire within our legal system. Our judicial role should be to reform poor behavior, but not annihilate either party in the process. Punitive damages, in my estimation, become a bit like chasing a fly through your house with a sledgehammer in one hand and a chainsaw in the other. Do I make my point?"

Bell and Devlin both nodded. Devlin, literally, was holding his breath. Bell, too, was tense and working his fingers like a bloodhound twenty yards from a treed fox. The judge took a deep sigh and flipped through Devlin's seventeen-page legal version of *Please-Please-Please-With-A-Cherry-On-Top*. The extended silence that emanated from the bench stretched into a painful eternity. Devlin finally drew in a long, slow, silent breath and closed his eyes for whatever came next.

"This motion," the judge said, leaning forward, "This motion makes a compelling argument… but I'm afraid this motion is… actually, counselors, my position today…"

The lawyers leaned forward in perfect unison, straining for the answer and equally terrified by the middling fifty/fifty odds appropriated to each. The judge sighed again and shook his head.

"This motion," the judge said again. "I'm afraid counselors that this motion is…" he looked up at Devlin and then Bell, shaking his head. "This motion is not yet ripe for a decision. I will need to take this under further advisement. In the interim, I am ordering a final mediation conference in this case to be completed before our scheduled trial date. That is all."

The judge rose, and everyone stared in disbelief. After the judge left, Devlin looked at Bell and both lawyers shook their heads. At least on this one point they could agree: Judge Stearns was playing games, by withholding his ruling on punitive damages, to keep both sides motivated to settle. As an instrument of slow legal torture, few were more painful and effective than what the judge had just done to both sides. Devlin and Bell looked at each other and offered similar shoulder shrugs without saying anything. It was a rare moment when, for a brief few seconds, the two were oddly in unison in their thoughts and feelings.

Back at the office, Devlin asked Nadia Flores to call Kay Pearson and see if she would come by after work. Devlin had already decided, during Judge Stearns' diatribe against Bell, that he was going to give Kay Pearson the $10,000. If nothing else, it would cover the funeral expenses and some of her mother's medical bills she still had not been able to pay. Devlin knew he should credit the judge's gift against the almost $50,000 in expenses he'd already racked up, but he wanted to get something on the scoreboard for Kay Pearson. Then Devlin looked at the calendar and grabbed a legal pad to outline a trial preparation strategy. He had already asked Nadia to start handling what she could on his forty-some other cases: making calls, handling correspondence, and letting both opposing counsel and clients know that Devlin was about to drop out of sight for sixty days. He needed the next month, full-time and more, to prepare, and then a second month for the trial itself. He couldn't imagine Judge Stearns letting a trial drag out into December.

Other than Flynn Winston and the mystery nurse, Devlin had finished all his depositions: fifty-six people total. Likewise, Bell had deposed all of Devlin's witnesses and experts. In total, Devlin had some 6,000 pages of deposition testimony, on both sides, to review, understand, and assimilate into the framework of his case. There were also some 500 exhibits to create, and he needed to start writing and rehearsing his opening and closing statements until he had them cold. He continued his list on the legal pad: witnesses to prepare for trial, financial records from Flynn Enterprises to decipher, and preparing his *voir dire* for jury selection. There was also a long list of medical issues, terminology, and chronology Devlin needed to understand well enough to translate into plain speak for the jury.

There was more: He would need to prepare cross-examination questions for all of Bell's witnesses and experts, and he needed to write his *Motions In Limine*, which was Latin for trying to fuck up the other side's case. In considering everything on his slate, Devlin decided he'd establish the war room at his condo, where the office phone wouldn't ring and his witnesses and experts would have access to food, drink, and the comforts of home. Devlin, too, could annex the entire condo and, literally eat, sleep, and breathe the case.

A week later, Devlin stepped from a shabby rental car into the humid stench of the pickle factory next to Flynn Enterprises. It was another cloying, muggy day in Texas, with air so wet and thick Devlin had been soaked again five minutes after drying himself from his shower. He'd dispensed with the hassle and logistics of any entourage and had, instead, come solo for this final deposition before trial: Flynn Winston. Bell hadn't wasted any time after the pre-trial conference, and he was now greeting Devlin in the lobby as he'd done the first time. Bell smiled and opened his arms as though the two lawyers were college pals reuniting to reminisce.

"Mr. Devlin. Good morning, and welcome to Texas again."

"Like I said the first time, place still stinks, Richard. I can see why Flynn Winston is never here."

"Yes, well, I can assure you he's here today and eager to help you however he can."

"I'll believe it when I actually see the man in the flesh." Devlin smiled as they walked and then waited at the elevator. Richard Bell smiled, too, without saying a word. Thirty minutes later, they were seated around the same conference room table with the same cigarette smoke and rotten-pickle stench as last time: Devlin, Bell and his two associates, the court reporter, and the video technician. The elusive man of the hour had not yet appeared.

As Devlin started to wonder whether this was going to be another round of lawyer hide-and-seek, an impish figure came through the door. If this was Flynn Winston, his reputation on paper far exceeded the man himself. As the introductions began, Devlin was surprised to see such a mousy-looking industrialist. He might be five feet tall if he stood on a box, with short, thinning grey hair, and skin that was beyond pale: The man looked positively embalmed. Yet, dress-wise, he had the appearance of having just stepped off one of his yachts: He wore a billowy, long-sleeved white shirt with navy slacks, deck loafers, and no socks. The red silk ascot and dark sunglasses perched atop his head completed the boating ensemble. The overall impression was that of a misplaced Oscar Wilde.

The mogul smiled a lot, too, like he was either genuinely nice, a bit feeble-minded, or had something to hide. Devlin tended toward the last in the list, but couldn't deny that Flynn Winston was likeable, in a fairy tale sort of way, a ghost captain at his empire's helm. Finally, after everyone took seats, the long-awaited deposition began. And, unfortunately for Devlin, it wasn't really worth the airfare from Phoenix even though it was Bell's dime.

Flynn Winston was, or at least claimed to be, a devout Christian. He was an honest businessman who believed in the American Dream and worked eighteen-hour days to build his first company. He was a devoted husband and father, and now patriarch to fourteen grandchildren and four great-grandchildren. He was a master at delegating, of course, which explained how something so ghastly went awry without his knowledge. Of course, he knew nothing, saw nothing, heard nothing. He had entrusted and empowered his employees to manage the day-to-day and month-to-month details. He was nineteen layers removed from anything unseemly that (allegedly) transpired at one of his facilities (allegedly). And at the first whiff of impropriety, he'd swept in with a crack team to right wrongs and punish wrongdoers in his employ. In three hours that was about all Devlin could pry out of the guy. He was well-schooled, well-prepared, and well-versed in the dance and vernacular of being simultaneously forthright and tight-lipped.

"So it is your testimony that you had no knowledge of this incident anytime prior to learning of the lawsuit against your company?"

"Yes, exactly, Mr. Devlin. I'm committed to helping the elderly. Ask anyone who knows me. Shoot, I'm practically an elderly myself." He chuckled along with his trio of lawyers. Even this far in, Devlin still couldn't believe this goofy little boat captain was the almighty industrialist he had feared.

"You had no personal knowledge?"

"None. Did my lawyers here tell you the idea for me getting into nursing homes came to me in church?"

"No, they did not."

"Well, the good Lord Himself is the one who put that bee in my bonnet."

It went like this for the rest of the final hour. Flynn Winston was folksy. He was mildly charming, but not nearly as clever as he imagined himself to be. He came off as slightly cheesy, polite, and solicitous to the point of being annoying. He was well-coached and used his "Aw-Shucks" *shtick* to hide a calculated smoothness. Devlin could see it there, right below the surface, but couldn't crack anything open. Flynn Winston repeatedly said that he wanted to find out exactly what had happened and bring justice and closure for the family of Ann Pearson. Right up front, he'd even personally offered the $25,000 to Ann Pearson's daughter, long before all this litigation or any official suit had been filed. He was an open book, or so he said, and ready and willing to do the right thing.

Behind all the canned words was the assured smugness that no sleazy ambulance-chaser from Phoenix was going to get one over on the old fox here, in court, or in life. Devlin knew it, too, and only stretched his questioning to the full four hours in hopes that Winston might grow weary, or slip, or snap, and say something incriminating. But he never once strayed near the edge in deviating from the script Richard Bell had taken all these years to craft. Devlin guessed right: Neither he nor the defendants would have much use for the old man on the witness stand. Ultimately the buck stopped with Flynn Winston, but he'd carefully constructed his business and orchestrated his days and years to insulate himself from any charges of wrongdoing.

That night back in Phoenix, Devlin studied the impossible to-do list again. Maybe, he thought, he could be prepared and ready for trial if he didn't sleep for the next month. And even then, the odds were steep. At the heart of things, really, was a cold nugget of doubt and insecurity that had solidified inside Devlin ever since he'd found his way onto the lawyer track, a fear that he simply couldn't compete at the rarefied level of brilliant academics like Richard Bell. Devlin's intellect was founded on his intuitive gifts and ability to understand human nature. So for Devlin, bookish lawyers like Richard Bell always seemed to hold a trump ace that DNA and destiny would forever dangle just beyond the Buffalo kid's reach.

To keep pace with Bell, his otherworldly academic underpinnings, and those vast legal resources, Devlin was prepared to live on the Other Side, the eerie netherworld all trial lawyers come to know in varying degrees. While

Nadia Flores began stacking sandbags to insulate Devlin from the whole of any other reality, the Ann Pearson case crystallized into the epicenter and totality of Devlin's universe, like some glowing deep-space phenomenon stronger than the sun itself. The fear that his opponent might somehow be smarter or more prepared meant only one thing to Devlin: He was about to take his trial preparation to a new plateau, a level one step beyond sanity, and then another step or two beyond that.

Chapter Twenty-Five

IF THE JURY LIKES YOU and your story, they'll go with you.

Now ensconced at his condo—amid the thousands of pages of deposition testimony and legal filings and complex neuropathology analyses—Devlin never lost sight of that most important element of every case. At its heart, he had to tell a captivating story that would move this group of eight random people to his side. That jury, he knew, must hear everything from him first. *Everything.* If the jury were surprised by what Richard Bell brought out, they'd take it out on Devlin. Winning a trial was about creating a bond of trust with the jury. So Devlin's idea was to create a blueprint for the entire trial. He would review and know what every witness had said in every deposition. He would remember and understand every detail of every exhibit. He would assimilate the chronology of Ann Pearson's decline in health with all the medical foundation, and tie everything together as he moved toward his closing statement. He would, in short, become a slave to preparation.

And just to be sure, he did something his own experts and every lawyer he knew said was crazy: Devlin began scripting, by hand, the entire trial onto legal pads. From the opening statement to every witness, direct, and cross, right through to the closing. Devlin wanted to capture on paper how he wanted it to play. He would never read from this script—that would come off as stilted and robotic—but he would be able to draw from this inner narrative throughout the proceedings. And as he implanted into his mind every fact, detail, and arcane document related to the case, he was drawing out what he needed to make the story burst to life for the jury. Like all people, the members of a jury wanted to hear a taut tale packed with drama, pathos, a few cliffhangers and, for relief, humor. No one wanted to sit through a boring trial, and by nature most trials were painful processions of tedium. Devlin wouldn't let that happen.

For the month of October 1979, the outside world ceased to exist. By mid-month, Devlin had scripted 500 pages of the trial. Tacked to every wall were large sheets of paper reinforcing the various elements of his case. The kitchen table morphed into the deposition arena, with all the three-ring binders spread open and stacked about. To get from the living room to the bedroom, Devlin had to tiptoe around and over all the boxes and documents. Avram Barak and Ford Rockwell were each visiting the condo every few days to review the technical aspects of the case (at their respective jaw-dropping hourly hits) and guide Devlin through the medical basis and theories. Each of his witnesses, too, spent a day or two in the war room going over testimony and mock cross-examinations from Devlin.

"Nursing homes are supposed to help people," Barak said, staring out at the golf course in his thick wool suit as Devlin took notes. "The defendants will contend that Ann Pearson was in a nursing home because she was, in fact, very sick. They are not to blame for that simple reality." Barak paused. He was going over the themes he thought Devlin might want to include in his opening statement. "Every time you mention the placement of Ann Pearson, say 'rehabilitation center,' not 'nursing home.' She went there because she was on the upswing, not on the decline."

Good, Devlin thought as he nodded. "What else?"

"Ten days," Barak said, now turning and looking at Devlin. "You must impress upon the jury that Ann Pearson's daughter only had that short amount of time to react to what was happening to her mother at Mercy Care Center."

"I don't quite follow you."

"Think about it… in litigation years, this is a long, drawn-out process. But in reality, going back to what happened, Kay Pearson only had a window of ten days.

That should lessen any potential for the jury to assign blame to the daughter for being a *schlub* and not watching her mother more closely."

Devlin smiled. "Not bad for an old man."

"Where there's smoke there's fire," Barak said. "Hammer this home to the jury. There's a long history of problems at Mercy Care Center, including trying to cover this up. Watergate is still fresh in everyone's mind. If there's one thing this jury can do, it's expose this cover-up and hold Flynn Enterprises accountable. Also, show them how the business model at Flynn Enterprises works, that the nursing homes are simply widgets and a means to an end, a grand real estate endeavor in which patients are simply moving parts to pay the monthly bills as Flynn Winston's land values and financial wealth grow."

Through the immersion process, Devlin missed running back Earl Campbell's MVP glory season with the Houston Oilers. The World Series came and went—with the "We Are Family" Pirates beating the Orioles in seven games—without a single inning appearing on Devlin's TV. Truly, the totality of his being was in a place inaccessible to all outside the chalk lines of this case. Somewhere in that blur, Devlin scribbled *Rule #7—Know the other side's case better than they know it themselves.*

By Halloween, sleep deprived and existing on adrenaline, Devlin had a 1,200-page handwritten script of the trial. He'd distilled Ann Pearson's wrongful death into three key elements: the conflicting medical charts, Debbie Kelman's deposition testimony about doctoring records, and the state report on Mercy Care Center.

Sometime during the month, Ann Pearson's medical chart began haunting Devlin in his dreams: He'd read all the versions so many times that the text was synthesized into his being. And then it happened: a little gem sparkled off the page after his being nudged awake by his own thoughts. He picked up the chart, turned right to the page, and saw it. *What the fuck. How had they all missed that up until now?*

Devlin, without thinking, reached over and started to dial Ford Rockwell. Then he realized it was 3 in the morning and hung up. He turned on the light and scrambled around the stacked boxes and papers collecting what he needed. He didn't even notice he was still wearing his pants and socks, no shirt, and had collapsed again while reading. Waking up in odd sleeping ensembles was now routine. He checked what he saw against the previous versions of her medical chart, and what he'd discovered wasn't on either. Devlin could barely contain his excitement, and he was sure no one over at Bell & Bauer had made a similar discovery. The source of his joy: a small, handwritten number "2" awkwardly squeezed in where the chart referenced how often to reposition Ann Pearson.

"Those bastards are trying to cover their tracks," he said aloud, smiling. Devlin barely slept that night. Several hours later, on Friday morning, November 2, Devlin and Kay Pearson stepped off the elevator at Bell & Bauer for the court-ordered, and final, settlement conference. Devon McCoy barely looked up from her desk in directing them down the hallway. Her allure and pulsing presence was no less palpable, but trial preparation had a way of tinting gray anything outside the case. Even Devon McCoy's primal pull had been relegated down the hierarchy. Devlin noticed her, of course, but the dizzying call of the wild was much more subdued. In the conference room, only Richard Bell sat waiting. No associates. No mediator. It looked informal, so Devlin wondered if the probe was coming out again.

"Where's Judge Nash?" Devlin asked.

"Please, come in. Would you like something to drink?"

"No thank you," Kay Pearson said.

"I'm fine, too. Where's our mediator?"

"Miss Pearson, Mr. Devlin, as you well know we're scheduled to start trying this case on Monday. And if you've been preparing as hard as we have then you're certainly also very tired." Devlin was thinking, *Bell sure loves the sound of his own voice.* "Rather than adding to that fatigue with another long day of trying to mediate this case, I would like to propose we cut right to the number that will get this resolved. Otherwise, let's save our time and breath for Monday."

"Richard, once again, I don't think this is what Judge Stearns had in mind when he *implored* us to settle this case. We can't negotiate a settlement without a negotiator."

"I would beg to differ. I seem to remember a certain well-heeled and eloquent lawyer explaining the merit of old-fashioned values and the lost art of, say, a handshake deal. Does this not qualify?"

Devlin turned to Kay. "Would you excuse us for just a few minutes?"

"Sure." She stood and walked out, and Devlin closed the door behind her.

"So what's your number?" Devlin asked.

Richard Bell reached into his pocket and pulled out a white business envelope. He set it on the table. "My client's carrier has given us authority up to this figure today. Your client can put this entire ordeal behind her right now, and you can go home and enjoy your weekend without the bother of having to prepare for trial Monday. It can all be over right now."

Devlin walked over and picked up the envelope. Devlin looked up and studied his adversary. "I think the only thing that's relevant right now is whether or not you're serious about settling. If this is another low-ball play, then maybe I'll take it up with the judge."

"Is that so?"

"Yeah. That's so."

"Fine. Shall I call Judge Stearns and request a conference, and we can ask him to decide the relevancy of various topics before us?"

"Be my guest. You're the one he's already slapped with $10,000 in sanctions. I'm sure Judge Stearns has clerk interns with better credibility than you right now."

Devlin desperately wanted to know what Bell knew about the case, or didn't know, and how he planned to play it. But he couldn't show even a hint of such longing.

"I think my credibility is the absolute least of your concerns right now, Mr. Devlin. Let's focus, as you say, on the settlement offer. Accept it, and the slate is wiped clean. All of this goes away." Bell smiled the wicked smile of The Evil One closing the deal on another bartered soul as he swept his hand through the air.

"Fair enough." Devlin pried open the envelope and peeked at the check. He swallowed hard. The first offer had been $25,000; the second was $35,000. The check amounts were headed in the right direction. This one: $150,000. Devlin did a double take and counted the zeros just to be sure. If no one had ever wrenched such a settlement from the tight grip of Richard Bell or anyone else at Bell & Bauer, this was a stunning and total victory on the eve of trial. But such an amount might also indicate at least a modicum of distress, a faint little pulse of possibility that the plaintiff's lawyer had stirred up some serious and nagging concerns.

"You're a smart man, Mr. Devlin, so you know that the figure is roughly what the case has cost us to date, plus our time for the folly of spending the next month in court winning a favorable verdict. Although I'm certain Judge Stearns will never allow punitive damages anyway, we must nonetheless protect ourselves from that potential fiduciary exposure. Be smart here. Given the facts, there isn't a whiplash lawyer in this county who wouldn't take $150,000 for this case and consider it a landslide victory. I told you at the outset of this case that you wouldn't get a penny out of us; I humbly stand here corrected. You have proven a worthy adversary and, obviously, you motivated us to settle. Congratulations; this is a career-making victory for you. And it's at my expense."

Bell was right on numerous levels: The case might have been worth $50,000 tops at the outset, and Devlin had tripled that with this offer. Plus, Devlin was considering the problem areas he still had: Max Daniels had been to all seventeen hospitals and clinics without turning up the second nurse. Kelman's testimony alone may not convince the jury. Another biggie: keeping Ann Pearson's gambling history out of evidence. If Devlin slipped and opened that door, Richard Bell would carve up the decedent's reputation without remorse. Then there was the question of punitive damages: Devlin was unlikely to get more than $150,000 out of a jury.

$150,000.

Subtracting expenses and dividing by three was one skill every plaintiff's attorney mastered early. After expenses, Devlin was looking at $65,000 to his client and $35,000 for himself. For 1979, this was watershed stuff and a get-out-of-jail card across the board. Devlin could hear all the voices clamoring in his head: Avram Barak, Nadia Flores, One-Armed Lucky, David Nash, Ford Rockwell and especially Trevor Walsh.

Take the money and run, kid! You took down Richard Bell.

Devlin peeked inside the envelope again—*yes, he'd read it right: $150,000.* Clearly, Bell had underestimated the Irish kid from Buffalo. Devlin could almost see the maniacal grin of Satan warming right now into a grudging countenance of respect. Almost, but not quite.

Devlin nodded. "Obviously, I need to confer with my client."

"Is that a 'yes' then?" Bell asked, his poker countenance slipping for the first time in all these years.

"No, it's a 'maybe' until I confer with my client." Devlin already knew what he was going to recommend.

After leaving Bell & Bauer and dropping Kay Pearson at her apartment, never did the Porsche seem to handle so well. It was a perfect November Friday afternoon in the desert, with sparse clouds and crisp air swirling through the open windows. "Le Freak" by Chic was booming from the car's speakers. After almost four years on this case, Devlin finally felt an overwhelming sense of relief, an unbridled freedom. He had poured all he had into getting a favorable verdict for his client, and in the process he'd squared off and backed the best defense firm in town into a six-figure settlement corner. In a career, a lawyer might get ten, twenty, maybe thirty days like this: when the dice landed square and the years of hard work coalesced into righteous justice on behalf of clients. Not to mention the fat payday.

For Devlin, later that day, there was only one fitting destination to celebrate: AAA Bail Bonds. After settling in and relaying the story, from his upturned plastic bucket, Devlin took a slug of cold beer. It was dark now. One-Armed Lucky was standing, pacing almost, as he drank. "So what'd you do, Big-Time?"

Devlin looked up and saw the concern etched in Lucky's deep wrinkles. Devlin wasn't sure which answer the gambler wanted to hear: that he took the guaranteed victory, or walked away and doubled down in honor of Ann Pearson.

"C'mon, Lucky. How long we known each other? He called me a whiplash lawyer. You believe that?"

Lucky eyed the lawyer. "This ain't no time to play, Big-Time. Tell me."

"There was one thing Bell said that cinched it for me. All of his points, of course, were right on. But that one thing in particular did it. He said they had to protect against 'potential fiduciary exposure.'"

"Meaning what?" Lucky said, not following the lawyer.

"Meaning they're scared they might have to write a much bigger check."

"No, I know that. I mean what did you do?"

"Oh that. I did the only thing I could do."

"C'mon, Big-Time."

Devlin smiled, took a drink of beer and said, "I told the smug bastard to go fuck himself."

A broad smile spread across Lucky's face. "No. You didn't say that to Richard Bell."

"Well, not those exact words, but, yeah, I talked to Kay, and we agreed to roll the dice and see what happens at trial." The Big City Auto Sales case still lingered in Devlin's mind—a victory on paper, but one that let the defendant off with just a wrist slap. Not this time. "I can't believe I just walked away from $150,000, my friend, and I'll tell you what: never felt better. They're scared, Lucky, but they don't care one whit about Ann Pearson. 'Potential fiduciary exposure.' Fucking lawyers. If he had just communicated to me on a human level and been real about what this loss has meant to Ann's daughter, hell, I probably would've told Kay we should take the settlement."

"No shit?"

"Probably, yeah. I truly don't know if we're going to do much better than that at trial." Devlin studied his bottle. "We start jury selection on Monday. You coming?"

"I'll be there when I can, you know, with work and all. You done moved on, Big-Time, grown up right before my eyes. But us little people still got to keep springing the accused every day."

Devlin nodded, wondering again about the settlement. There was always the second-guessing and anxious doubt that, if left unabated, would devolve into debilitating fear. Already he was thinking he should have taken the money. Maybe he'd violated his own code: *Rule #4—The goal is to win the case, not particular points with the client, opposing side, judge, or a witness.* Was he selling out his case and client just to get one over on Richard Bell? Had he pushed aside certain victory simply because he wanted a crushing defeat of his opponent? *Shit.* He'd never know. The only sound now was the hum of traffic filling the space between the buildings and the roar of his growing doubt. He shivered in the cold. Devlin felt oddly panicked and wondered if he might still be able to reach Bell at his office and undo the damage.

"No sir, Big-Time," Lucky said, startling Devlin. "There ain't gonna be none of that."

"What?"

Lucky snapped his fingers at Devlin's face to properly rally his charge: "You done the right thing, Big-Time. For Annie. Now what's done is done, so get on back to your fancy Big-Time lawyer crib and get your mind right. You got a trial starting Monday. I ain't want to be seeing none of that sad-faced shit around here."

Devlin looked at Lucky and smiled. The old dog was right. The lawyer wanted to thank him, maybe give him a hug, something to demonstrate his gratitude for always being there all these years. It was Lucky who'd seen something in the 0-1 Devlin ten years ago and had been imparting his odd brand of mentoring ever since. But when Devlin stood he just said, "I know I'm in trouble when I need a broken-down bail bondsman, with one fucking arm no less, giving me advice. Jesus Christ, Lucky, my case must be for shit."

Lucky shook his head and concealed his smile, "Get out of here you silver-spooned, fucking crybaby. I'll see you in court."

"Yes you will." Devlin turned to leave.

"And Big-Time?"

"Yeah?"

"Don't be fucking anything else up."

Part III

The Trial

Chapter Twenty-Six

"LADIES AND GENTLEMEN OF THE JURY, we are here to prosecute a civil case of elder abuse and neglect of Ann Pearson, a 76-year-old woman," Devlin said. From his first words, he would always speak of Ann Pearson as Avram Barak had suggested.

"Ann Pearson died an agonizing, unnecessary death on April 4, 1975, after a ten-day stay at Mercy Care Center, a rehabilitation center in the Phoenix area owned by Flynn Enterprises, Inc. which is the defendant in this case." Devlin paused briefly. He didn't want to confuse things just yet with the second named defendant. He quickly scanned and took in the jury, judge, opposing counsel, and gallery; everyone was with him. Of course, the real test would be in the days and weeks ahead, as medical and forensic experts droned on about the intricacies of Ann Pearson's decubitus ulcer and advancing sepsis.

"We will prove that Ann Pearson died of a massive infection that she developed as a direct result of the gross negligence, abuse, and neglect that she suffered while in the care of Mercy Care Center, a facility with a long history of systemic problems. We will prove that Ann Pearson died as a result of callous disregard for the health and safety of residents in Mercy Care Center, with features of patient neglect…" Devlin paused at each and numbered the offenses with a finger count.

"Falsification of medical records…"

"Misleading patients and their families…"

"And violation of basic hygiene and health-care standards…"

"All of which was done with the knowledge of the parent corporation, Flynn Enterprises, whose leadership and employees chose to allow substandard patient care to exist as these elderly residents suffered."

Devlin's body pulsed with that rare energy that only fully came to the fore during trial. His senses were simultaneously assessing the tension of every unseen string and every chord and pressure point along the continuum of the courtroom. However menial a gesture or movement or eye roll, Devlin caught and catalogued it into his own mental database without any perceptible pause. Over the weekend, he'd barely slept and ate little. He'd written and re-written his ninety-minute opening statement and practiced it until he no longer needed the script. To further eliminate any worries or hassles, he left the Porsche parked at the condo and hired a car service to drive him to and from court throughout the trial. No detail was too small, and every variable he could control and eliminate freed up valuable capacity.

Now he was center-stage. In this moment, Devlin knew every word on every document related to this case, and he was ready and able to cross-reference whatever detail, fact, or conclusion he needed. The amount of energy it took to do this would, out of necessity, be shifted and allocated elsewhere immediately upon the conclusion of the trial. A month after the trial, he might retain half the information he now held in suspended animation in a three-dimensional matrix. In six months, maybe ten percent. A year after the trial, he'd remember the name Ann Pearson, the last names of a few key witnesses, the basic facts of the case and not much else. But right now, all the data was inseparable from his being. So much so that, as he made his final preparations yesterday afternoon and late into the evening, Devlin missed the report that a group of 3,000 Iranian radicals had stormed the U.S. Embassy in Tehran and taken ninety hostages, including sixty-three Americans. For litigators like Devlin, not even an unfolding national crisis had the power to pierce the trial bubble.

Seated at the plaintiff's table was Kay Pearson, dressed in a dark blue skirt and jacket with a white blouse, a conservative look recommended by Devlin. At the defense table, Richard Bell sat with three associates. Bell wore his best Western suit with his boots polished to mirror-like military perfection. Jeffrey

Redmond sat with an associate behind the defense table. High on his bench was Judge Stearns, with his glasses perched at the end of his permanent scowl.

Galleries at most trials were largely empty. Especially at civil trials with complex and dry testimony about decubitus ulcers. But on this morning, word had spread among the big defense firms as this odd case against a nursing home in Arizona went to trial. Richard Bell, of course, was a local legend, and what better way to sharpen young associates and partners than to send them to watch the mustached master deconstruct a lowly plaintiff's attorney. Front and center were two other keen observers: One-Armed Lucky and Vera.

Outside, with October's passing, the long, brutal desert summer was, mercifully, over. The unending string of 100-degree days gave way to mild, sunny days and crisp evenings. As the usual throngs of court staff, families, and lawyers made their way to the Old Courthouse this morning there was a fresh chill in the air. Fall in the desert came late, but when it finally did it signaled a rebirth.

The large windows in Judge Stearns' courtroom allowed a full measure of diffuse morning light, which gave the space a warm glow. In a momentary flash, Devlin recalled his first day as a real lawyer in Judge Stearns' previous, and windowless, turn-and-burn courtroom across the street. Devlin could feel the full weight of how much was riding on this opening statement. He looked at Kay Pearson and smiled. Next to Kay on the table, spread open, was a large three-ring binder. Just as he'd practiced night after night, Devlin looked to the jury and said, "I have prepared an opening statement, but…" He reached down and closed the notebook. "I think I'd rather just talk to you, informally, about this case." Now he continued with a fluid ease born only out of his maniacal preparation.

"Our state legislature has passed broad protections for people like Ann Pearson. The elderly. The incapacitated. The indigent and vulnerable. We will prove that Ann died as a result of violations of basic, common-sense, and common-decency standards of care. We're here to seek justice and damages as the law allows, and as the judge will instruct you at the end of the case."

"In this case, you are going to learn about the nursing home business and how, in places like Mercy Care Center, terrible things happen every day. In order to understand how and why Ann Pearson suffered and died, you will learn about the standards and systems that must be provided in nursing homes, standards and systems mandated by law."

Devlin was in that magical flow. Already he was extending his hand to the jury and asking them to join him in doing the right thing. The jury, subconsciously, was already appreciative of his preparation. It wouldn't be until later in the trial that they would fully understand that, but for now they were listening intently.

"Sometimes we have a picture of a nursing home as small, quaint, a welcoming place where the elderly receive proper care on an interim basis. Or one of our elderly parents or grandparents may peacefully live out their days in such a facility." Just a few moments for the jury to conjure and survey various versions of that visual. Now to have the defendant step in and poison that lovely scene.

"The nursing home business we're dealing with in this case is much different. Mercy Care Center is a seventy-six bed facility with twenty-four hour nursing care. Patients come into the facility for several reasons. For example, patients who are unable to ever care for themselves who require, in varying degrees, assistance with activities of daily living and medical care. Number two, patients who are terminally ill and require total assistance and medical care. And three, there are patients like Ann Pearson who arrive at a facility for a short stay of rehabilitation, physical therapy, nutrition support, and rest before returning to their normal life. This third reason was the case for Ann Pearson. She was not placed at Mercy Care Center by her loving daughter to live out the rest of her life. She was already living independently in her apartment before she went to Mercy Care Center. Her doctor at Phoenix Municipal Hospital sent Ann Pearson to Mercy Care Center to rehabilitate after a bought of anemia and dehydration. Her loved ones visited every day, but were not aware that she was not getting the care she needed until it was too late." Devlin looked at the jury, several of whom were shaking their heads. All of them, every one, was with him. Time for the bad guy again.

"Mercy Care Center is owned by a large corporation based in Dallas, Texas, called Flynn Enterprises. This company owns, controls, and manages Mercy

Care Center and more than seventy similar facilities around the country. Flynn Enterprises is owned and controlled by one man: Flynn Winston. Nursing homes are licensed by the Arizona Health Services Department. This agency acts on behalf of the state and federal Medicare programs as the agency in charge of inspecting nursing homes. During complaint investigations, the agency does an inspection and issues a report. If cited for a deficiency, the facility must prepare a plan of correction. It's a promise that the facility makes to the government that the problem has been resolved. If deficiencies are consistent and persistent or not corrected, the facility may be sanctioned, from fines all the way to prohibition of accepting new Medicare patients."

Devlin paused. It was time to, ostensibly, review the medical jargon for the jury. But what he was really about to do was start planting seeds about what went on inside Mercy Care Center that led to Ann Pearson's death. This was a subtle art. He didn't want to be too overt or come off as blatantly trying to interject evidence and finger-pointing. The judge would not tolerate that in an opening statement. For now, he simply wanted to drop subtle possibilities into the mind of each juror.

"Let's review some of the terminology you'll be hearing in this case. We'll start with two of the more important tools of nursing care. A medical chart is not only a road map, it's the Bible of patient care. It must be accurate, complete, and contemporaneous. It's not supposed to be subject to alteration, moderation, additions, deletions, post-dated notes, false entries, and multiple versions. All are serious violations of regulations and the law."

"The chart is a medical record that the members of a treatment team can rely on to keep track of a patient's progress, shift by shift, day by day, involving different personnel and disciplines. Any doctor or nurse coming in to see the patient must be able to rely on the chart. It's vitally important in sub-acute care because of changes in conditions that require the care providers to act. If the chart is incomplete, or worse, if it's fabricated, then a nurse's word as to what happened cannot be trusted and one can assume that something was covered up. This case involves that kind of intrigue." Time for a little more emphasis.

"Post-dated entries..." Pause.

"Added and cleaned-up notations..." Pause.

"Notes and an absence of notes that don't support the overall clinical course of Ann Pearson and her outcome." Pause.

"Mercy Care Center has an abysmal record of performance in every category of patient care. It is a facility marked by high turnover, staffing issues, poor morale, and poor patient care. The facility has been fined for Federal compliance violations. The facility has been cited by the state's regulatory agency."

"Administrator Rupert Styles testified under oath in deposition that when he came to Mercy Care Center, the facility was in a state of what he called 'meltdown.' He testified that Mercy Care Center as a facility, and its systems, were massively broken. He will testify that he tried to implement new systems and training, but by the time he left there were still significant breakdowns of systems."

"During 1975, there were complaints from residents, family members of those residents, and nurses at the facility. There were more than thirty deficiencies cited. These complaints involved wound-care monitoring and assessment, dieting issues, inaccurate and incomplete medical records, materially false resident assessments, internal memos and surveys, and residents being pulled out of the facility with massive pressure sores that were toxic from infection."

"Unfortunately for Ann Pearson and her daughter and loving friends, they did not know that the systems of care were in such disarray, or that the types of deficiencies that had resulted in sanctions over the preceding year still had not been corrected. The problems that existed at Mercy Care Center were veiled behind a thick curtain of secrecy, not only from Mrs. Pearson and her family, but from regulatory agencies. There was a climate of concealment: don't chart pressure sores, because surveyors may find out, and fabricate patient charts if necessary. Low morale, high turnover, and poor care equaled, sadly for Ann Pearson, needless suffering and her eventual death."

"You may be asking yourself, 'How could these problems go on for so long?' That's one of the things you'll evaluate in this case. 'Why did Flynn Enterprises and its sole owner, Flynn Winston, allow the problems to persist without correcting them?' In this case, you will also learn about a condition known as pressure sores, bed sores, decubitus ulcers, pressure ulcers. They can be nasty, painful holes that may develop in a patient at risk: patients who are bedridden for periods of time, elderly, thin-skinned, overweight, nutritionally deficient, and suffering from any physical condition that inhibits good circulation, such as diabetes or hypertension."

"These risk factors are universally known, especially to nursing homes that hold themselves out and accept our tax money as places that care for the chronically ill and rehabilitate those with short-term problems. Pressure ulcers and decubitus ulcers are the most common and recognizable problems for skilled nursing facilities, and recognition of those at risk to develop these conditions is obvious and mandated. Nurses must be vigilant and proactive in preventing them from developing, and if sores do develop, swift in their care and treatment. We will present evidence of the breakdown in systems of patient care at Mercy Care Center that led to this continuing problem of pressure sores in the facility. Inadequate assessment of patients, lack of turning and repositioning adequately, inadequate nutrition and monitoring of patient conditions, failure to report to doctors, inadequate charting—these types of problems form the background of a facility that was understaffed, undertrained, and employed personnel who were lackadaisical in prevention and treatment of pressure sores. Sadly, it was against this murky backdrop that Ann Pearson entered the rehabilitation facility in March 1975."

Devlin looked at the jury: He had them. The orchestration of a trial was critical. Opening statements won and lost cases. The order of proof won and lost cases. The plaintiff, with the burden of proof, presented first. For Devlin's case, he planned to call twenty-five witnesses. With cross-examination by both Bell and Redmond, this was going to be at least a month-long trial. But these opening moments were critical in hooking the jury for what would be a long proceeding. Devlin continued his opening with a detailed history of Ann Pearson's life, and emphasized that, right up to the day she went to the hospital, she was living independently and driving herself to church. He also had to tell the jury about her pre-existing health conditions. There could be nothing surreptitious or Devlin would lose their trust.

"As Ann Pearson aged, as is the case for most of us, she developed conditions that required medication. While Ann was not overweight in the slightest, she did have hypertension and high blood pressure, for which she took medicine. This condition was well under control. It sounds ominous, but it is not."

Devlin looked at the jury and explained why it was not the cause of death. The rarefied levels of his preparation had paid off: He was fluid, confident, and pulling from his mental notes with ease. "Now, the defense is going to spend a lot of time telling you that it was these various conditions, not their client's own negligence, that took Ann's life. For now, I will just say that on her autopsy report, there was no evidence of a heart attack. No evidence of any stroke or congestive heart failure. And no evidence of a heart murmur. None."

Devlin told the jury, in detail, about Ann's ongoing fainting spells. He was stealing any dramatic thunder Richard Bell had planned. And once again, he told the jury why it wasn't important in this case. He paused and took in all ten people in the jury box—civil cases in Arizona were tried with an eight-person jury and two alternates—he'd selected this morning. Judge Stearns had brought up a jury pool of seventy-five people and got things rolling right at 8:45 a.m. Then, in an unprecedented nod to Devlin, he'd let him go all the way to lunch with his *voir dire*.

Judge Stearns hammered through his own *voir dire* like a union riveter building a ship's hull: fast, mechanical, and efficient, with no emotional effect. He excused fifteen people with his general strikes and turned it over to Devlin. The lawyer's ideal jurors were those with close ties to their parents, and especially people who had personal experience with caring for an elderly relative. Anyone who'd had a negative experience with a nursing home would also be a plus. He wanted people who viewed the elderly as equally valuable as anyone else in society. It was important to find jurors who would not judge Kay Pearson harshly for allowing her mother to be sent to a nursing home and not being attentive to her care. A good juror need not have medical training, but a certain level of intelligence would be required to understand the pathology and complex jargon.

Devlin looked at the courtroom packed with prospective jurors, all people who didn't want to be there. "I've got great news," he said. "Someone just told me disco is dead."

The eruption of laughter, he knew, was more from nervous relief than his comedic patter. But it had the intended effect. While the judge would not tolerate a lawyer trying to endear himself to the jury, even the old, rumpled Stearns seemed to appreciate the tension-breaker. From there, Devlin started asking his questions and used his unlimited Strikes for Cause to start eliminating jurors, the same people Bell would want to keep: nurses (they would always side with the care facility) and engineers (usually anti-lawyer, and generally didn't connect well with the emotional aspects of injury and wrongful death).

After Bell took his Strikes for Cause, there was a panel of twenty-three people remaining. From there, Devlin and Bell each got four peremptory challenges. The ten who survived were, in Devlin's estimation, good for his case except for two: juror #43, sitting at the left of the bottom row, an automotive product engineer who was already barely paying attention and doodling on his legal pad. And then in the top row, on the far right, juror #20: He, too, didn't seem that interested in being here. He worked at a lumberyard during the day and was going to an electronics school at night. Devlin hoped that both didn't end up on the final jury of eight.

FOR the next forty minutes of the trial, Devlin went over a detailed and graphic timeline of events from March 22, 1975, to April 1, 1975. For the first time, the jury saw a large, color photo of Ann Pearson's exposed buttocks and the huge, infected sore that had developed. Several jurors turned their heads; Kay Pearson wiped her eyes with a tissue. Devlin was already establishing Ann Pearson's condition when she left the hospital and then the conflicting record at the nursing home only thirty minutes later. The surging adrenaline and nervous excitement had settled into a calm confidence that would be Devlin's demeanor throughout the trial. He would never slip into optimism or arrogance, even when he sensed he was making points with the jury. He would never relax, and would proceed methodically like a trusted centurion at his outpost. He would be up at 4 every morning to begin preparing, in court all day without leaving the room even at lunch, and collapse into bed by 10 p.m.

Next, Devlin presented and refuted each of the defense arguments. The jury, even the two doodlers, were right with him. Time to bring it home: "I'm confident that when you hear all the evidence in this case—from those who were there to give you eyewitness accounts of Ann Pearson, her care, or lack thereof, and her condition at various points along this continuum—that the following will be self-evident..."

"... That this facility was a disaster waiting to happen. That poor treatment and neglect at Mercy Care Center led to an increase in the severity of Ann's wounds, creating a condition totally unnoticed by anyone at Mercy Care Center of a rotting wound, massively infected, foul-smelling, and covered in pus and feces, a wound that because of neglect carried infection close to the bone and into the bloodstream. That coupled with no catheter care, no change of a catheter that, as noted on April 1 Phoenix Municipal Hospital records, was filthy and covered in stool, leading to an additional massive urinary tract infection."

"Ann Pearson died as a result of neglect. Her infections and life-saving surgery drained her and led to the ultimate final event of a fatal arrhythmia brought on by the effects of infection. The evidence will show that what happened to Ann Pearson is apparent. Behind that, the more interesting question will be: How did Mercy Care Center and its owner, Flynn Winston, allow this and other atrocities that you will hear about—alteration of records, a cover-up, misleading Ann's daughter, and misleading state investigators? The evidence will show that at this facility this was indicative of Mr. Winston's corporate empire. Built on Medicare dollars, he and his corporation have amassed seventy facilities. I believe the evidence will show that the corporate mentality of putting profits over people was embodied in the care of Ann Pearson. You will hear momentarily from lawyers hired by Flynn Enterprises. I'm certain Mr. Richard Bell will articulately set forth their position."

Devlin turned and looked in the direction of the defense table and smiled at Richard Bell like they'd just gone fishing together yesterday. Then to the jury he said, "But, in the end, the thing I'm most confident about is that the facts you will hear from the witness stand are irrefutable, and the legacy of Ann Pearson will not soon be forgotten." Devlin gave a humble nod to the jury and the judge and then returned to the plaintiff's table, where he took Kay Pearson's hands.

Richard Bell paused before standing to give his opening statement. Devlin had just spoken for an hour and a half without so much as a glance at his notes, and clearly he'd captured the jury. It was, without question, the best opening statement the veteran defense lawyer had ever heard. This kid was good, and Richard Bell fully realized that whatever he might have thought about Devlin almost four years ago no longer applied. This was going to be a bloody, bare-knuckled showdown.

"Ladies and gentlemen of the jury, good morning. I am going to be very brief in my remarks, because the real issue at the heart of this case is quite simple. We lawyers tend to complicate things, so instead I want us to remember why we are here this morning and for the next days and weeks. We are here to answer one very simple question. As jurors in this case, no matter how many different witnesses and experts and charts and medical terms we throw at you, remember that all you have to do is answer this one question."

Bell walked to the edge of the jury box and rested his right hand on the railing. Devlin studied the jurors again. From the bottom, left to right: the product engineer, who was doodling again; a female secretary in a conservative suit; a male mechanic in jeans and a wrinkled, collared shirt; a Hispanic who was a personnel executive at a discount tire company; and a housewife who wore Western shirts, jeans, and cowboy boots and always had a warm smile. The back row, left to right: a male car salesman, in his 30s, who did a lot of community volunteer work; a retired teacher in his 60s; a woman in her mid-50s who used to work as a nursing home assistant and quit because of what she saw; a university professor in his 40s; and the young Hispanic kid who worked at the lumberyard and was not paying attention again.

"Without question, Ann Pearson was a wonderful person. She was a churchgoer. She loved her daughter. She was a good citizen of our community. We do not dispute these facts. Ann Pearson was also 76 years old and, unfortunately, had a multitude of health issues, as Mr. Devlin already outlined for you. She had hypertension and high blood pressure. She had congestive heart failure. Despite what Mr. Devlin said, these are serious health conditions and were the main precursors to her death. She was not a strong, healthy, vibrant woman in her 20s or 30s; she was an elderly woman in the twilight of her time here. As you will hear, her mind was still strong, but her body was not."

"Throughout this trial, Mr. Devlin is going to want you to believe that Ann Pearson died from some dark plot of abuse and cover-up and neglect. The simple truth, we believe the evidence will show, is that Ann Pearson passed away because she was old, which is the natural order of things for all of us. She was elderly, she was frail, and her heart gave out. It happens every day in every country on our planet. It will happen today here in Phoenix. It will happen in Monroe, Louisiana; Santa Rosa, California; and Austin, Texas. It is not some conspiracy against the elderly; it is simply the inevitable and final chapter in our shared human experience. We get old, our hearts give out, and we die."

"That, then, is the one question you must answer as jurors in this case: Why did Ann Pearson die? That's it. Put aside everything and focus on that single question: Why did Ann Pearson die? I've just told you what we believe is the answer to that question, and our evidence will support that theory. Mr. Devlin will have a very different tale, which I'm sure will be quite exciting and full of drama and twists and turns, like a good piece of fiction: allegations of chart fabrication, dark plots, conspiracies to increase profits, this alleged cover-up. He is quite talented and, I'm certain, his story will be captivating. Unfortunately, his story will also ask you to put aside two simple facts: Ann Pearson was a 76-year-old woman. And Ann Pearson had a long history of health issues."

"None of us here in this courtroom has the power to bring Ann Pearson back. That is out of our hands. You as jurors do not have that power. Our esteemed judge does not have that power. Nor do I or Mr. Devlin or anyone else involved in this case. Nothing we do in this courtroom will bring back Ann Pearson. Nothing."

Devlin watched the jury. No doubt, Bell was as good as billed. Already Devlin was nervous; the jury was completely rapt.

"You as jurors, however, are the ones in this courtroom with an immense power within your grasp, and that power is to do what is right. Supporting Mr. Devlin's version of things will not bring back Ann Pearson, but it will allow Mr. Devlin and his client to, essentially, profit from her death. Or you can decide that a far better way to honor Ann Pearson's memory is to let the natural order of things simply be. Despite the valiant efforts of hard-working nurses and doctors like the ones you'll be hearing from in this case, elderly people die. The nurses and doctors at both Phoenix Municipal Hospital and Mercy Care Center did everything in their human power to save Ann Pearson. Just as they are no doubt doing today and will do tomorrow and the next day and so on. Should these people be punished for doing their absolute best when, sometimes, the natural order of things is beyond human control? I think not, and after hearing the evidence, I am confident you will have no choice but to agree."

"Mr. Devlin and I are about to start marching out all our witnesses with fancy titles, and experts who are so smart we pay them $200 an hour and more just to come here and tell us their opinions. Can you imagine? We're going to go through long and detailed explanations about every detail in this case. We're both going to do our best to sway you to our version of the facts. But as you sit as jurors in this case and take in the information, keep that one question at the fore of your mind: Why did Ann Pearson die? That answer is where you will find your verdict."

Chapter Twenty-Seven

"SIR, WOULD YOU PLEASE tell the jury your name and occupation?"

It was day two of the trial, and Devlin was energized by yesterday's opening salvos. Bell's introduction and defense strategy were articulate, reasonable, and exactly as Devlin had predicted. Bell hadn't told the jury anything Devlin didn't tell them first. If he'd been scoring the opening day as a boxing match, he'd put it down as a 1-1 draw, both sides getting in their shots without taking any fatal blows. While that was only the first half-day, Devlin had set the stage well to call his first witness: Dr. Wayne Michaels from Phoenix Municipal Hospital. Devlin spent twenty minutes establishing the doctor's credentials and bringing him up to the time of Ann Pearson's arrival at his hospital.

"Doctor, I'm going to put before you what has been marked and received into evidence as Exhibits 1 and 2, which are the medical records of Ann Pearson's first hospitalization at *Phoenix Municipal* as well as her second visit. Doctor, you've treated thousands of patients, have you not?"

"I have, yes."

"Out of those thousands, do you remember Ann Pearson?"

"Yes, I do."

"Would you please tell the jury why you remember Ann Pearson?"

"I remember Ann Pearson vividly from her second admission to our hospital on April 1, 1975."

"Why is that?"

"The reason I remember her is that she presented to the emergency room from the nursing home in a very serious condition because of an enormously huge, astonishing, appalling decubitus ulcer on her coccyx area. I've been practicing medicine a long time and have not seen anything that dramatic and that large and that infected in all my time as a doctor."

Keeping in mind that the hospital was actually a co-defendant in this lawsuit, Devlin's strategy was on target. It was as though the doctor was his witness, not the defense's, in attacking the nursing home. Then Devlin elicited testimony to establish Ann Pearson's condition upon her first admission on March 19, 1975. It was a slow and painstaking trip back through the medical chart that had the potential to completely put the jury to sleep. Devlin kept his yes-no questions short so that he and the doctor settled into a steady, quick rhythm.

"Anything about a heart attack here?"

"No."

"Anything about a stroke here?"

"No."

"And, of course, you're looking for those things?"

"Yes."

"Did you note on Ann Pearson's chart any signs or symptoms of hypertension or high blood pressure?"

"No."

"Anything to indicate she'd suffered a stroke or any kind of brain hemorrhage?"

"No."

"Was her heart beating normally?"

"Yes."

"No need to call in a cardiologist?"

"No."

"Now looking at her chart, under the heading 'History,' it's noted that she had high blood pressure and congestive heart failure. Correct?"

"Yes."

"No surgeries, not a smoker, not a drinker, and not a drug user; is that fair?"

"Yes."

"Was there anything, doctor, during your first examination and testing of Ann Pearson that suggests she was suffering from a terminal disease?"

"No."

"Anything to suggest that she was in failing health and dying?"

"Objection," Bell said, rising from his chair. "With all due respect, the decedent did in fact die."

"Overruled."

"She wasn't dying," said the doctor.

"She was a 76-year-old woman in relatively good health, but for the underlying conditions that were under control by medication. Isn't that fair?"

"Yes." There were more technical details Devlin had to get into evidence: hemoglobin counts, B-12 deficiencies, dehydration. Once he did that, he moved on to a key line of questions.

"Doctor, you noted on your chart a small blister on her backside. Is that correct?"

"Yes. There was a blister in her perineal area."

"Were you alarmed at this condition?"

"No."

"Why not?"

"It's common for older people who sit for long periods to develop pressure sores."

"What was your treatment for this blister?" Devlin asked.

"I think at the time it was just to keep repositioning her to keep the pressure off."

"OK, let's reference the chart again on March 21, 1975, 2030 hours, the nurse requested a PT consult to assess care of lesions to inner buttocks, one and a half inches in diameter—"

"Objection. Counsel is testifying."

Judge Stearns looked at Devlin. "Ask your question, counselor."

"Yes, your honor. Doctor, we've created a graphic illustration of the nurse's note of March 21. Does this approximate, from your best recollection, what the sore looked like on March 21?"

"I can't remember exactly. That was almost four years ago, but that looks pretty close."

"Can you explain the stages of decubitus ulcers to the jury?"

"Yes. Stage 1 is just a reddened area from pressure. Stage 2 presents denuded skin, but not into the fat or muscle at all. Stage 3 means the sore has migrated from the top down through the skin and into the fat and near the muscle. Stage 4 can go through muscle all the way to the bone."

"And at discharge, on March 22, 1975, you noted a Stage 2 decubitus ulcer on Ann Pearson's coccyx. Correct?"

"Yes."

Devlin was in that place of effortless flow. All the practice, all the scripting, all the endless data from fifty-plus depositions were melding together now in a smooth, evenly paced give-and-take. Any good trial lawyer knew well this heightened place of perfect rhythm and the attendant sense of an almost out-of-body experience.

"And the coccyx, is that a bone?"

"Yes, a bony prominence."

"Doctor, when you discharged Ann Pearson, did you have any reason to believe the pressure sore would not heal with proper treatment?"

"None whatsoever. I felt it would heal with proper treatment."

"As she was leaving Phoenix Municipal Hospital on March 22, was she septic?"

"No."

"Was she suffering from any problem, any disease, any illness for which you thought she was in imminent danger of death?"

"Absolutely not."

"When you signed Ann Pearson's discharge papers from this facility, doctor, on March 22, was it your understanding and your intention from a medical standpoint that within days, a week or two at most, she would return home to independent living?"

"Yes."

"At this point, you were transferring the care of Ann Pearson to the physicians at Mercy Care Center. Correct?"

"Correct."

"Even so, you wrote your telephone number on the discharge papers, didn't you?"

"Yes."

"Doctor, from March 22 when you discharged Ann Pearson, until April 1 when she was brought back to Phoenix Municipal Hospital, did you ever receive a single phone call from anyone at Mercy Care Center about Ann Pearson?"

"No, I did not."

"From the director of nursing?"

"No."

"From any doctor?"

"No."

"From any administrator alarmed at the condition in which Ann Pearson had arrived at their facility?"

"Objection, your honor. Asked and answered."

"Sustained. Move along, counselor."

"OK, let's now talk about April 1, when Ann Pearson returned to your hospital. Tell the jury again what you saw."

"Quite frankly, I was totally shocked and appalled. She had an extremely large decubitus ulcer that was open and foul-smelling and draining a mixture of stool and purulent material. I would say it was one of the worst sights I've seen in all my years of practicing medicine."

"What actions did you take?"

"I recommended a surgical intervention to try to stem the infection."

"Did she have to have the surgery?"

"Yes, it was the only chance we had to try to save her life."

"Was Ann Pearson in pain those final three days of her life?"

"Objection. The witness cannot testify as to someone else's experience of pain."

"I'll withdraw it, your honor. Doctor, was Ann Pearson crying, screaming?"

Bell rose again. "Objection. Your honor, the defense would ask the court to direct Mr. Devlin to stop offering his own testimony."

Judge Stearns nodded and scowled at Devlin. "You know the drill, counselor. Doctor, you may answer the question."

"Yes, she was moaning, crying, in much distress."

"Doctor, what happened to Ann Pearson, clinically, during those ten days?"

"She deteriorated rapidly."

"Why?"

"There was continued pressure on the wound."

"Objection, your honor," Bell said, standing again. "Foundation."

"Sustained." Devlin paused and took a deep breath. Bell, too, had sensed and disliked the perfect rhythm of a few minutes ago. Now he was undoing that very rhythm. It was a good time to wrap up anyway. Devlin smiled, "I'll withdraw, your honor. Last question: Did you discharge Ann Pearson in the condition that you saw her in on April 1?"

"Absolutely not. Her sore was not that size and not that deep. No."

"If you did that, you wouldn't be much of a doctor, would you?"

"I would not have sent her out our doors if she looked like that."

Devlin was surprised, and pleased, that he'd slipped that last question through with no objection. "Thank you, doctor. No further questions."

"You may step down for now, but we'll need you back for cross examination," Judge Stearns said. "Based on the hour of the day, we will take our noon recess and reconvene at 1:15. Please report back to the jury room."

At lunch, Devlin found a pay phone and called Max Daniels. As usual, there was no answer, but the lawyer needed to know if he was any closer to finding the nurse. He'd have to try again later.

"Welcome back," Bell said after lunch. Devlin was already nervous. Cross examining witnesses, both an art and a science, was the key to victory in most trials. And Richard Bell, no doubt, would be as adept as any at simultaneously eliciting agreement and chipping away at the credibility of each witness. Bell was too smart to debate a doctor on issues of pathology and internal medicine, but he would carefully stalk and attack elsewhere.

"Dr. Michaels, good afternoon. Thank you again for being here."

"Good afternoon."

"I'd like to start with just a small point of clarification with you. Let's call up the nursing note from the first day you saw Ann Pearson, March 19, 1975." Bell's associate put the transparency on the overhead projector, which cast an image on the screen for the jury. "Do you see this 1800 hours nursing note?"

"Yes."

"See where it says, 'Dr. Michaels examined patient, orders received, requested IV for fluids.'?"

"Yes."

"OK, it says 1800, which is what time for us civilian types?" Bell looked at the jury and smiled as if he and they were all getting together later to make chocolate-chip cookies from scratch.

"Six in the evening."

"OK. Six in the evening. But what is the time of your dictation?"

"Well, it says 17:10. That's ten past five in the evening."

"So what's this fifty-minute discrepancy in time?"

"I dictated my note at 5:10 and then the nurse transcribed it into the chart at six."

"I see. So there was no intention on your part or by the nurse to mislead anyone by this fifty-minute discrepancy in the medical chart?"

"Mislead, no. And I don't know that I'd consider it a discrepancy. It's just a normal timeline of how things happen when you're attending to multiple patients at any given time."

"Hospitals and care facilities are busy places?"

"Yes, very."

"With lots of patients who simultaneously need lots of different things from doctors and nurses?"

"Yes."

"Which can be stressful for doctors and nurses?"

"Definitely, yes."

"You do the best you can to meet every patient's needs, but sometimes there are delays such as in this charting procedure?"

"Happens all the time."

"Something like this in a chart certainly would not, in your opinion, indicate any sort of falsification of the record?"

"Absolutely not."

"As you say, 'It happens all the time'?"

"Objection, your honor. Asked and answered."

"That's fine," Bell said, knowing he'd already scored the point anyway. "Doctor, I'd like to get your expert opinion on something. If we could put up the final autopsy report for Ann Pearson. Have you seen this, doctor?"

"Yes."

"In this autopsy report, could you read for the jury what the pathologist listed as cause of death?"

"*Most likely cause of death in the patient is cardiac failure with arrest, most likely a terminal arrhythmia.*"

"Thank you. Do you disagree with that?"

"No," the doctor said. Devlin, without looking, sensed the jurors all looking to him. He knew this was coming, but he wasn't worried.

"If we could see the death certificate for Ann Pearson. Can you see the signature there?"

"Yes."

"And who signed this death certificate, Dr. Michaels?"

"I did."

"Would you read to the jury what you wrote, please?"

"First line, immediate cause of death is acute myocardial infarction."

"And what does that mean?" Bell asked as though he truly did not know.

"A heart attack."

"OK, so it is your testimony that you wrote the immediate cause of death of Ann Pearson was a heart attack?"

"Yes."

"OK, please continue."

"Second cause of death was acute pulmonary edema, which means the lungs are filled up with fluid. That's what happens with a heart attack. Third was congestive heart failure, which means the heart was not working and fluid was backing up."

"And what was last in that series, doctor?"

"Fourth was infected decubitus ulcer."

"Objection on foundation grounds," Devlin said. Bell wasn't wasting any time in trying to destroy his case. There was no wrongful death if the jury decided Ann Pearson died of a heart attack.

"I'll sustain the objection," Judge Stearns said. "And let you ask in some other way."

"Is it still your opinion, doctor, that the most likely cause of death here is a terminal arrhythmia with those underlying factors?"

"That's what is the terminal cause of death for everybody. When their heart stops."

"Dr. Michaels, with all due respect, we're not concerned with anyone in this case except Ann Pearson. So what does the death certificate, that you signed, list as the terminal cause of death for Ann Pearson?"

"If you want to get really specific, yes, terminal arrhythmia with those underlying factors."

"Yes, Dr. Michaels, I think it's imperative that we get really specific here. She did not die, if we could be really specific, from sepsis shock syndrome?"

The doctor glared at Bell, who'd painted him into legal corner. "Not specifically, no."

"There's simply no evidence in this record of ever having the criteria that are required in terms of vital-sign changes to support that diagnosis?"

"Objection," Devlin said, standing. "Asked and answered."

"Overruled."

"Doctor, let me repeat the question: There's simply no evidence in this record of ever having the criteria that are required in terms of vital-sign changes to support that diagnosis?"

"No," said the doctor.

"Nothing further, your honor."

"Mr. Devlin. Redirect."

Devlin stood and smoothed his tie. "Just one question, Dr. Michaels. If an Olympic athlete like Bruce Jenner, vibrant, robust, and at the peak of his fitness and strength, died in a car crash, what would you list as cause of death on the——"

"Objection, your honor. Relevance? References facts not in evidence. Foundation. Shall I continue?"

"Sustained."

It didn't matter; Devlin had already put it out there for the jury, who weren't stupid. "Doctor, isn't it true, based on your thirty-plus years of experience, that the official cause of death for most of us will be a terminal arrhythmia?"

"Yes."

"At some point, our heart stops?"

"Yes."

"And Ann Pearson's heart gave out, in your opinion, because of the stress of the systemic infection and the stress of the surgery. Correct?"

"Yes, that's correct."

"Objection, your honor. Leading."

"Sustained. The jury will disregard the previous question and answer."

But again, it was too late; Devlin had already slipped it into their minds. "No further questions, your honor."

The first week of the trial followed the same pattern. Devlin called each of the doctors and nurses from Phoenix Municipal Hospital who attended to Ann Pearson. And, as predicted, their testimony didn't produce any surprises for either Devlin or Bell. Devlin spent time with each witness establishing the chronology and charting of Ann Pearson's two separate stays at the hospital. The surgical doctor, Jeremy Sanford, held his own as Richard Bell exhausted every possibility that the surgery might not have been necessary, might have somehow contributed to her death or, possibly, was the actual cause of death. Bell also continued raising the possibility that Ann Pearson was discharged from Phoenix Municipal Hospital in much worse condition than what they had documented on her chart.

With the trial fully in its throes, Devlin tapped his endurance training from basketball and running. He was down to about five hours of sleep on a good night, two or three hours when the insomnia hit. A trial lawyer's body might be trying to find sleep, but the brain never stepped off the information treadmill. Though he wasn't eating much, he wasn't hungry, either. The nervous tension in his stomach, rather than a hindrance, was fueling his drive. Devlin didn't live through the 1930s Great Depression, but he'd absorbed the mentality from a father who had: *Yesterday in court might have been good, but what are you going to do today?*

"Would you please tell the jury your name and what you do, sir?"

"My name is Wilfred Roberts, and I'm an internal medicine physician and the medical director at Mercy Care Center." It was Monday, November 12, and week two was underway. Devlin could see that, after four and a half days of medical terminology and graphic discussion of Ann Pearson's pressure sore, he was on the borderline of losing the jury. Sheer adrenaline and the excitement of a trial energized the jurors for the first day or two. And since most trials only lasted about a week, at the mid-point jurors could already see the rapidly approaching moment when they would render a verdict.

This trial, however, was probably going to last at least a month, and would test the focus and enthusiasm of even the most ardent jurors. This week, especially, was the no-man's-land of the trial, with the initial excitement gone and no finish line in sight. This was a key witness, however, and Devlin's chance to establish the conflict between the hospital and nursing home. Some fireworks along the way to keep things interesting certainly wouldn't hurt. After leading Roberts through his medical credentials and employment history, Devlin placed papers in front of the doctor.

"I've placed several exhibits before you, which are the various versions of Ann Pearson's Mercy Care Center chart. Feel free to refer to those at any time."

"OK."

"Would I be correct, doctor, to say that in March 1975 it was your normal routine to visit Mercy Care Center three times a week?"

"That's correct."

"And was there a policy or practice at Mercy Care Center as to how much time would elapse between a new admission and when a doctor would first see a patient?"

"I'm not clear on what the policy or law might say, but I always strive to see a patient within seventy-two hours of their admission."

"All right. And you also had responsibilities at other hospitals and clinics, correct?"

"Yes."

"So when you went to Mercy Care Center on one of those three days each week, how would you know which patients you were supposed to see?"

"The nurses laid out the new-patient charts for me. I'd eyeball the chart rack and know which names were not familiar to me. I'd always start with the new patients unless there was an emergency. Beyond that, it would just be a matter of talking to the nurses."

"Let me make sure I'm clear. You really relied on the eyes and the ears of the nurses to pull those charts of new patients, and those charts of patients that needed to be seen because of their critical conditions?"

"Correct."

"And if the nurses did not bring a particular patient to your attention, then you wouldn't know about it, would you?"

"I think that's a fair characterization unless, like I said, I saw an unfamiliar name."

"In addition to your three-times-a-week visits to Mercy Care Center, you also carry a beeper. Is that correct?"

"Yes. It's my worst enemy." A few chuckles from the jury, anything to break the monotony.

"So when the nurses needed to reach you about Ann Pearson's condition, at any time day or night, all they had to do was dial your beeper number?"

"That's correct."

"You were responsive, you were competent, you were caring, you were empathetic—"

"Objection," Bell said. "Counsel is testifying again."

"I'll rephrase," Devlin said. "Did you, doctor, understand the issues involved in elderly care?"

"Yes, that's correct."

During his deposition of Dr. Roberts, Devlin had quickly uncovered an ego big enough to derail a train, which of course the lawyer would now use against the doctor. The idea was to feed out a lot of rope to Roberts, then let him drift way out there on his own before snapping the line tight. "And you were, in fact, at Mercy Care Center on March 25, 1975, which was three days after she was admitted?"

"Yes. I do recall that is the date we discussed and clarified at my deposition."

"We also discussed and clarified that you were in the facility on March 27 and March 29. Correct?"

"That would be 1975, yes?"

"Yes, doctor," Devlin said.

"Yes, I was there on those dates."

"We also know from your records that you only saw Ann Pearson once on March 25. Correct?"

"Yes."

"No nurse, no director of nursing, no unit coordinator, no administrator from Mercy Care Center asked you to see Ann Pearson on March 27 or March 29 while you were physically present at the facility?"

"I have no independent recollection of encounters matching that description."

Devlin paused to let the pomposity fully settle in among the jurors. "Doctor, did you ever get a page on your beeper or a phone call from anyone at Mercy Care Center telling you that Ann Pearson had high fevers from March 27 to April 1?"

"My notations don't indicate any such calls."

"Ever get a page or call from anyone at Mercy Care Center that Ann Pearson's decubitus ulcer was worsening and getting larger?"

"Again, I have no notes to say that I did."

Normally Devlin would ask the judge to instruct the witness to simply answer "yes" or "no." But the pontificating was exactly what Devlin wanted.

"Ever get a page or call from anyone at Mercy Care Center that Ann Pearson's decubitus ulcer was foul-smelling with purulent drainage?"

"There are no notes to reflect such calls, no."

"Did you order a cardiac consult for Ann Pearson?"

"She seemed to be clinically stable based on my exam."

"That would be a 'no,' doctor?"

"Yes…no." This got a good chuckle from the jury. Roberts' face was red.

"Which is it, doctor," the judge asked.

"No, I did not order a cardiac consult."

Devlin let the interruption stand. Then he established the admitting doctor: Thomas Wu. "Did you see any notes on Dr. Wu's admitting form from March 22, or did you observe on March 25, anything that described the following: a large, foul-smelling, draining, Stage 2 or 3 decubitus ulcer that extended hip-to-hip on Ann Pearson, the borders of which had necrotic tissue?"

"No. I mean, I noted Stage 2, but not foul-smelling."

"And yet, you never got any written notes or recorded information from any nurses at Mercy Care Center indicating a condition as I've described it?"

"There are no notes indicating I was told of that type of condition."

"OK, doctor, let's try to move through this quickly, because the jury's heard a lot about this. Based on your notes of March 25, is there anything to indicate that Mrs. Pearson was anything but a short-term patient admitted for monitoring, rest, and rehabilitation?"

"It appears that was the... sometimes patients come in and wind up staying long-term, depending on the living situation that awaits them upon discharge."

"So you're agreeing that she appeared, at the time of your initial examination, to be a short-term patient?"

"I find nothing in my notes to disagree with that statement."

"OK, referring again to your notes, did you not order an egg-crate mattress to relieve pressure for Ann Pearson?"

"That's correct."

"No one from Mercy Care Center told you any time after March 22 that Ann Pearson was in dire health and should not have been admitted to Mercy Care Center?"

"I don't recall that happening."

"And we know from your records that you recorded a large decubitus over the sacrum and over the coccyx. Is that true?"

"That's correct."

"But you did not measure the wound. Correct?"

"I don't normally do the measurements."

"And you did not order Ann Pearson to be seen by a plastic surgeon, a general surgeon, or a wound specialist?"

"There were no such orders."

"From your records, doctor, did you indicate whether or not the pressure sore was infected?"

"There's no indication in my records that it was infected when I saw her."

Devlin spent another twenty-five minutes reviewing every order Roberts detailed in his notes: physical therapy, occupational therapy, medications, a thyroid test, and some routine blood tests. But he ordered no further tests and no nutritional consult. "Doctor, was there anything about Ann Pearson on March 25, 1975, from your review of your records, to suggest that she was dying?"

"Not from my review of my records, no."

"Anything to suggest she was at risk of imminent death?"

"Not imminent death. Obviously she had multiple medical problems, with low odds of long-term survival."

"I don't think you'd want to tell that to Ann Pearson's mother, my client's grandmother, who lived to be 96, would you?"

"I suppose not."

Bell had been unusually quiet. He sensed the damage being done, but Devlin wasn't giving him many openings to object. Devlin, meanwhile, was not out to humiliate the doctor. He'd learned early to never intentionally embarrass, ridicule, or destroy a witness. Ultimately it reflected on the attacker, too. But Devlin was pleased with the points he was making with the jury.

"Ultimately, Dr. Roberts, you are a good doctor, and if you felt this woman was in serious trouble you would have immediately addressed it. Correct?"

"That's correct."

"OK. We're almost done here. Tell the jury, please, what you ordered on March 29?"

"It says to reposition every two hours. Give a pressure relief mattress and barrier cream each incontinent episode."

"This is a nurse's order you signed off?"

"Yes."

"Why, doctor, would a nurse ask you for an order to reposition a patient every two hours a full seven days after admission?"

"I don't know."

"OK, let's talk about the pressure-relief mattress. If one was ordered by Dr. Michaels prior to discharge from Phoenix Municipal Hospital, why would your nurse be ordering one seven days after admission to Mercy Care Center?"

"I don't know."

"OK, let's talk about your final order on April 2. What does that say?"

"Just says to send her to the emergency room."

"A telephone order on April 1 at 6:45 p.m., and it says OK to send patient to the ER for evaluation, which you signed the next day when you came in, on April 2. Correct?"

"Yes."

"That day, April 2, were you told by anyone at Mercy Care Center the condition in which Ann Pearson left your facility the previous night?"

"I don't recall having any such conversations."

"And we've already established that you never spoke to anyone before, during, or after at Phoenix Municipal Hospital?"

"That's correct."

"When did you find out that Ann Pearson had died?"

"When I heard about this lawsuit."

Devlin let that answer hang there for a few seconds, nodding. From his peripheral vision he caught several jurors shaking their heads, grimaces on their faces. "One final thing. Could we put up the letter that's already in evidence? This is a letter dated April 21, 1975, signed by Rupert Styles from Mercy Care Center. He signed this as administrator for Mercy Care Center. Correct?"

"Correct."

"This is a letter he sent Maricopa County investigators in response to a letter of inquiry about Ann Pearson. Do you see that?"

"Yes."

"Before your deposition, had you ever seen this letter?"

"Never."

"Let's read the description of the wound as described here as of March 22: *butterfly shape, hip-to-hip, down over the anus, up into the vulva, wound not dressed, 10 inches by eleven inches on the left, gray tissue with pink tissue on the surrounding edge of gray tissue, edge of the decubitus black and separated.* Doctor, is that the condition of this Stage 2 decubitus ulcer that you described for the jury based on your examination on March 25?"

"No. Absolutely not."

"No one ever told you this woman's condition was worsening?"

"No."

"Or that she had a foul-smelling wound for days on end?"

"No."

"Your honor, leading." Bell finally stepped in, but it was mostly too late.

"Sustained."

"One last question, doctor: Mr. Styles never asked for your input, as the treating doctor, before he wrote these statements to Maricopa County investigators, correct?"

"I don't recall that he did."

"Thank you for your time, doctor."

Bell did what he could to rehabilitate Roberts: as medical director, he would be removed from the day-to-day decisions and any investigations involving nursing care. Rather than an uncaring physician who was detached from the well-being of his patients, Dr. Roberts was a caring professional who did all he was asked.

As Devlin stood, unbeknownst to anyone in the courtroom, President Jimmy Carter was issuing an order to halt all oil imports into the United States from Iran. Around the courthouse all last week, Devlin had heard mention about the worsening hostage situation in Tehran, but hadn't read a single newspaper story or seen a TV report.

The next day, Devlin called the ex-nurse, and now waitress, Debbie Kelman to the stand. An hour into her testimony, he methodically worked toward the real meat of what he wanted the jury to hear.

"Who was your boss at Mercy Care Center, Miss Kelman?"

"I don't remember his name, but I have a description for you." She rolled her eyes at the jury. Devlin caught their reaction: They seemed intrigued by this woman and her dramatics.

"OK, how would you describe this person?"

"Big, fat white guy with glasses, gray hair, always had his nose in the air. You know the type?"

"Miss Kelman, please," the judge said. "Just answer the question."

Devlin smiled and said, "Does the name Rupert Styles refresh your memory, the administrator during your employment at Mercy Care Center?"

"That's right: Rupert Styles."

"Please tell the jury what it was like working under Mr. Styles at Mercy Care Center as a nurse?"

"Let me extrapolate that one out for you, if you know what I mean: being dropped into the middle of Vietnam on the wrong side."

"It was unpleasant?"

"Very."

"Stressful?" Devlin asked.

"Very."

"Why, in your opinion, was Mercy Care Center such a difficult place to work?"

"Why do pork chops taste so good?"

"Excuse me?" Devlin said.

"Who knows, really? Just the way it is. Where do I begin? Not enough staff. Not enough nurses. Too many damn patients. Poor management. No support from corporate."

"And you told us you would often leave work crying?"

"Yes."

"Why was that?" Devlin asked.

"How long you got?"

Devlin smiled. "We have as much time as you need."

"Well, basically I just felt so overwhelmed, overworked, and over-everything. You ever heard the one about being a one-legged man in a butt-kicking contest?" The jury laughed.

"So you were extremely busy?"

"Beyond busy."

"And eventually, Mr. Styles fired you, didn't he?"

"Yes."

"Prior to your termination, did he ever bring you into his office and discuss your performance with you?"

"No."

"Did he ever give you any verbal or written warnings about your performance?"

"No."

"How exactly were you terminated?"

"He just came up to me on duty one day and did it right there in front of the patients and other nurses."

With some theatrics thrown in for good measure, Devlin said, "He just walked up and, without any prior warning, said, 'We are terminating you'?"

"Yes."

"And then he escorted you out of the facility?"

"Yes."

"Do you know, to this day, why you were fired?"

"Not a clue. I'm such a pleasant person to be around." She couldn't hold back her smile.

"Prior to your termination, what other problems did you see at Mercy Care Center?"

"More like what didn't I see. How about a breakdown in communications between the multidisciplinary units and lack of cooperation among the staff."

"Did you observe these problems during March and April of 1975?"

"Yes, I did."

"OK, switching gears, in this case, Miss Kelman, we've taken deposition testimony about a conversation on April 1, 1975, that took place between you, the administrator Rupert Styles, and the executive director of the facility, Miss Pilar Moreno. Do you recall that meeting?"

"Yes, I do."

"Were you instructed during that meeting to fix Ann Pearson's chart?"

"I guess I don't remember anyone saying anything about 'fixing a chart.'"

"What do you recall?"

"They said they needed a more complete description for the chart."

"And did you agree with them that a more complete description was needed for the chart?"

"I did."

"And why was that?"

"Basically to cover my butt. I'm a nurse, you know, so if you got busy and forgot to chart something because they have you doing a hundred different things at once and then they tell you we need a more complete description, then that's what you write."

"Why didn't you write this entry sooner, Miss Kelman, at any time from March 22 to April 1?"

"Like I said, you get busy. Things fall through the cracks. You ever try to keep fifty bedpans clean at once? Damn near impossible."

"Miss Kelman," said the judge, putting on his glasses. "Again, let's let the lawyers ask the questions, and you just stick to giving answers, OK? And watch the profanity in this courtroom."

She nodded. Devlin continued: "But when you had an admonition from your two superiors, Rupert Styles and Pilar Moreno, you wrote the entry into Ann Pearson's chart?"

"Let's just say I was strongly encouraged, yes."

Bell did a reasonable job on his cross-examination of attacking Debbie Kelman's credibility—*Why hadn't she ever logged any formal complaints or talked to her superiors if conditions were so deplorable at Mercy Care Center?*—and portraying her as the clichéd "disgruntled whistle-blower." Devlin, therefore, scored her testimony as another draw, which was not a good trend. A tie might go to the runner in baseball, but in this arena a close call usually went to the defense. Devlin had to start making better headway, or this case would be over in the next few days.

Chapter Twenty-Eight

ON WEDNESDAY, PRESIDENT CARTER ISSUED an executive order freezing all Iranian assets in the United States. It was the president's first public statement on the tense situation. The Iranian students, meanwhile, were upset that Carter had allowed Mohammad Reza Pahlavi, the Shah who ruled Iran for forty years with a brutal and oppressive regime, to seek cancer treatment in New York.

But the dramatic interplay between that history and the breakdown in diplomacy did not exist at this moment inside the Old Courthouse. In Judge Stearns' courtroom, while the jury was out for a recess, Bell, Devlin, and Jeffrey Redmond were all nervously waiting the ruling on punitive damages. Kay Pearson was the only other person in the courtroom.

"Counselors, where are we on reaching settlement in this case?"

"Your honor," Bell said, "our last offer just prior to this trial, which was triple any previous offer, was rejected by plaintiff's counsel."

"Is that true, Mr. Devlin?"

"Your honor, in all fairness, the defendant's offer increased only because during discovery it had become more and more apparent that gross negligence is at work and, I believe, the defendant is trying to protect against the potential fiduciary exposure of punitive damages." Bell, at least, thought it was clever the way the gadfly had turned the senior lawyer's own words; this kid was nimble on his feet.

"All right, counselor, we're not trying the case here. I'm just trying to find out where we are."

"We have been, despite our best efforts to be reasonable, your honor, unable to reach an amicable settlement," Bell said.

"All right," Stearns said, putting his glasses on. He picked up some papers. "Let's clear up this motion on punitive damages. I've read the motion by plaintiff's counsel, and I must say that my personal bias in these matters is to rule against punitive damages, which as I've said can grossly exceed what I would constitute a fair and reasonable punishment. However, last week in this case we heard some compelling testimony entered into evidence regarding the conduct of defendants." The judge sighed. "By what I would consider the narrowest of margins, the court finds that plaintiff's 'Motion for Determination of Prima Facie Case for Punitive Damages' is accepted. Now…"

Devlin could barely contain his excitement, and he glanced over at Bell, who was stoic and staring straight ahead at the judge. In fact, neither really heard the judge ask, "Where are we with jury instructions?"

When the jury returned, Devlin called Fay Fancher, the unit manager at Mercy Care Center. As she walked toward the witness stand, she already had a firm scowl in place. She was at least thirty pounds to the bad, and wearing a white skirt and jacket that both accentuated her girth. Her blue high-heel shoes echoed as she strode across the wooden courtroom floor. After she wiggled into the witness stand and was sworn in, Devlin stood up.

"Would you please state your name for the record?" She paused before saying something imperceptible under her breath.

"Ma'am, please lean closer to the microphone and speak up so the court reporter can hear you." She leaned forward and in a booming voice said, "Fay Fancher. Is that better?"

Again, Devlin let the jury soak up her already-obstinate demeanor. Bell had, no doubt, tried to prepare her and had warned repeatedly how much of what she communicated to the jury would be non-verbal. Devlin led her through her credentials as a registered nurse and then back through her employment history.

"In March of 1975, you were the unit manager at Mercy Care Center?"

"Yes, sir."

"And during March 1975 Rupert Styles was the administrator?"

"Yes, sir."

"And during March 1975 Debbie Kelman was the director of nursing?"

"Yes, sir."

"And you are a registered nurse?"

"Yes, sir."

"And the difference between a registered nurse and an LPN is, briefly, what?"

"An RN is little higher level and can give certain medications. LPNs can't give out meds."

"And at Mercy Care Center in March of 1975 there was also something called a 'charge nurse.' Is that right?"

"Yes, sir."

"What did the charge nurse do?"

"Charge nurse makes sure you know what staff you have, give them their assignments, carry out doctor's orders. You know, call the doctor if there's a problem with a patient. Things like that."

"OK. Let me show you Exhibit 219, which purports to be the Flynn Enterprises' Clinical Services Policies and Procedures for Nurses, Volume I and Volume II. Have you ever seen these documents?" She wrinkled her nose and made a face as though Devlin had made her smell a bowl of rancid garlic. "No."

"So in your duties, you were never given these policies, procedures, and protocols from Mercy Care Center so you could understand how the facility worked?"

"I think I might have seen manuals like this at the nurse's station collecting dust."

"At any time, did you ever read, look at, utilize, or consult these manuals?"

"I'd probably take the easy way out on something like that. In my position I could make an RN read them and ask them what we were supposed to do."

"Did you ever do that?"

"No, sir. You ever been on a care ward? No one had time to read manuals. And if we did, we wouldn't anyway."

"As the charge nurse, you were responsible for all the nurses in your unit during your shift. Is that correct?"

"Yes, sir."

"You would be responsible for making sure that patient care was being given?"

"I would hope so."

"You would hope. Does that mean yes?"

"We both know it does."

Devlin looked at the judge, who was already saying, "Ma'am, please listen to the lawyer's question and just answer yes or no."

"Is one of the charge nurse's responsibilities to make rounds of the patients during your shift?"

"Supposedly, yes."

"Supposedly?" Sometimes witnesses just make it easy on a lawyer.

"Sometimes I made rounds and sometimes I didn't. I worked the graveyard 8 at night to 8 a.m., so it was always quiet. I liked to read a lot when the patients slept."

"Fair enough. Let's switch gears for a minute: What were your responsibilities related to patient charting in March 1975?"

"I oversaw the nurses from each unit who were supposed to do the charting. I mean, I could help as charge nurse, but it's not necessarily my job to chart those patients."

"But a charge nurse could make entries on a chart?"

"Sure."

"In March 1975, what were the charting requirements at Mercy Care Center for each patient?"

"That was a long time ago, but I think we charted every shift."

"So at least once a shift, during the ordinary course of business, one could pick up a patient's chart and reasonably expect to see something about that resident, especially a resident such as Ann Pearson who was in a Medicare unit. Is that true?"

"I'd say that's pretty true."

"Pretty true? Does that mean yes?"

"Yes, pretty true means pretty true, which is pretty much yes."

"Would it be unusual, then, for a patient at Mercy Care Center in March 1975 to go an entire shift, twelve hours, without a single nurse's note about the condition of that patient?"

"I'd say likely."

"Likely?"

"Likely means yes."

Judge Stearns rolled his eyes, but didn't say anything.

"OK, would it be even more unusual then for a patient at Mercy Care Center in March 1975 to go two shifts, or a full twenty-four hours, without a single nurse's note about the condition of that patient?"

"That would be unusual."

"Can you think of a reason you can give to this jury why Ann Pearson, in March 1975, in the Medicare unit at Mercy Care Center, can you think of any reason why, twelve, twenty-four, forty-eight hours would go by, four complete shifts, during which time there's no charting about Ann Pearson?"

"Not really."

"Pardon me?" Devlin had heard her fine; this was for emphasis.

"No, I'm sorry. I have no idea why that would happen if it did happen."

"Prior to March 22, 1975, which is the day that Ann Pearson came into the facility, had you ever in your career as an admitting nurse felt that a patient's condition was such that the patient couldn't be cared for properly in your facility?"

"Oh, sure. We end up sending them out immediately. Usually respiratory patients."

"On March 22, 1975, Ann Pearson came into your facility. Correct?"

"Yes, sir."

"She came from Phoenix Municipal Hospital?"

"If you say so."

"Well," said Devlin, "we'd like you to say so, either 'yes' or 'no' for the jury, please."

"We both know the answer is 'yes.'"

"The hospital is pretty close in proximity to the facility, isn't that right?"

"If you say so, but I'm not walking it." Devlin didn't have to pause or even respond; she was doing great all by herself.

"And when Ann Pearson came to your facility on March 22, 1975, around 6 p.m., you were the charge nurse on duty?"

"Yes."

"And you, in conjunction with nurse Debbie Kelman, admitted Ann Pearson that evening?"

"Yes, sir."

"And why, if you remember, did Miss Kelman ask you as charge nurse to help admit a patient?"

"Probably because I'm so easy to talk to." From any other witness, the response would have been deadpan sarcasm. But Devlin knew that the irony was lost on her and, incredibly, she actually believed what she'd just said. Without looking, Devlin could feel the energy of disbelief from the jury box.

"Aside from being so easy to talk to, can you think of any other reason?"

"I don't know. Probably I'm the first person she saw."

"It was Miss Kelman's job to assess the new patient, but she asked you to help her?"

"I guess."

"You guess?"

"That was four years ago, you know what I'm saying? So I guess that's what happened."

"Did Miss Kelman then tell you that this was the biggest, largest pressure sore that she had ever seen in her career?"

"She probably mentioned it, but I don't remember."

"Did Miss Kelman tell you the patient should have never been discharged from Phoenix Municipal Hospital?"

"I don't remember."

"Did Miss Kelman tell you that Ann Pearson was an inappropriate transfer?"

"Not that I remember."

"Did Miss Kelman tell you that Ann Pearson could not be adequately cared for at Mercy Care Center?"

"Can't remember."

"If she had told you that, do you think that would be something you would write in the chart?"

"I would think no."

"Do you think, out of all the new patients you might see, that you would remember one that presented with the largest pressure sore Miss Kelman had seen in her career?"

"Objection, your honor," Bell said. "Calls for speculation and hearsay."

"Your honor, Miss Kelman's deposition testimony has already been admitted into the record."

"I'll allow it."

"Do you think it would be something you'd remember?"

"I wouldn't know."

"Would it have been Miss Kelman's job or your job to pick up the telephone that night and call Dr. Roberts to confirm the Phoenix Municipal Hospital orders?"

"Her job."

"But she didn't call, did she?"

"You'd have to ask her, I guess."

"And you didn't call either, did you?"

"I guess not if it's not in the chart notes."

"OK, so we can set the story for the jury: When Ann Pearson came into your facility on March 22, 1975, around 6 in the evening, she arrived with transfer documents from *Phoenix Municipal*. Correct?"

"Yes, sir."

"At any time that evening, did you ever pick up the phone and call Phoenix Municipal Hospital or Dr. Michaels to tell them that you felt Mrs. Pearson was in a dire condition that, A, the facility could not properly address and, B, she needed emergent medical care? Did you ever do that?"

"No, sir."

"Was the pressure sore that you evaluated on March 22, 1975, the largest pressure sore you had ever seen in your nineteen-year nursing career?"

"I believe it was."

"And you made a note of that pressure sore on the interdisciplinary records, correct?"

"Yes, sir."

"But yet you admitted Ann Pearson like any other patient and put her on a ward that evening without so much as a phone call to any doctor about this allegedly record-sized and grotesque pressure sore?" She looked away and shifted a bit. "Ma'am?" Devlin asked.

"Yeah, that's pretty much it."

"Let's fast-forward. On April 2, 1975, Rupert Styles, the administrator, told you he wanted you to write another note about what you recalled about the admission of Ann Pearson. Is that true?"

"Yes, sir."

"In your career as a nurse, spanning nineteen years, had you ever been asked to do that before?"

"No."

"In your career as a nurse since that day, have you ever been asked to post-date a note like that again?"

"Not that I remember."

"Tell the jury, please, why on April 2, 1975, the day after the discharge of Ann Pearson, Rupert Styles told you to write this post-dated note?"

"I don't really remember what he told me about why. I just remember he said, 'Write everything you remember about this patient Ann Pearson.'"

"Where you curious why he was asking you do to this?"

"Not really. I normally don't ask why. When you start as a nurse you ask 'why' a lot, and then you quickly learn doctors and administrators don't really want women asking them 'why' all the time. You learn to just do what they say. 'Why' just gets you into trouble."

"Let's also clarify, for the jury, that when Ann Pearson came to your facility on March 22, she didn't have diarrhea, she didn't have any bloody stools, and she was not incontinent. Can we conclude that since you didn't write it in the chart?"

"If that's what it says."

"In other words, don't nurses say, 'If it's not written down, it didn't happen'?"

"Objection, your honor. Misleading."

"Overruled."

"You've heard that, right?"

"Yes, sir."

"It's a very common expression in nursing, right?"

"Yes."

"Do you believe in it?"

"No," she said, shaking her head.

"Your honor, this would be a good time for me to stop." Devlin returned to the plaintiff's table as Bell stood and walked forward.

"Mrs. Fancher, in your nineteen years working at different nursing homes, you've become pretty familiar with how most nursing homes do things?"

"Yes. You figure out the system, and that's how you do it."

"And for the most part, don't things run similarly from one facility to the next?"

"More or less. People is people."

"And as a nurse with almost twenty years of experience, wouldn't you say you know how to do your job without reading a policy and procedure manual?"

"Yes."

"Most of what you do to care for patients you learned in nursing school and over many years of daily care, not from a policy and procedure manual, right?"

"Yes, sir."

"So even though you may not have needed to read the policy and procedure manual at Mercy Care Center, you knew they had one. Is that right?

"That's right."

"You could also ask other nurses if you had a question, right?"

"Yes."

"Wouldn't that sometimes be easier, with so many patients to see, than thumbing through a big manual?"

"Of course."

"In terms of the charts that were kept on a patient at Mercy Care Center, there are lots of different documents in a patient's chart, right?"

"Yes."

"You have doctor's orders?"

"Yes."

"You have medication administration sheets?"

"Yes."

"You have a treatment record?"

"Yes."

"You've got CNA records, flow sheets?"

"Yes."

"There are just a whole lot of pieces that make up the complete picture of the care the patient is getting. Correct?"

"Yes, sir."

"In addition to keeping track of all that documentation, there were patients to provide care to, right?"

"Yes."

"Is it fair to say, over the course of a twelve-hour shift, that things happen that are out of your control?"

"Happens every day."

"And with all the responsibilities that you had as a charge nurse, there were just certain times when things didn't get recorded because you were too busy giving the patients care?"

"Yes, sir."

"So when Mr. Devlin asked you about the expression about things not existing if they're not documented, that's why you said you don't believe in it, right?"

"Yes."

"It's just not realistic to think that every day, every shift, you will always be able to have a perfectly documented record?"

"Objection," Devlin said. "Leading the witness."

"Overruled. You may answer."

"There's no such thing as a perfectly documented chart."

"Thank you," Bell said. "Now, switching to the chart that Mr. Devlin asked you about. You wrote 'large wound.' Correct?"

"Yes."

"When did you write that?"

"The same time I wrote the admission note."

"Everything we see on your note was written on March 22, 1975, around 6 p.m.?"

"Yes."

"You didn't come back later and add in the word 'large'?"

"No."

"Were you busy the night of March 22, 1975, the night Ann Pearson was admitted?"

"Yes."

"And how do you recall that now some four years later?"

"When were we not busy? So if you ask me if I was busy that night, the answer's always, 'yes.'"

"How many nurse's notes have you written in your almost twenty-year career?"

"No idea."

"If you have to estimate? Ten, twenty, 100?"

"More. Thousands and thousands."

"And part of your training at nursing school is writing accurate nursing notes. Correct?"

"Yes."

"And when you wrote this note on the night of March 22, 1975, while busy with numerous other things, you tried to be as accurate as possible, didn't you?"

"Yes."

"And this note would then reflect your best observation at that point and time. Correct?"

"Yes."

"Now, you didn't grade the wound for a particular stage. Are you familiar with the stages I to IV?"

"Yes. Of course."

"And the wound you saw on Ann Pearson that night was what stage—if you would have given it one at the time, what stage would you say it was?"

"Objection. Calls for speculation."

"Sustained."

"As the charge nurse, you have no choice, or decision-making authority, as to what patients you receive at Mercy Care Center, do you?"

"None. We're one step above the janitor and some days probably one step below."

"And you felt like Mercy Care Center would be able to provide care for the large wound you observed on Ann Pearson's buttocks. Correct?"

"I did."

"You and the other nurses and doctors cared for Ann Pearson during her ten days there as best you could. Correct?"

"Yes."

"Now, Mr. Devlin asked you about April 2, 1975, and a conversation that took place between you and Rupert Styles. Do you remember that?"

"Yes."

"And did you write a note in Ann Pearson's chart based on that phone call?"

"Yes."

"And you wrote this note because your superior asked you to, right?"

"Yes."

"Did Mr. Styles tell you why he was asking you to write this note?"

"I don't remember, no."

"And he asked you, I believe you testified, to write everything you can remember about Ann Pearson. Correct?"

"Yes."

"Did he tell you what to write?"

"No."

"Did he tell you to embellish or make Ann Pearson's condition sound worse that it really was on March 22, 1975?"

"No."

"Did he tell you to lie?"

"No."

"You simply did as asked by your superior and wrote a note based on what you remembered about Ann Pearson on March 22?"

"Yes."

"And the note you wrote, based on that request, is accurate to the best of your recollection, isn't it, ma'am?"

"Yes."

"You've been a nurse for a very long time, haven't you?"

"Yes."

"And while you were at Mercy Care Center, you never ignored any patients, and you never ignored Ann Pearson, did you?"

"No."

"You provided the very best care your nineteen years of nursing experience could offer for Ann Pearson while she was at Mercy Care Center, didn't you?"

"Yes." Bell turned to the judge and leaned forward slightly. "Thank you, your honor." The judge nodded and looked at Devlin.

"Hello again," Devlin said, smiling and he stood.

"Hello."

"I'm like a ghost," Devlin said. "I keep coming back."

"You scary all right." The jury, along with Judge Stearns, laughed.

"When you and Miss Kelman admitted Ann Pearson to your facility on March 22, did you consider yourself a wound specialist?"

"No."

"Do you have any recollection whatsoever of ever calling Kay Pearson, the decedent's daughter, to tell her that her mother's pressure sore was getting worse?"

"No recollection."

"Kay Pearson visited her mother every single day. Did you ever express your concerns to her?"

"Not that I remember."

"How about Ann Pearson's close friend Larry White, who goes by the nickname One-Armed Lucky due to his war injury, who also visited every single day. Did you tell him about the worsening pressure sore?"

"I guess not."

"So you have no recollection over those ten days of telling either Ann Pearson's daughter or closest friend, daily visitors to her bedside, about this pressure sore that was the largest you've ever seen?"

"Yes."

"Excuse me?"

"Yes, I have no recollection, is what I meant."

"Can you explain to the jury why you wouldn't have told her loved ones about this condition?"

"Objection, your honor. Calls for speculation."

"Sustained."

"No more questions, your honor." The week concluded without any real breakthroughs or fireworks on either side.

OVER the weekend, on Saturday, Iranian leader Ruhollah Khomeini ordered the release of thirteen hostages, bringing the number still being held to fifty-three. The females were allowed to leave along with—in a show of solidarity for their own racial oppression at the hands of the U.S. government—all the black American hostages at the seized U.S. Embassy.

Although Devlin was at the condo all day preparing for Ford Rockwell, the first witness he planned to call on Monday morning, he never once turned on the TV. Through two weeks of trial, Devlin felt relatively good about how things had progressed. But he was as anxious as ever: The jury was always the wild card. It was obvious the jury didn't like the hospital's doctor, Dr. Wayne Michaels, whose personality wouldn't get him invited to many parties. But he had proved a good and credible witness in establishing the nursing home as the more shadowy of the two care facilities.

Devlin had planned the pattern that was now forming after two weeks of trial: The doctors and nurses from the hospital gave consistent testimony. Everyone from Mercy Care Center, however, was giving conflicting stories and variations about Ann Pearson's ten days in their care. Then, during a long afternoon of mostly repetitious testimony from Mercy Care Center's assistant director of nurses, she talked at length how state investigators had noted Ann

Pearson's high-grade fever while Mercy Care Center's own nurses had not charted that fact.

Both Bell and Jeffrey Redmond, however, were doing a good job of presenting their respective defenses: that the doctors and nurses had done the best they could. They might have different versions of the chart leading up to her death, but the two defendants did agree on one thing: In the end, it was the heart attack that killed Ann Pearson. There was enough doubt there, Devlin knew, that the jury might not find that Mercy Care Center's actions, while perhaps objectionable, constituted neglect.

The condo was awash in papers, court documents, transcripts, and file boxes. Large charts detailing case elements hung from every wall like cultish religious affirmations. He glanced at his clock—4:10 p.m.—and then realized he was still in his pajamas. Ford Rockwell would arrive at 5 to spend the evening practicing his testimony. With court recessed Thursday and Friday for Thanksgiving, Devlin anticipated Rockwell being on the stand, including cross and redirect, for all three days of the shortened week. Devlin looked out to the golf course and watched a duo searching for a ball in the long shadows near his back wall. He couldn't remember the last time he'd picked up a golf club. In fact, he couldn't remember the last time he was outside for more than the walk to and from his Porsche.

Still entrenched on the Other Side, his days were like living a scene from an old movie. The colors were muted, shapes flattened into two dimensions. Surrounding the golfers were apparitions of each juror's face, one by one, bottom row left to right, then the top row. Then the jury faded from view and a golfer found the ball, hit it, and walked away. A large, beady-eyed grackle landed on the railing at Devlin's patio and cocked its head several times. Then a second grackle swooped in and the two birds pecked and squawked at each other a few times before flying away. Without knowing how long he'd been sitting there staring at nothing, Devlin finally got up to shave and shower before Ford Rockwell's arrival.

Chapter Twenty-Nine

"DR. ROCKWELL, I RETAINED YOU to perform expert services as a pathologist in this case. Is that right?"

"Yes, it is."

Ford Rockwell had a movie-star quality, the thick black hair and moustache, and even created a few murmurs and raised eyebrows from the female jurors as he entered the courtroom. Throughout the preparation session Saturday night and all day yesterday, Devlin sensed his expert would shine on the witness stand.

"And what might those services be?"

"To evaluate the case from the pathologic point of view. That is, cause of death, changes that were present in the body at the time of surgery, and ultimately at time of death. My job is to figure out how those changes related to the patient's ultimate demise."

Devlin asked the questions as though they were occurring to him spontaneously, but he and Rockwell had practiced this script eight, nine, ten times. "Just so the jury understands, would it be fair to characterize what you do as part doctor and part detective?"

"Yes. I would say so."

"So you're like Marcus Welby, M.D., and McCloud combined?"

"I would say that's a pretty accurate way of describing a pathologist." The jury, obviously, were lockstep with Rockwell.

"Where did you go for your undergraduate studies?"

"I went to Dartmouth in New Hampshire."

"And what did you study there?"

"Molecular biology as my pre-med."

"That sounds difficult. How were your grades?"

"All A's, actually." When Rockwell smiled, it dissolved any possibility of ego or arrogance.

"Wait," Devlin said, playing it up as planned, "you're telling this jury that you got a four-year degree in molecular biology from one of the top universities in the country without getting any grade less than an A?"

"Yes, but actually I completed my studies in three years."

"All A's. Three years. With that track record I'm guessing you didn't go to just any medical school?"

"No."

"And where did you go to medical school?"

"I went to Harvard Medical School."

"Of course you did. And did you knock that out over a long weekend?"

"No sir. Medical school was four years."

"After completing your studies in molecular biology and getting your degree as a medical doctor, did you do any other training?"

"Yes. I did four years of residency, which was two years in anatomic pathology and two years in clinical pathology."

"Let's see, that's eleven years. Did that about do it, or is there more?"

"There's more. I did an additional year of medical microbiology. Then I did a year of dermato-pathology, which is the study of the skin and how disease affects it."

"So you have thirteen years of schooling and residency in the field of pathology?"

"Yes."

"How long have you been practicing as a pathologist?"

"Twelve years now."

"So in total, between your education and professional experience, you have twenty-five years of knowledge and expertise?"

"Yes."

"In this case, you reviewed Ann Pearson's records from Phoenix Municipal Hospital and Mercy Care Center. Is that right?"

"Yes."

"And you reviewed the pathology report of the autopsy performed on Ann Pearson?"

"Yes, I did."

"You are licensed as a pathologist in the state of Arizona?"

"Yes."

"And as part of your expertise you sometimes testify in trials such as this one, is that correct?"

"Yes." It was better for Devlin to bring it up, to soften the blow when Richard Bell attacked Rockwell as another $200-an-hour mouthpiece.

"How much am I paying you to be here, Dr. Rockwell?"

"One hundred and seventy-five dollars an hour." The jury visibly reacted to this news.

"That's a lot of money. How many pathologists in this country, Dr. Rockwell, do you think have credentials similar to yours, including getting your degree in molecular biology in three years with nothing less than an A?"

"None that I know of," he said, smiling and looking almost embarrassed.

"Objection, your honor," Bell said. "Calls for speculation and facts not in evidence."

"Sustained."

Devlin nodded. "Let me restate: Do you believe your hourly rate is commensurate with your highly unique and very rare knowledge, expertise, and ability?"

"It still seems like a lot to me, but yes."

"OK, shifting gears: Upon my request, Dr. Rockwell, did you review all of Ann Pearson's medical records in February 1976?"

"Yes."

"And also upon my request during February 1976, did you review pathology tissue slides from her surgery at Phoenix Municipal Hospital?"

"Yes."

"And did you review those medical records and tissue slides again in the last few days in preparation for this testimony?"

"Yes."

"Dr. Rockwell, have you formed an opinion concerning the cause of Ann Pearson's death?"

"Yes, sir, I have."

"And do you hold that opinion to a reasonable degree of medical probability?"

"Yes, I do."

"Would you please tell the jury your opinion as to the cause of death for Ann Pearson?"

"I believe that the cause of her death related to an infection originating at the site of the decubitus ulcer and spreading to other areas of her body." There was a bit of rustling in the courtroom.

"And Dr. Rockwell, did you consider the possibility that Ann Pearson died from a myocardial infarction, or heart attack?"

"Yes, sir, I did."

"And what did you conclude?"

"I could find no evidence, either in the slides or her history, that would support her having a primary myocardial infarction." More rustling. This was always the wild card: Devlin and his experts had one version of the events while Bell and his team had a very different story altogether. Both believable, both credible, both backed up by intelligent experts. It would all come down to the subtleties and intangibles that might sway the jury to one side or the other.

"What do you mean by 'primary myocardial infarction'?"

"Ultimately everybody dies because the heart stops. In theory, that's an infarction because the heart stops. The heart infarcts itself. But it's not the primary cause of death."

"Dr. Rockwell, in your deposition testimony you also said that Mrs. Pearson's health deteriorated precipitously during her ten-day stay at Mercy Care Center, is that right?"

"Yes. Definitely."

"Well how do you, and I guess this would be the McCloud part of your job, but how do you know that with any degree of medical certainty?"

"If you look at the last two days of her admission, her vital signs spiked, her temperature was over 100, and her white blood count went to 20,000."

"And what is the significance of Ann Pearson showing these signs in March 1975?"

"These vital signs indicate an infectious process, meaning the infection spread to the bloodstream. This leads to peripheral vascular dilatation, which drops blood pressure and blood return to the heart and cuts off blood circulation throughout the body. The vital organs, without adequate blood supply, start to die off, and then the body can no longer survive."

From there, Devlin had to lead Rockwell through a grisly and graphic account of how the actual bacteria entered the bloodstream and began doing its damage. There were more exhibits showing the final, decaying stages of the wound. Devlin also had to cover a lot of ground he had already gone over with the other doctors: the stage and treatment of the wound, a line-by-line analysis of the medical records, the surgery and its aftermath, and the autopsy report and tissue analysis. It took Devlin two full days to get through everything he wanted to cover with Rockwell. And when Devlin saw he could take Rockwell to the end of Tuesday, he dragged his feet with some superfluous questions. Devlin didn't want to overload the jury with technical information, so this way they could get a good night's sleep before Bell began his cross Wednesday morning.

In almost ten years of practicing law, Devlin had learned only one irrefutable truth in cross-examining experts: It was more art than science. The experts themselves were a necessary evil, on both sides, in civil litigation. The liability and damage issues in most plaintiff cases were simply beyond the scope of the lawyers themselves and normal witnesses. These highly paid experts were the legal equivalent of Himalayan sherpas guiding everyone—lawyers and jurors—safely through complicated terrain.

And like people in every other profession, paid experts ran the gamut from dedicated, honest professionals to some of the slimiest, quick-buck prima donnas who would squawk any needed opinion with an upturned palm. Richard Bell would attack Ford Rockwell's credibility just as Devlin would attack the experts Bell was going to call. But it was a delicate balance: neither wanted to alienate the jury with such tactics. And each lawyer also relied on the very same brand of experts they would attack for being less than credible.

On Wednesday morning, a rare cloudy day with a dark sky threatening rain, the jury took their seats and Ford Rockwell entered the courtroom. Devlin turned and noticed something odd: The gallery was, in contrast to most trials, actually growing in size. There were now twenty-five or so men and women in suits scattered along the fixed wooden rows. The reality fully struck Devlin for the first time: A win would be groundbreaking, and a loss embarrassingly played out before a growing audience of his legal peers. Just what he needed: more pressure. Ford Rockwell took the stand and nodded to the jury with a smile.

"I will remind the witness that you are still under oath. Mr. Bell, cross-examination." Judge Stearns barked his commands like an elementary school teacher directing 4th-graders.

"Good morning, doctor. When Mr. Devlin originally asked you to review the medical records of Ann Pearson, did he suggest that he wanted you to focus on Phoenix Municipal Hospital or Mercy Care Center in particular?

"No. He just asked me to look at the pathology issues and try to determine the most likely cause of death."

"I see."

"During your twenty or thirty meetings with Mr. Devlin, did he ever share his legal theories with you regarding this case?"

"Sure."

"And did your pathology opinions generally support his legal theories in this case?"

"I think it's the other way around."

"How so?"

"My pathology opinions were the basis for his legal theories. His legal theories didn't influence my medical opinions."

"I see." Bell had to be careful, but he'd already slipped it in there like the old pro he was: This guy will say whatever gets him paid.

"Mr. Rockwell..." Now Bell was intentionally dropping the "doctor" prefix to subtly lessen the expert's credibility. "In your opinion, is it possible for a patient to develop a pressure sore like the one Ann Pearson had without any medical negligence?"

"Objection! Beyond the scope of his expertise, your honor." Bell was barreling down a road based on Devlin's own *Rule #8—Only ask questions that you don't care how the witness answers—The message is in the question.*

Judge Stearns considered the objection. "Restate the question."

"Your pathology opinions about how the pressure sore developed and Ann Pearson's primary cause of death are separate from, and do not include any connection to, the care she might or might not have received. Is that true?"

"I'm a little confused by your question."

"Let me try it this way: What the jury has to decide in this case is whether there was medical negligence on the part of either or both defendants."

"Objection, your honor. He's testifying now."

"Sustained. Ask your question."

"In your opinion, doctor, could Ann Pearson's condition and ultimate death have transpired even with the best possible care in the world?"

"Your honor, same objection. Beyond the scope of his expertise and calls for speculation."

"I'll allow it."

"I think your question is more of a clinical issue. If I can't put something under a microscope, it's impossible for me to render an opinion."

"Fair enough."

Devlin was scanning the jury. The product engineer on the bottom left seemed to be a lost cause, because he was doodling again. Same thing with the young Hispanic kid, top right; he was always writing. The housewife on the bottom row still had a warm smile, but the other jurors looked only vaguely interested and also distant. There had been a lot of medical jargon and testimony, and it was just impossible to gauge if the jurors were absorbing it all sufficiently.

"Mr. Rockwell, you have testified here today and established an impressive educational background and professional career. Is that true?"

"Well, I don't know if I'd call it 'impressive,' but I did testify as to my background and credentials." Rockwell was one of the rare expert witnesses: He said things like that without any coaching or direction from Devlin! He was simply a smart guy, not a hint of false modesty or smug arrogance, who also happened to look like Burt Reynolds. He was a rare package indeed.

"Fair enough. And with your impressive credentials and knowledge, you've testified in this case as to the primary cause of death for Ann Pearson. Is that right?"

"Yes."

"And you stated that opinion with what we call a reasonable degree of medical probability? Is that right?"

"Yes."

"Could you explain what that means to the jury?"

"As I've said, as a pathologist I rarely deal with living patients. So I look at the evidence, if you will, and render an opinion. But even with all our science, we can never be 100 percent sure. We are, after all, only human."

Devlin concealed his frustration at that answer, which he'd specifically walked Rockwell through and warned him about. But Rockwell had just put into evidence that he himself could never be 100 percent sure about his own opinion. Even the best witness slips.

"Yes, we are, Mr. Rockwell. So if we know, as you've just testified, that you can never be 100 percent certain of your own opinion, what percentage accuracy would you assign to it?"

"I'd say in this case 99.9 percent."

"That's pretty close to 100, isn't it?"

"Yes."

"So you are saying, then, with a reasonable degree of medical probability, that if there is a 99.9 percent chance you are correct in your opinion, there is also a corresponding .1 percent chance that you are incorrect?"

"I'm a pathologist, not a mathematician." There were chuckles, which Bell took graciously and let subside.

"Mr. Rockwell, if you rendered a medical opinion in 1,000 wrongful death cases and were right 99.9 percent of the time, in how many cases would you be flat-out wrong?"

"One," Rockwell said.

"So you're testifying that, mathematically, even the best expert in the world over a career will probably render an opinion that's wrong at least once?"

"Maybe or maybe not. You're asking me about statistical likelihood of future events, but each case in an independent event. So it all depends."

"But scientifically, it is possible that this is the one case in which your opinion is wrong?"

"Scientifically, yes, it's possible."

That was only the beginning. Richard Bell spent the rest of the morning taking Ford Rockwell through the same wringer on every medical fact and opinion he'd rendered. Throughout, Devlin studied the jury. There seemed to be a balance between moments of fatigue from Bell's plodding strategy of "But isn't it possible…" and stretches of real head-nodding that maybe there was something to all this doubt Bell was stirring up. Devlin thought back to his own initiation into Walsh's grind and the unending drumbeat of bringing out Mr. Reasonable Doubt. Now here was Bell, the seasoned pro, who didn't have to prove a single fact; he only had to keep chopping at the legs of Devlin's precarious three-legged table. One decisive whack and everything fell over. The thought completely deflated Devlin for a moment before he caught himself.

Devlin's redirect didn't come until well after lunch. It had already been a long trial. The jury was tired and was already thinking about tomorrow: eating turkey and pumpkin pie and falling asleep on the couch with the football game at low volume. There were grocery store trips to be made and airport pickups. Devlin had debated throughout Bell's cross: He could go back and resurrect Rockwell on each point, but that would mean having to carry Rockwell over into Monday, *four days* after hearing Bell's cross-examination. Devlin feared the jury wouldn't recall Bell's specific points by then and might even turn against Devlin if he put them through the same tedium again.

Instead, Devlin decided to pin his strategy on the intuition that Rockwell's inherent likability had already won over the jury. If that was the case, Devlin could plant one simple seed and send the jury home for a well-deserved Thanksgiving weekend. Outside, the dark clouds had coalesced to produce a steady drizzle that in the last few moments had subsided. As Devlin stood for his redirect, the ambient light in the courtroom was visibly, and slowly, increasing. Devlin smiled at the jury. It was just one of those synchronous moments that he couldn't let pass. With upturned palms he said, "Let there be light."

It was a hit with the jury, all laughing, but not Judge Stearns, who rapped his gavel and barked: "Counselors, approach the bench." Huddled at the bench, Judge Stearns said, "Mr. Devlin, you will not continue to endear yourself to this jury. Is that understood?"

"Yes, your honor. I'm sorry. It was very inappropriate."

Judge Stearns eyed Devlin. "You started this little charade during jury selection with your 'disco is dead' remark, which seemed innocuous at the time, but I should have nipped it in the bud then. If it happens again, you'll be in contempt. Now let's wrap this up quickly, shall we Mr. Devlin?"

"Yes, your honor." That tenuous balance of momentum had just violently shifted. As he began his redirect, Devlin was afraid to even look toward the jury for fear of crossing the line.

"Dr. Rockwell, Mr. Bell asked you a lot of questions about probability and medical certainty, and you stated that in this case you are 99.9 percent certain as to the cause of death for Ann Pearson. Is that right?"

"Yes."

"And what is that cause of death, in your 99.9 percent opinion, just to refresh for the jury?"

"After studying this case, I listed the cause of her death related to an infection originating at the site of the decubitus ulcer and spreading to other areas of her body."

"And as a man of medicine and science, is there anything about which you can ever be 100 percent certain?"

"Objection. Calls for speculation."

"I'll allow it since you opened this door, Mr. Bell."

"I'd say there's only one thing, medically, I can say with absolute, 100 percent certainty."

"What is that, Dr. Rockwell?"

"That we will all die." It was one of those questions Devlin had alerted Rockwell to during their weekend of trial preparation.

"That's it? Nothing else?"

"Everything else is open for interpretation," Rockwell said.

"Everything?"

"Objection. Asked and answered."

"Sustained."

Devlin nodded and paused. He had the jury laughing, and now they were going to love him for keeping this so short. Time to send them home for the long weekend. "Just one final question: If you are 99.9 percent certain about a particular medical opinion, then any other opinion is possible but, in your best estimation, highly unlikely."

"Yes," said Rockwell. "Highly unlikely. Just like it's possible that this building will be hit by a meteor in the next five seconds, but also highly unlikely."

"It's highly unlikely, in your opinion, that there is any other justifiable cause of death for Ann Pearson?"

"Correct."

It was a perfect ending to the trial's shortened third week, but Devlin was already thinking about the pink message slip from earlier: Max Daniels called and said he found the missing nurse.

Chapter Thirty

"THE BROAD YOU'RE LOOKING FOR is Barbara Reynolds."

It was Friday night, almost midnight, and Devlin was feeling buoyed after sleeping sixteen hours straight, right through Thanksgiving, and any attendant festivities. Today, Iran's new leader Ayatollah Ruhollah Khomeini ordered the return of the Shah or he said he'd put all the American hostages on trial as spies. In a heated back-and-forth, Carter promised that if a single American hostage was killed the U.S. would strike militarily. Devlin missed all the details, but someone had told him there were still fifty-three captives.

Max Daniels had insisted they meet here, at the Playboy Club, because Daniels had never been. But Daniels, ever the pragmatic one, wasn't going to pay the lousy $25 membership fee just to get beers served by women dressed like rabbits. Devlin was his free ticket to the carnival. If disco was dying, no one here had gotten the memo: "You Should Be Dancing" by the Bee Gees was playing to a sparse crowd. Devlin glanced around and wondered whether he'd see Jessica Jean. Scanning the smoky and lonely room, what had seemed so alluring to the young Devlin now seemed contrived and out of step with the changing outside world.

"So what do we know about her?" Devlin asked.

"Good news and bad. Which you want first?"

Devlin took a drink of club soda and, glancing down, nodded. "Good news first."

"Let's see. Licensed nurse for fourteen years. Worked at Mercy Care Center for three years, from 1974 to 1977. Remembers One-Armed Lucky visiting Kay Pearson every day. Stellar performance record. Quit of her own volition."

"Sounds pretty solid. How'd you find her?"

Daniels smiled. "After going through all the hospitals and clinics and turning up squat, I got another long-shot idea: Maybe she was a patient at one of those same places?"

"That is a long shot."

"There was this one personnel manager at the first place I originally checked, Phoenix Municipal, that was a little sweet on me, so I set up another meeting with her. From there it was like shooting fish in a barrel: At the risk of getting canned, she pulled the patient roster and brought it to her apartment for me to scour."

"To her apartment?" Devlin asked. "You dog."

"Like I said; she was sweet on me. Obviously we eliminated the men. There were only three nurses who were also patients. First one deceased. Second one easy to eliminate. So I went and talked to the third one. Bingo: Barbara Reynolds."

Devlin nodded. "Impressive." He took a drink of beer and smiled at a bunny, in her green satin one-piece, as she passed their table. "So what's the bad news?"

"She's in rough shape. Advanced stages of leukemia. She could barely talk."

"Shit. Poor girl. She's in no shape to testify?"

"Well, I did ask her that. She said she does want to get this off her chest before the final bell. She wants a clean slate."

"I hate to be that goddam intrusive."

"Believe me, she wants to do it. She's got something important to say."

"OK. I'll set it up. This will be a nice mid-stream surprise for Bell. I'm sure he thought we'd never find her, and there she was all along at the defendant's hospital."

"It is quite a twist."

"So what about this personnel manager, Daniels? What happened there?"

"Oh, Kelly? Turns out Kelly is quite fond of former-law-enforcement types."

"Is that right? You lock her up with your handcuffs, kinky shit?"

Daniels smiled and glanced around the room. "Let's just say she gives new meaning to the phrase 'unlawful search and seizure.'"

After leaving the Playboy Club around 12:30 a.m., Devlin drove the Porsche the short distance to Phoenix Municipal Hospital. He left his suit jacket in the car and found Barbara Reynolds' room. It was an odd time for an unannounced visit to someone he didn't know, so he was formulating an answer when he saw that it didn't matter.

There wasn't much left of Barbara Reynolds: The hospital bed seemed to engulf her small, frail body, which was plugged with various tubes and wires. She was either asleep or in some other deep, distant state. Seeing her now, he knew he could not ask her to go through a deposition. He knew what the jury would think about him as a lawyer and, more importantly, a human being. *Ambulance chaser. Bloodsucker. Money-grubbing worm.* As the bedside machines beeped a steady, soothing rhythm, Devlin made his decision. He would only ask her once and, without any pressure or an ounce of persuasion, stand by her decision. Then he whispered a prayer for her and left.

ON Monday morning, November 26, Devlin filed the motions he'd spent all weekend writing. He was asking the court for a continuance, as well as further sanctions against Bell & Bauer for blatant obstruction during discovery. Clearly, Sniff and his team at Bell & Bauer had disregarded the court's previous orders to provide this nurse's name and make her available for deposition. Once in the courtroom, with the gallery growing to about forty or so people now, Devlin made his case.

"Counsel, anything before we bring in the jury?"

"Your honor, we have filed two motions with the court this morning based on evidence obtained over the weekend that defense counsel has further obstructed discovery in this case. We are asking the court for a brief continuance so that we may depose a witness that until now had been intentionally hidden from us."

Judge Stearns wrinkled his nose and put his glasses on and looked at Bell. "Mr. Bell?" Getting stared down by Judge Stearns was like standing under a bank of heat lamps.

"Your honor, we are unaware of any witness of substance in this case whom we have not made readily available."

"Barbara Reynolds—does that ring, no pun intended—a bell, Mr. Bell?" Devlin asked.

"Counselors, you will not bicker in this courtroom. Let's recess through the lunch break. I will read and then rule on all outstanding motions at a conference with counsel in my chambers at 1:30 p.m. Mr. Devlin, I trust you have brought copies of these two motions with you?"

"Yes, your honor."

"Very well. Bailiff, please so instruct the jury. Court adjourned."

That afternoon, the judge had to leave on some urgent family matter, which delayed his ruling until the next morning. The jury, meanwhile, was sent home for the day and instructed to be back in the jury room at 8:30 Tuesday morning. As the jury was filing in on Tuesday with their Styrofoam coffee cups, Judge Stearns, Bell, Devlin, and Jeffrey Redmond were gathered in chambers. The judge, seated behind his desk, folded his hands.

"I will be brief, counselors. The conduct in this case, apart from you, Mr. Redmond, has been suspect at best and deplorable at times."

"Your honor—"

"No, Mr. Bell. You will not speak. None of you will speak anything further. If you have something to say to me, put it in a motion and file it with the clerk. Beyond that, I am ruling on what's before me, and we are returning to the courtroom to move this trial along. Understood?"

The three nodded in unison. Devlin was, inwardly, praying to Jesus, Mary, and Joseph, and any other celestial entities who might be listening. "Now, if I may indulge a gross sports analogy, are you all familiar with the concept of 'no harm, no foul'? Well, in that spirit, plaintiff's motion for sanctions is denied. But because Mr. Devlin's claims do hold merit, I'm granting the motion for a continuance so plaintiff's counsel can properly depose Miss Barbara Reynolds as they should have been allowed to do long ago. OK, Mr. Bell and Mr. Devlin, you may now each acknowledge your understanding of what I've said here with a simple head nod and nothing more." Each lawyer did as told, without so much as a sideways glance. The bailiff went to the jury room and told them to return on Monday morning. None of the jurors were told why court was being recessed for the remainder of the week, but none complained, either.

On Thursday morning, as scheduled, Devlin, Bell, and Redmond gathered around Barbara Reynolds' hospital bed for her deposition. When Devlin had asked her, she had been adamant about saying her piece. But she was too frail to leave her bed. Now, the video technician had the equipment set up, and the court reporter sat bedside to transcribe the proceedings. Due to her state and difficulty in speaking, Devlin had suggested reducing the deposition's maximum time allowed from four hours to a single hour. Bell, obviously, welcomed the suggestion without objection. As Devlin began asking her questions, with the beep of the machines clearly audible, he wondered again if the jury was going to hold this against him no matter what Barbara Reynolds might say. He was doing it because she insisted, but it was a calculated risk.

Tomorrow was the last day of November, which Devlin and the other lawyers would use to prepare for next week. The hopes of finishing the trial in a month had been dashed, and the jury wasn't going to be happy to know the proceedings were going to drag out at least until the days before Christmas.

On Monday, with a gallery of more than fifty people now, the judge explained why the jury was going to watch videotape of Barbara Reynolds' deposition. The bailiff dimmed the courtroom lights, and as Barbara Reynolds' frail figure appeared on the TV screen, several of the jurors covered their mouths. They would see and hear her, but only hear Devlin's voice. After the formalities of establishing her name and career, Devlin went to the heart of what she needed to say.

"While employed at Mercy Care Center, did you determine it was an unwritten policy that when facing legal liability with a patient, it was okay to change or alter or modify or make late entries in charts to protect Flynn Enterprises?"

She nodded, struggling to speak, and finally whispered, "Yes."

"How did you make that determination?"

"When you complete… an MDS assessment… you need documentation for the chart. MDSs are how the facility gets reimbursed for funds from the government. Without documentation you get paid less. Corporate sent some people from Dallas… to ask why our reimbursement levels were so low."

"Who came from corporate and asked you that?"

"Ava Quinn."

"What else did she say?"

"She used the word 'skewed.' She said our reimbursement levels were skewed. Said we needed to provide the documentation to get them up."

"The corporate representative from Flynn Enterprises, Ava Quinn, asked you to provide this documentation?"

"Yes."

"What did you tell her?"

"I explained I wasn't comfortable documenting something when there was nothing to support it in the chart."

"And what was Ava Quinn's response?"

"She said the documentation had to be there."

"And if it wasn't there, you were being asked to make up those records after the fact?"

"She didn't exactly word it that way. But it was clear that it was part of my job to make sure the documentation was there. They didn't care how it got there."

"And eventually, is that why you quit, because you didn't want to make up records?"

"Yes."

"You became a nurse because you have a commitment to caring for people?"

"Yes."

"And you felt, based on that commitment, that you were in an ethical and moral dilemma based on what Miss Quinn told you about charting?"

"Yes."

"What did you do?"

"I refused to lie. I have my own morals and ethical code, and I sure didn't become a nurse for the money. I just hoped I could make a change. I felt bad for my patients there."

"Did you tell Miss Quinn that you would not lie and make up medical evidence to go into a chart?"

"Yes."

"Do you remember being at work on April 1, 1975?"

"Yes," she said, nodding.

"And do you remember a conversation you had with Rupert Styles, the unit administrator?"

"Yes."

"Can you tell the jury the sum and substance of what you said to him and what he said to you?"

"I asked him what was going on in his unit that a patient could develop a wound like that. He oversaw the unit. I screamed at him, 'How could you allow nurses to be slapping zinc ointment on a wound that deep?' I asked him what the hell he was thinking."

"And his response to you?"

"He finally said, 'Yeah, oh my God, this does look pretty ugly. We better do something about it.'"

"Any other explanation?"

"No."

"Did you talk to anyone else about it?"

"Yes."

"Who was that?"

"Debbie Kelman. She was a nurse there, too."

"What did you tell her?"

"I apologize for my language."

"That's fine."

"We were in a closed room, not where family or patients could hear us."

"I understand," the jury heard Devlin say.

"I said, 'Goddammit, Debbie, what are you thinking? Where are the treatment orders? How did we let this go on for so long?'"

"Did anyone in your presence order you to make late entries in the chart of Ann Pearson?"

"At the meeting the next morning after Ann got sent back to the hospital, Rupert Styles told Debbie Kelman, 'You need to get that chart fixed, and I mean now.'"

"Do you remember any other instructions Mr. Styles gave Debbie Kelman, in your presence, about fixing this chart?"

"No, I left."

"Disgusted?"

Richard Bell's voice said, "Objection. Form."

"I was very disgusted."

"Is that why you finally quit working at Mercy Care Center?"

"Yes."

Devlin also elicited testimony similar to that of Debbie Kelman: The routine back-to-back double shifts, 128 hours worked in eight days, the lack of charting as Ann Pearson slipped toward oblivion. The jurors, all of them, were shaking their heads and sighing, tearing up.

"Miss Reynolds, why are giving this testimony now?"

She paused for a long time, and then there were tears in her eyes. "I just, it just wasn't right what happened. They lied to cover their own butts. I tried to help. I... I just hope it never happens to anyone else. That's all."

By the time the lights came back up, there were tears in many of the jurors' eyes. Unlike Debbie Kelman, Barbara Reynolds came off as anything but a disgruntled whistle blower. She painted the picture perfectly for the jury: Mercy Care Center was always short-staffed. Nurses didn't care. No one ever reported what was going on to the medical director, who, by the way, only came in once a week. No one ever reported what was going on to Ann Pearson's friends or daughter. There were gaps in her chart for twenty-four, thirty-six, even forty-eight hours. Without looking like an evil bully, there wasn't much Bell could do to refute the testimony, and there was no way he could diminish the image of Barbara Reynolds as an honest, hard-working caregiver who was just trying to do the right thing. That night, Devlin had the TV on while he thought about her testimony. But he was in his own world, and missed the news report from Cincinnati where an ugly incident at Riverfront Coliseum, a stampede for general admission seats, killed eleven fans who had come to see a concert by The Who.

The next morning and into Wednesday, Devlin put Avram Barak on the stand, followed by Kay Pearson. Both performed brilliantly. Kay Pearson, especially, as the last witness for the plaintiff's case, brought home the close connection she and her mother had developed, including the daily morning phone calls. After her testimony, much of it tearful, Devlin helped her off the stand and back to her seat. Then he turned to the judge and said, "The plaintiff rests, your honor."

Chapter Thirty-One

IN EARLY DECEMBER, the wife of one of the hostages tied a yellow ribbon around a tree at her Maryland home and sparked a trend that swept across the nation in a matter of days. Jurors, court staff, and people in the gallery started showing up at court with small, yellow ribbons pinned to their dresses, shirts, and jacket lapels. But other than those bantam bursts of color, the embroiled international standoff barely pierced the drama unfolding within the Old Courthouse.

For the next ten days, Richard Bell and his team of associates, along with Jeffrey Redmond, began disassembling the case Devlin had put forth. They, too, called respected doctors and nurses who testified to a different set of facts about what had happened in the days preceding Ann Pearson's death. Witnesses explained away charting discrepancies as a necessary evil in the fast-paced, twenty-four-hour-a-day world of life and death in which they always did the best they possibly could. Witnesses filled in the gaps Devlin had intentionally skipped over, about their dedication to caring for people and the high success rate of rehabilitation in places like Mercy Care Center.

Bell called an expert pathologist who didn't have the credentials or Burt Reynolds good looks of Ford Rockwell, but who scoffed at Rockwell's "99.9 percent" notion as to cause of death. Further, two other expert pathologists testified to six other possible—and likely, given Ann Pearson's health history—causes of death with the same degree of medical certainty Rockwell had held about his opinion. The jury seemed to take in these differing accounts with the same level of interest they'd granted Devlin. The two lost jurors, at least, ignored the defense lawyers as much as they had Devlin. One victory for Devlin was the advantage of having two defendants and the large measure of finger-pointing that arose. Pull two bloodied patrons out of a bar brawl and, regardless of who might have been more righteous, both get kicked out along with their excuses and oozing cuts. Each defendant's zeal to protect his own client—either would feel victorious if absolved while the jury nailed the other—diluted the credibility of both.

Devlin, too, held his own with the cross-examination skills he'd honed side by side with Walsh in the trenches of criminal law. When to be gentlemanly, when to go hard. When to hammer something home, when to back off. Devlin had learned to approach cross-examination with a respect for each witness and a willingness to reach common ground. Before starting, he would imagine himself sitting in the jury box. Then he would open with innocuous questions to get the expert agreeing with his theory in its broadest sense.

You'll agree the patient died? You'll agree she died after a short illness? You'll agree that when she arrived at the nursing home, the description of the nursing home records is diametrically opposed to the discharge note written thirty minutes prior?

Devlin would never debate an expert witness in that person's area of expertise because, quite simply, he'd lose that battle. He was a trial lawyer; Devlin was never going to know everything the experts knew. Bell had taken that bullheaded approach with Rockwell by questioning his professional certainty about cause of death. For Devlin, that was one of the first mistakes he thought Richard Bell had made.

Instead, Devlin would chip away at the expert's credibility on more peripheral issues. One of Bell's medical experts, Percy Masterson, wanted to be the boss and star of the courtroom. And he loved to give his opinions, at every opportunity, in pontificating speeches. He purported to know everything, had done everything, and so who was this lowly lawyer to challenge his vaunted expertise and sacred opinions? With a guy like Masterson, nothing was easy.

"Dr. Masterson, can you restate for the jury your generic, or overall, opinions in this case related to Ann Pearson's health on or about March 22, 1975?"

"Well, when you say 'generic' I don't even know what that means." He acted as though Devlin had switched to Farsi. Simple answers to simple questions were not an option with experts like Masterson. Instead he'd make the lawyer drag it out of him just so Masterson could savor the succulent strains of his own utterances and the grand breadth of his sprawling genius.

"Just your area of opinions, doctor."

"But you specifically used this word 'generic,' as opposed to trademarked opinions or what? I'm not sure what that means. What am I missing here? I mean, to me, you're asking for something that may not even exist."

Devlin had quickly, and covertly, taken in the jury's reaction to this $300-an-hour windbag, and they didn't like him, either. Devlin had tried to be a gentlemen, but now it was gloves-off time.

"Doctor, let's strike that question and try it this way: What is your medical opinion of the treatment to Ann Pearson provided by Dr. Wayne Michaels from March 19 to March 22?"

"Well now, Connor, for what year in particular are we inquiring?"

"Your honor, I would ask the court to instruct the witness to please refer to counsel as 'Mr. Devlin.'"

Judge Stearns nodded. "Sir, you are testifying in a jury trial. This is not a conversation between Mr. Devlin and you, so please just listen to the questions he asks and then answer them without the extended narrative each time." Masterson looked aghast, as though he'd been unjustly humiliated by some sub-standard public servant who had no right to do such a thing. He even shook his head in defiance of the judge.

"Sir, did you understand me?" the judge said.

Masterson nodded.

"For the record, sir, please say your answer."

"Yes," he said in barely a whisper.

"Would you like me to restate—"

"I'm certain I can remember your little question, Connor—I'm so sorry. Mr. Devlin. I do have an opinion, but just to be sure, I don't believe we established the year for the dates you gave me?"

"1975."

"OK, so you are asking me for my opinion of the treatment to Ann Pearson provided by Dr. Wayne Michaels from March 19, 1975 to March 22, 1975?"

"Yes."

"May I refer to the document provided to me by counsel?"

"Yes."

Masterson opened the three-ring binder and began slowly reading and leafing through it page by page. Then he handed it to Devlin and said, "Mr. Devlin, I don't recall where my notes for that are. Would you find that for me?"

Devlin paused and turned toward the jury. "How much are you being paid to testify here today?"

"That would be $300 an hour."

Then Devlin spun back around and flipped the binder toward Masterson, who grabbed it and bumped the microphone in the process. "For $300 an hour, find it yourself."

"Objection, your honor."

"Sustained."

Didn't matter, Devlin thought; message sent. Throughout the rest of it, the substance of Masterson's testimony made strong points. But the filter of his pomposity was so offensive Devlin suspected he was actually a liability for the defense.

Each night, back at Devlin's condo, Avram Barak spent a couple hours helping the lawyer plan his cross-examination tactics for the next day. Part consultant and part mentor, Barak had also become the lawyer's unofficial motivational coach. At midnight, when Devlin insisted he could not go another five minutes, Barak would remind him the *schlubs* over at Bell & Bauer were at that moment bringing in fresh associates to work through the night. Devlin, somehow, would summon another hour or two of preparation time before collapsing into his bed. One night, after Barak had left and Devlin fell asleep on the couch surrounded by deposition testimony, the phone startled him awake. He awoke saying, "Move to strike, your honor" and then realized where he was. He answered the phone.

"Devlin. You lazy Irish fuck; it's early. You already sleeping?"

Devlin squinted at the clock: 1 a.m.

"Who is this?"

"Ungrateful hack. What are you up to, Irish, bottle a day now?"

In his half-slumber state, there was a vague familiarity to the voice booming through the phone, but Devlin couldn't place it. "I'm sorry, I—"

"Fucking lawyers, I tell you. Just like street whores: only in it for the cash."

"Walsh?" As Devlin said it, he knew. "Trevor Walsh, holy shit."

"Jesus, kid. Thought I was going to have to come through this phone and pistol-whip your shanty-Irish mug."

Trevor Walsh. Razor-sharp and elusive. Devlin couldn't remember the last time they'd talked. "How'd you get my number?"

"Yeah, fuck you too, Devlin. That's how you greet an old pal? I'm an ex-prosecutor, what do you think? Anyway, I don't have all night to circle jerk with you here."

"You called me, Walsh."

"I know, I know. Give me a second here."

Devlin shook his head. "So you can insult me some more?"

"Yeah, and what are you going to do about it, you ungrateful potato farmer?"

The man did have a way with words.

"Look, kid, I just wanted to say, you know, I been following you in the papers and all that with this trial. Hey, you like football right? Christ, what am I saying, silver spoon-Notre Dame brat, of course he likes football. Probably has a framed poster up of Knute Rockne."

"Walsh, it's late." And clearly at this hour Walsh was more drunk than sober. Devlin felt a twinge of sadness for his old comrade as he imagined how far down Walsh had slid.

"Just shut up for a minute, kid, and let an old broken-down lawyer say his piece. Anyway, I was reading about you and made the football connection the other day with you and your dad and all, and I'm a big Raiders fan, silver-and-black and all that—Kenny Stabler, now there's a fucking hard-core grunt if I ever saw one—and I was thinking it was John Madden, or maybe Al Davis, but one of them said whichever side makes the fewest mistakes wins. I was thinking maybe it's like that for you in court, too. You know?"

Decorum and diplomacy had never evolved as full possibilities for Trevor Walsh. But somewhere in there, interwoven with the folk wisdom and ethnic slurs and football-as-life metaphors, was a genuine nod for the rising lawyer. It was oddly touching.

"Thanks, Walsh. You drunk?"

"Oh fuck you, Irish. You're the one's drunk, I'm sure. In fact it's getting late, time to refill your vodka IV. Look, I gotta go. Just remember it's late in the game now; protect that ball, kid."

"I will, Walsh. And you should come down to the courthouse and watch me in action. Or when it's done let's go grab a bite sometime and catch up." Silence. "Walsh?"

But Trevor Walsh was gone. Devlin hung up and thought about those first days and weeks with Walsh, slapping together pleas for Lucky's miscreants. Still half asleep, Devlin picked up a legal pad and, laughing, scribbled: *Rule #9—The side that makes the fewest mistakes wins.*

Chapter Thirty-Two

THE LAST DAY OF THE TRIAL was Wednesday, December 19. Devlin was relieved that, after closing arguments tomorrow, the jury would get the case. A quick verdict tomorrow or Friday would wrap things up before Christmas next week. Devlin feared that the pressure to finish before the holiday might work against the plaintiff: an indecisive jury might err on the side of caution. However, the court would be recessed all next week for the holidays, and he didn't want them returning to deliberate after seven days of too much holiday revelry and forgetting half the testimony. The timing, it seemed, benefited the defendants either way.

The gallery now was full and festooned with the small yellow ribbons. Word had continued to spread about the precedent possibilities of this obscure plaintiff's case against a nursing home and hospital. The buzz was that some upstart soloist was taking on Richard Bell himself and hanging in there. Lawyers and students and curious retirees were turning up now, some lawyers from out of state, even, to see how it played out. Judge Stearns grudgingly allowed a single TV camera at the back of his courtroom to provide a feed for all the local stations. Wearing his favorite gray suit, with a crisp white shirt, red tie, and his shoes buffed to a ridiculous gloss, Devlin was commanding the attention of everyone in the courtroom.

"Fair enough," Devlin said. "If you would, in your role as corporate representative, what has Mercy Care Center done independently to investigate the allegations of chart fraud, altering of charts, and falsification of records alleged in this case from April 1975 to the present time?"

"Objection," Bell said. "Beyond her scope as a witness."

"Overruled."

She was the last witness in the defendant's case: Ava Quinn, the chain-smoking Flynn Enterprises executive Devlin had deposed in Dallas amid the humid stench of smoke and sour pickles. The trial was in its seventh week now. Barak had reminded Devlin that most people couldn't remember what they had for dinner three nights ago, much less testimony specifics going back seven weeks. In these final days, Devlin had to try to elicit something that would really stick with the jurors as they went into their deliberations.

"I know our attorneys conducted interviews with some of the staff. Other than that, I cannot address that. I simply do not know."

He knew, of course, exactly where he was taking her. "Let's go to the issue of charting, if we could for a minute. Is it your opinion that during 1975 Mercy Care Center was experiencing a systemic failure of charting and documentation, especially as it related to pressure sores?"

"Throughout 1975?"

"Yes, ma'am."

"No, I'd say we were showing a significant improvement."

"Your testimony is that things were improving?" Devlin asked.

"Yes, for the most part."

"Well how about the other part, then?" A few laughs from the gallery.

"You're asking me for a 100 percent 'yes' or a 100 percent 'no,' and it's not that simple."

"The truth is, Miss Quinn, that the charting issues and documentation issues during 1975 at Mercy Care Center were constantly the subject of inquiry, complaint, investigation, and remedial measure by you and Mr. Styles. Is that true?"

"I would say... I would say yes."

"Do you know Barbara Reynolds?"

"I know of her, yes, but not personally."

"She was a nurse at Mercy Care Center?"

"Yes."

"Any reason to suggest to this jury that she wasn't a competent, honest employee? Anything from your personal knowledge?"

"Not from my personal knowledge, no."

"Why, if there was not a systemic failure of charting within Mercy Care Center, did you issue this memo dated July 1, 1975?" Nadia Flores laid the memo transparency on the overhead projector.

"I can't respond to that."

"Why is that?"

"I can tell you skin care is a constant issue in all our nursing facilities, and we are constantly educating our employees in this area."

"OK, we'll come back to this. Would you please tell the jury what a CNA flow sheet is?"

"A CNA flow sheet is a record that the certified nursing assistants use to document the care they provide."

"So I would be correct, then, to say that if we look at Ann Pearson's chart, we would find a CNA flow sheet on which instructions are given for taking care of her. Correct?"

"That's correct."

"These CNA sheets are important, right?"

"Sure."

"So why, if we look at the CNA instructions and internal memos during this time period, weren't the weekly skin assessments occurring per schedule? Do you know?"

"I do not."

"So if skin sweeps are not happening, then every resident is at risk to develop pressure sores. Correct?"

"You could assume that."

"Would you also assume that incomplete documentation of a patient's records means inaccurate medical records?"

"That's correct, yes."

"You then issued memos stating that effective immediately the level of scrutiny and intensity would continue until there was 100 percent compliance with accurate documentation. Correct?"

"Correct."

"This is pretty strong stuff, isn't it?"

"It is."

"It would take some severe, serious, immediate problem for you to have been alerted and then written a memo from your Dallas office. Correct?"

"I would say it would take me finding out a facility needed some extra encouragement to complete documentation."

She could answer however she wanted. Regardless of her qualifiers and hedges, Devlin was leading her down the path to a place she didn't want to go. She was powerless to stop the direction and momentum.

"Let's bring up another document," Devlin said. "This is dated April 2, 1975, the day after Ann Pearson left your facility, and it's titled, 'Ulcer Prevention and Treatment Action Plan.' Correct?"

"That's what it says."

"Authored by you?"

"Yes."

"OK, let's read it. *Problem: facility not treating pressure sores in a timely manner after identification. Goal: residents will receive orders for treatment within four hours of identification.* True?"

"That's what it says."

"Why did you write this the day after Ann Pearson left?"

"I don't recall."

"Well, you identify a problem in this memo and give goals to solve that problem. Correct?"

"Correct."

"But you still can't tell this jury what triggered you to write this?"

"I cannot."

"And you can't tell this jury whether or not this was in response to Ann Pearson's case?"

"I can't. I don't have... I can't tell you any specifics."

"How many other residents at Mercy Care Center in March and April of 1975 did you determine were not being properly treated for their pressure sores?"

"I can't answer that just from—this memo doesn't say."

"Would you generate such a memo, all the way from Dallas, if it was one isolated case?"

"Yes."

"You would?"

"Yes."

"With all your various administrative and managerial responsibilities overseeing seventy nursing facilities across this country, you're telling this jury you would write this memo based on one isolated instance at a facility 1,000 miles from your office?"

"Yes."

"OK." Again, the right questions reduced her answers to superfluous strands of nothing. "Or it could have been many cases?"

"Could have, yes. But I don't believe it was."

"We've already heard testimony in this case that Ann Pearson never had a care plan until March 25, even though she came into your facility on March 22. True?"

"Apparently so."

"And because she did not have a care plan, you said in your deposition that was a violation of Mercy Care Center's policy, practices, and protocols?"

"Yes."

"OK, let's look at that initial care plan, written on March 25. There are no measurements or reference to her pressure sore; no mention of whether it's a Stage 1 or Stage 4; no depth of the wound; no description of the odor; no description of drainage. There's nothing there, right?"

"I wouldn't say 'nothing.'"

If only Walsh could see the kid now: *Rule #8— Only ask questions that you don't care how the witness answers—The message is in the question.* Devlin was killing it right now in a way Walsh would truly admire.

"But on April 1, 1975, at the behest of management, Barbara Reynolds sure did a complete documentation. We've got the stages, we've got dimensions, we've got the depths, we've got the treatments. She did a good job on April 1, didn't she?"

"It does not—her care plan does not make the first one any less relevant."

"But if a doctor or nurse looked at the original care plan, they can't tell anything about this large wound, can they?"

"No, but they can refer back to the medical record, where they would find that information."

"Exactly, Miss Quinn, which is why the sanctity of the medical record is so important, because it ensures continuity of care. Correct?"

"That's correct."

"And that's exactly the reason you don't mess with the medical record?"

"No."

"You don't alter it?"

"No."

"You don't modify it?"

"No."

"You don't make fraudulent entries into it?"

"Of course not, no."

It was as though he was a painter who had glimpsed the finished canvas in the ether, long ago, during her deposition in that dingy, yellowed conference room in Dallas. Now he was near completion of his masterpiece, brush stroke by brush stroke. He was in that pure creative flow, out-of-body, where the edges around everything blurred into a cohesive whole. Devlin could almost take a seat himself, in the gallery, and watch the performance unfold, the ecstatic synergy that every trial lawyer craves but cannot access anywhere else but here on the main stage. Even when these triumphant passages rushed forth, they could not be held or savored except as fluid moments.

"OK. Let's pull up the final version of Ann Pearson's medical chart. Now, I want the record to be clear. You're looking at the fourth and final version, provided to us by your legal counsel. Correct?"

"Yes."

"And this version is dated some two years after Ann Pearson was discharged. Do you see that?"

"Yes."

"Tell the jury please what instructions the nurses had for turning and repositioning Ann Pearson?"

"Q2 hours."

"What does that mean?"

"It means they should reposition her every two hours."

"Does this support Mercy Care Center's argument that she was being turned and positioned every two hours?"

Miss Quinn smiled. He was a gentleman, and she couldn't deny he looked fabulous in that suit. These questions only seemed to help her side, and it would soon be over. Testifying in open court hadn't been nearly as bad as she'd feared. "Yes, it does."

"Who had access to this chart after Ann Pearson left?"

"That would be difficult—the medical director, the executive director, director of nurses, myself, obviously."

"I've asked counsel to bring in the assembled original chart. Counsel, can I have a stipulation that I'm now looking at what purports to be the original chart?"

"We have no objection to that, your honor," Redmond said.

"So stipulated," Bell said.

The judge chimed in with, "I am instructing the jury that all counsel stipulate that that's the original."

The afternoon sun streaming through the windows warmed Devlin's face and cast the unfolding scene with an incandescent glow. The gallery was riveted to his every word. The witness, opposing counsel, judge, and jury all seemed to acquiesce to his power to steer this massive vessel right where he needed. In his first real case as a lawyer, across the street before this very judge, Devlin could barely find his own ass in the courtroom. But after almost ten years of practicing law, here he was playing out this shining moment of drama and revelation with the subtle touch and dynamics of a seasoned craftsman. His unsuspecting prey had willingly skipped along to this place, and she still did not realize it was a darkened dead-end lined with razor wire. Nor did she realize Devlin was now unsheathing a glistening blade.

"Take a look, Miss Quinn, at the original document and tell the jury what the original document shows as Mercy Care Center's support that Ann Pearson was turned every two hours."

"Nothing."

"Pardon me?"

"It is not marked," she said.

"Not marked?" Devlin acted astounded, as though learning this for the first time.

"It's not marked."

"It's empty, isn't it?"

"Yes it is," she said.

For the last week, in every spare moment outside the courtroom, Devlin had been champing at the bit to get to this moment, wherein he would bring forth his discovery of the seemingly innocuous little entry: that someone had written the number "2" on the final version. And so it was time. Without even raising his voice, Devlin slowly pushed the hard steel all the way to the hilt. The imagined sensation of warm blood pouring forth was palpable.

"Who perpetrated this fraud on the court?" Devlin said.

"Objection, your honor," Bell yelled, leaping out of his seat.

"Who added the '2' after the fact and ordered a cover-up?" Devlin said, raising his voice.

"Your honor," Bell pleaded.

Devlin jabbed in a third shot, before the judge could even respond, with a measured and loud cadence: "Who—cooked—this—chart?"

"Objection sustained. Mr. Devlin?"

The courtroom was abuzz—bustling, shifting, humming. Judge Stearns rapped his gavel several times without saying anything. Finally, the hushed murmuring abated but did not end. Devlin could restate the question for emphasis, but he would never elicit such a dramatic response again. And Bell's reaction alone spoke volumes. Although it was somewhat risky, Devlin decided to trust that the jury had in that moment fully absorbed the weight of doctoring charts and engaging in an obvious cover-up. Nothing more needed to be said. "No further questions, your honor."

As he returned to the plaintiff's table, smiling at Kay Pearson, he was thinking they'd just won the case. A direct report to Flynn Winston had admitted in open court that someone at the corporation had falsified a subpoenaed document. Bell would have to settle before closing arguments tomorrow. If the defendants let the case go to the jury, they'd be facing each juror's wrath in the form of punitive damages. No one likes a liar. And Bell knew, too, that he wasn't going to get out of jail now for a measly $150,000. For the first time, Devlin was about to enter the hallowed sphere where it would take a check with a lot of zeroes to make the annoyance go away. After doing their best to resurrect Ava Quinn on redirect, *"Please tell the jury a little bit about yourself...,"* the defense rested. After court adjourned, Bell approached Devlin.

"Well done, Mr. Devlin. Well done."

Devlin nodded. It was no time to gloat: The race itself might be over, the horses lathered and slouched, but the day wasn't done until they were wiped down and safely in the barn and munching hay.

"In the spirit of compromise, is your client open to a new round of settlement discussions?"

"I will certainly take your question to my client and get back to you. May I reach you at your office?"

Bell nodded.

Later, Devlin retreated to his office and assembled his team: Kay Pearson, One-Armed Lucky and Vera, Nadia Flores, and his two experts and now friends: Avram Barak and Ford Rockwell. They ordered in pizza and had beers and sat around the conference room. It wasn't a premature celebration. Devlin viewed it more as a long-overdue gathering, and he wanted everyone there for mutual support. He'd talked it over with Kay and called Bell with the new settlement number: $3 million. The offer was good until midnight.

At 8 p.m., however, the office phones had been eerily silent. Periodically, Devlin retreated to dark corners and picked up receivers just to make sure there was still a dial tone. Just before 9 p.m., he called Bell & Bauer. No answer. His friends gradually started to drift away, and by 9:30 he said he should take Kay Pearson home. Everyone else was already gone.

As he drove her home in the Porsche, neither spoke. Devlin kept repeating the same questions: *Was Richard Bell really going to let this case go to the jury? And if so, did he know something Devlin didn't?* An hour later, back at his condo, as he replayed the day's proceedings in his mind, the phone rang. Bingo. It was almost 11 p.m. Bell's flair for the dramatic, it seemed, would play out right to the end.

"I am sorry to bother you at home at this late hour, Mr. Devlin, but we have spent the hours since court adjourned discussing your settlement offer." Devlin was feeling confident and energized, and had a good quip about whether this was another "informal settlement probe." But he let it go. He was staring out to the dark golf course.

"Our stipulation is that the specific terms of any settlement would remain sealed by confidentiality, with no admission of guilt on our part." *Of course*, Devlin thought, thinking about Kay Pearson and the apology she desperately wanted for what had happened to her mother. But Devlin knew he was powerless to ever wrench contrition or accepted responsibility from the lips of defense lawyers on behalf of the corporate string-pullers lurking in shadow. It simply would never happen. Devlin's only instrument of recourse and leverage was cold, hard currency.

"Those terms would be acceptable to my client."

Bell sighed and then, without any further positioning or his standard extended explanation, quietly said, "Our settlement offer is one million dollars."

Chapter Thirty-Three

THE NEXT MORNING, AS DEVLIN WALKED up the steps of the Old Courthouse, a clutch of journalists and TV cameras migrated toward him. The case had started in anonymity and was now front-section news. Just an hour ago, after giving Kay last night to sleep on it, Devlin had called back Richard Bell with their decision: no settlement. The case would be going to the jury.

"Mr. Devlin, have you completely lost your faculties of reason and logic? You're advising your client to turn down a guaranteed million? This is absurd."

"Actually, I told her we should take a good, hard, long look at this and probably accept it, for obvious reasons. But you know what really bothered her?"

"I have no earthly idea."

"She wants your client to apologize and to openly admit they were wrong. It's not about the money. Never was."

"It's not about the money? Well, that's just naïve and preposterous, and you and I both know that. She's asking for something that, legally and contractually, we simply cannot provide."

"Well, I know. But she does make a good point."

"Have you also advised her that we will vigorously appeal any jury verdict and drag this out a number of years? How does that benefit her or anyone else?"

"Like I said, she wants you to say you're sorry. Your client killed her mother."

"Mr. Devlin, you have proven yourself capable, but you need to reel in this client of yours, along with your own ego, and convince her to accept this offer. She has to accept our offer."

"You know, Richard, there's an old Buffalo expression that really captures what we're talking about here." Devlin thought hard about it, smiling, but it just wasn't the time or place. "Never mind, Richard. I'll see you in court."

FOR closing arguments, the order of openings was reversed: Devlin would have the last word with the jury. As Redmond and then Bell spoke, Devlin was anxious about Kay's refusal to settle. Win or lose, it was only going to create more pain. *Rule #9—The side that makes the fewest mistakes wins.* They had made fewer mistakes and won, but the measure of the resolution they'd carved out was not enough for Kay Pearson. Bell's voice was a distant echo, and Devlin felt oddly alone now, as though he'd made a horrible misstep. The peak experience of yesterday's cross-examination was now an empty, dark void of doubt. A stunning victory had turned to certain defeat. Devlin felt a wave of nausea and heat flash through his body. *What had he done? What the fuck, Devlin?*

Then it was his turn, and he snapped back and was up and delivering the closing he'd been practicing for months. Devlin covered the points of the case again, slowly, one by one so they were fresh in the mind of each juror. Then the heart of his closing, which was to diplomatically explain the types of damages and how much the plaintiff was seeking. As a backdrop to that, he showed charts of Flynn Enterprises' corporate assets that approached $1 billion. The message: Anything less than a significant award of punitive damages would be nothing more than a wrist-slap for a man of Flynn Winston's obscene wealth.

After lots of talk about responsibility in preventing another wrongful death such as this one, Devlin had to put out the hard numbers: The plaintiff was seeking $250,000 in compensatory, or actual, damages, and $6 million in punitive damages (Devlin had decided if Bell was willing to cut a check for $1 million, then the case had completely rattled the defense and now represented a teeming black cauldron of "fiduciary exposure.")

The bigger number did raise some jurors' eyebrows, but overall didn't seem to knock anybody off their seat. After thanking the jurors for their time in performing their civic duty, he returned to the plaintiff's table and sat while the judge read the jury instructions he and the two co-defendants had written. The pit of despair, however, was growing in Devlin's stomach. Before lunch, the case went to the jury. After four years of living and breathing this case, the outcome was now completely out of Devlin's sphere of influence. There was, thankfully, nothing more he could do. Not one single thing.

Devlin returned to the office and tried to work, but could only think about the case. The verdict. The case. The cool million he'd turned down. *Had he completely lost touch with reality?* Throughout the afternoon, random points and clarifications he wanted to make with the jury popped into his mind. Questions he wanted to ask witnesses floated around in his head along with new motions he might have filed. The long procession of data, faces, testimony, and every other facet of the case just revolved through his psyche like a spinning carousel gone mad.

At 6:05, he knew Judge Stearns had sent the jury home, which meant sleepless night number one for the three lawyers awaiting a verdict. And behind those three men, all the others who were waiting and equally anxious: Kay Pearson, alone with her thoughts and strong in her resolve that win or lose, they'd done the right thing; Flynn Winston, sock-less and wandering his mansion in Dallas with a snifter of brandy and a feeling of victory after the news that the dumb plaintiff's attorney had turned down a seven-figure check; and One-Armed Lucky, headed to the Royal Palms Kennel Club to put a few bets down for good luck. For Devlin, the night was a fitful, thrashing affair. Finally, at 2:45 a.m., he pulled on gray sweats and went for a walk through the golf course. He thought about all the cold morning runs he'd taken through these familiar dark fairways thinking about the very same case.

Trying the case was officially over, but his mind, focus, and energy were still not acclimated to the speed of normal civilian life. Awaiting a verdict, for a trial lawyer, was the mental equivalent of being a hooked marlin hoisted toward the boat: as fate hung in the balance, the mind gyrated non-stop with violent and fruitless thrashing. Still unable to sleep, at 7 a.m. Devlin went out for breakfast although he didn't really eat. By 9:30 a.m. he'd showered and shaved, put on a suit and tie, and was posted outside Judge Stearns' courtroom for the vigil. If he was going to be worthless at work anyway, he might as well be nearby if the jury came back.

At noon, Devlin walked across the street to AAA Bail Bonds to kill some time with the one-armed oracle, but Lucky was out. Devlin returned to the courthouse and paced up and down the halls. At 3:10 p.m., he feared the worst: This jury wasn't coming back until after the holiday week. He'd lost miserably. He'd completely and utterly fucked this whole thing up. *One million dollars!* He should have insisted she take the million and been done with this. He was finished as a lawyer. He'd somehow managed to snatch defeat from the jaws of certain victory. At 4:45 p.m., Devlin started the slow walk to a week of exile. Just as he turned the corner in the hallway, the bailiff bumped into him. "Good news, huh?"

"What?" Devlin said, his mind ramping back up to warp speed.

"Jury's got a verdict. The other lawyers are on their way. Judge wants the jury and everyone assembled by 5:15 so we can all get home for the holidays. Merry Christmas, counselor."

This was it. The official and public proclamation of your new life as the permanent punch line in Richard Bell's cocktail-party anecdote. Devlin found a phone and called Kay, who'd posted herself at a nearby bookstore and left him the store's number and the manager's name.

At 5:35, the gallery was packed again, the judge and jury seated, and all the lawyers gathered at their respective tables. Devlin had not, could not, look at the jury when they came into the room. He was looking down at the table and holding Kay Pearson's hands with both his hands.

"Has the jury reached a verdict in this case?"

"Yes your honor." Unbelievable, but somehow that kid from the lumberyard, Mr. Doodler, had become the foreman. That was an odd choice. Devlin felt his spirits sink even lower.

"Go ahead, please."

"We the jury..." He stopped, cleared his throat several times, and began again. "We the jury, in case number PB1977-002736, find for the plaintiff, your honor."

Devlin squeezed Kay Pearson's hand. There was a little rumble of murmurs that rippled through the full courtroom, which Judge Stearns had to beat back with his gavel.

"And have you determined the allocation of damages against each defendant?" the judge asked.

"Yes, your honor. On the issue of compensatory damages in case number PB1977-002736, we the jury assess to each defendant in this case, Phoenix Municipal Hospital and Mercy Care Center, $100,000 each." Devlin's heart sank again. At least he had just recovered his expenses with a little left over for Kay, but he'd asked for $250,000 against each; the jury might be hard-liners. But the real wrecking ball was about to be unsheathed and released. Or not. Devlin could barely breathe.

"On the issue of punitive damages in case number PB1977-002736, we the jury assess no punitive damages against co-defendant Phoenix Municipal Hospital."

Not unexpected. Redmond did his job.

So Devlin's strategy—to pin the blame solely on the nursing home—was still in play. This was the moment, all or nothing. It was almost too much to bear: Whatever came next would validate or decimate the last four years of his life, represent the sum and total of his ten-year career, and, perhaps, define his entire future as a lawyer.

"And for the other defendant?" the judge asked.

"On the issue of punitive damages in case number PB1977-002736, we the jury assess against Mercy Care Center punitive damages in the amount of twelve million dollars."

Epilogue

ON MONDAY, NEW YEAR'S EVE, with the fatigued glow of the seminal victory still lingering, Devlin put on a suit for the first time in a week and drove the Porsche to the office with a satisfied confidence. There was a new case with some potential, and he wanted to check a couple leads. Since the verdict, he had ensconced himself at the Scottsdale condo, drawn the drapes, and unplugged the phone. Nadia Flores had strict instructions to act as though he had left for the jungles of Belize: He was simply unavailable. Devlin spent the first few days sleeping in the darkened cocoon. Then he opened the drapes and alternated the sleeping with some basketball and a few rounds of golf. He went to dinner by himself and then to see *10* with Dudley Moore and laughed himself silly. He sat and read the newspaper over leisurely cups of black coffee. Sadly, no end in sight for the hostages still being held captive in Iran.

Throughout these various indulgent diversions, Devlin's mind was still elsewhere. He simply couldn't shut off the flow of trial information; being able to do so was a function of time that could not be fast-forwarded. Every waking moment since hearing the verdict, Devlin never once stopped thinking about her. *Ann Pearson.* A life lived start-to-finish in quiet anonymity. She never got rich. She didn't build a business or invent a better television set, find a cure for wearing eyeglasses, or put down some other more permanent stamp to mark her existence. Maybe this one civil action changed all that. Maybe her influence and contribution to positive change would continue to grow beyond anything she might have ever imagined while living. Devlin thought, too, about One-Armed Lucky as the one who first got the ball rolling a decade ago.

Ten years. Jesus.

Together, the one-armed bail bondsman and the solo lawyer had shined the light on deeds that otherwise would have been forever hidden behind the corporate curtain. The other questions were always there, too. Was it ever enough? Would a chunk of money rectify anything, truly, for Kay Pearson, minus the apology she wanted? Those were questions he could never answer. Her tearful sobs after hearing the verdict would be, for now, the full measure of her relief and reconciliation, for Bell & Bauer had already started the appeals process and, if anything, could claim victory in buying more time. No money had yet changed hands. And over time, there was the likely chance they'd get the punitive-damages amount reduced and maybe thrown out altogether. Even now, the case dragged on with no final resolution, like some bloodied beast from a bad B-movie that just keeps coming back.

But still, Devlin wanted to believe that Ann Pearson somehow knew what they'd just done on her behalf. And the two doodling jurors, the engineer and the lumberyard kid who both made it onto the final jury, were actually keeping detailed notes of the trial! The kid especially: He had entered into his notebook every single exhibit in the case, some 900 of them, with its corresponding number. They'd elected him foreman because he had absorbed the case in its most infinite details. Who would have ever guessed. Jurors, in the end, always find some way to surprise.

Before going to the office, Devlin had one stop to make. He wheeled the Porsche into the dingy parking lot at a pawn shop called Super Place. The neon "r" had been broken and dark so long that everyone called it *Supe's Place.* Devlin needed to ask a potential witness a few questions. Once inside, he asked the slender man behind the counter, who disappeared through a red, velvet curtain.

Devlin browsed among the banged-up drum sets and guitars, eight-tracks in nice condition, power tools, and endless stacked shelves of junk. A glass case with vintage watches caught his eye. The man reappeared.

"She'll be right out."

"Great. Mind if I take a look at some of these?"

"No problem." He unlocked the case.

"How about that one?" It was an older Rolex, $300 and in great condition. The crystal didn't have any deep scratches, and the band was smooth and free of nicks. Devlin turned the watch over and ran his thumb over the back, which had an inscription. For someone, at one time, the watch had a lot of emotional value. Now it was just a $300 piece of collateral among all the other castoffs. Devlin had to strain to read the inscription: *To Trevor, Congratulations! Love, Mom.* Devlin dropped the watch, looked away, and then read it again. *Unbelievable.*

Devlin hadn't talked to his old protégé since that night the phone rang at the condo, but he'd heard what happened since. As his old friend slid further and further into dark obsessions, he was eventually working out of his house, eking out a few chump-change cases between broads and booze, and barely grasping reality. Then he got too close to a criminal client and brought cocaine to the client on a jail visit. That was the bottom of the barrel for Trevor Walsh's long descent into madness. He was looking at certain disbarment and a prison stint. Devlin had thought, many times, about stopping by the jail for a visit, but hadn't yet. And he didn't know if he wanted to see Walsh locked up, the same gritty confines from which he and his talented mentor had carved out their new practice all those years ago.

"I'll take this," he said, reaching for his wallet. And then, without prompting, added, "It's for an old friend."

As the man punched the buttons on the cash register, Devlin thought about The Hawaiian Champ and, although he was a complete and utter bust, how excited Walsh was to be a boxing promoter. Demons aside, Walsh's spark, his precision and unshakable confidence as a lawyer, had, without doubt, honed the young protégé. Walsh, along with a lot of other good lawyers, was all over that courtroom throughout this case and trial. Devlin still couldn't believe it: *$12 million.* Walsh would be, perhaps for the first time in his colorful life, completely speechless when he heard what the kid had done to those silver-spoon corporate robots. Devlin couldn't wait to tell him.

"Do you want me to wrap it?"

"Please." He'd already decided he would hold the watch for as long as necessary and return it to Walsh only after he was out of prison, cleaned up and back on the mend. It would be a fitting welcome-back gift to his old partner, an affirmation of sorts to help pull his buddy upright.

"I think I have a box for this. Be right back."

The man disappeared again through the thick curtains. Next to the red velvet was a tin sign that Devlin read, a simple sentence that captured his Irish heritage and everything he'd kept bottled up during the intense trial. He pulled out the crumpled index card he'd been carrying, the one with the other various hard-earned maxims. This stupid little sign in a pawn shop perfectly rounded out the list he'd been crafting for a decade:

The Rules of Action

#1   Preparation is not a punch line—It's a way of life.

#2   Never be surprised—Surprise is death.

#3   Show your opponent death, and they'll always accept sickness.

#4   The goal is to win the case, not particular points with the client, opposing side, judge, or a witness.

#5   Seek the unconventional.

#6   As you move through the case, the issues become smaller and smaller.

#7   Know the other side's case better than they know it themselves.

#8   Only ask questions that you don't care how the witness answers—The message is in the question.

#9   The side that makes the fewest mistakes wins.

#10 Never let them see you sweat. Or cry.

Then Devlin remembered Walsh's diatribe against algebra and, more specifically, polynomials. Christ, he hadn't thought about that in years, but he could remember every word as if Walsh had just said it yesterday: *Out here it's all meatball justice. And just like there's no such thing as algebra in the real world—trust me, you'll never see another fucking polynomial as long as you live—there's no such thing as nuance and strategy in this type of law. Factoring polynomials. Remember that shit?*

Devlin was chuckling to himself when the witness finally appeared. Devlin, ever the professional, tried several times to collect himself to speak to her, but he couldn't get Walsh's words out of his head. What started as a chuckle turned into fits of uproarious laughter. Like a child at church, the more Devlin tried to contain the laughter the stronger it surged forth.

Finally, after trying to keep it down, he just let go completely, of everything he'd been meticulously holding together throughout the trial, the million and one details he had to keep pinned down for weeks and months and years. He began laughing so hard that he had to lean over and support himself on the counter. In one beautiful moment, as the mix of euphoria and tears and relief and celebration poured out in healing gales, the long ten years and being a lawyer all made perfect sense. He had the odd sensation of making a shift as he finally crossed over the line into who he was always supposed to be. Tears in his eyes, he drew in a deep breath and felt a surge of energy.

They'd see the Irish kid in court again.

LANDON J. NAPOLEON is the award-winning and critically acclaimed author of fiction and nonfiction books. He has a bachelor's degree in journalism from Arizona State University, a master's degree from University of Glasgow in Scotland, and has been an author for more than two decades.

His debut novel *ZigZag* received starred reviews, was a Barnes & Noble "Discover Great New Writers" finalist (1999), was translated into multiple foreign editions, and was adapted for a motion picture (Franchise Pictures, 2002) starring John Leguizamo, Oliver Platt, and Wesley Snipes.

His nonfiction biography *Burning Shield: The Jason Schechterle Story* was the March 2014 "The Arizona Republic Recommends" selection. Interweaving narratives of human triumph, medical marvels, police procedure and high-stakes legal showdowns, this "inspiring true story" (Kirkus Reviews) chronicles the triumph of a rare human being with an undeniable will to live.

www.landonjnapoleon.com

Made in the USA
San Bernardino, CA
19 November 2018